MASTERING NATIVE AMERICAN LAW

CAROLINA ACADEMIC PRESS MASTERING SERIES

Russell Weaver, Series Editor

For other titles, please go to caplaw.com.

Mastering Administrative Law, Second Edition
Linda D. Jellum

Mastering Adoption Law and Policy
Cynthia Hawkins DeBose

Mastering Alternative Dispute Resolution
Kelly M. Feeley, James A. Sheehan

Mastering Appellate Advocacy and Process, Second Edition
Donna C. Looper, George W. Kuney

Mastering Art Law, Second Edition
Herbert Lazerow

Mastering Bankruptcy
George W. Kuney

Mastering Civil Procedure, Third Edition
David Charles Hricik

Mastering Constitutional Law, Second Edition
John C. Knechtle, Christopher J. Roederer

Mastering Contract Law
Irma S. Russell, Barbara K. Bucholtz

Mastering Corporate Tax, Second Edition
Gail Levin Richmond, Reginald Mombrun, Felicia Branch

Mastering Corporations and Other Business Entities, Second Edition
Lee Harris

Mastering Criminal Law, Second Edition
Ellen S. Podgor, Peter J. Henning, Neil P. Cohen

Mastering Criminal Procedure, Volume 1: The Investigative Stage, Third Edition
Peter J. Henning, Cynthia E. Jones, Ellen S. Podgor,
Karen McDonald Henning, Sanjay K. Chhablani

Mastering Criminal Procedure, Volume 2: The Adjudicatory Stage, Third Edition
Peter J. Henning, Cynthia E. Jones, Ellen S. Podgor,
Karen McDonald Henning, Sanjay K. Chhablani

Mastering Elder Law, Second Edition
Ralph C. Brashier

Mastering Employment Discrimination Law, Second Edition
Paul M. Secunda, Jeffrey M. Hirsch, Joseph A. Seiner

Mastering Environmental Law
Joel A. Mintz, Tracy D. Hester

Mastering Evidence
Ronald W. Eades

Mastering Family Law
Janet Leach Richards

Mastering First Amendment Law
John C. Knechtle

Mastering Income Tax, Second Edition
Gail Levin Richmond, Christopher M. Pietruszkiewicz

Mastering Intellectual Property
George W. Kuney, Donna C. Looper

Mastering International Sales Law
Herbert Lazerow

Mastering Interviewing and Counseling
Kelly M. Feeley, Rebecca C. Morgan

Mastering Labor Law
Paul M. Secunda, Anne Marie Lofaso, Joseph E. Slater, Jeffrey M. Hirsch

Mastering Legal Analysis and Communication
by David T. Ritchie

Mastering Legal Analysis and Drafting, Second Edition
George W. Kuney, Donna C. Looper

Mastering Legislation, Regulation, and Statutory Interpretation, Third Edition
Linda D. Jellum

Mastering Native American Law, Third Edition
Angelique Wambdi EagleWoman, Stacy L. Leeds

Mastering Negotiable Instruments (UCC Articles 3 and 4) and Other Payment Systems, Second Edition
Michael D. Floyd

Mastering Negotiation
Michael R. Fowler

Mastering Partnership Taxation
Stuart Lazar

Mastering Products Liability
Ronald W. Eades

Mastering Professional Responsibility, Second Edition
Grace M. Giesel

Mastering Property Law, Revised Printing
Darryl C. Wilson, Cynthia Hawkins DeBose

Mastering Sales
Colin P. Marks, Jeremy Kidd

Mastering Secured Transactions: UCC Article 9, Third Edition
Grace M. Giesel

Mastering Tort Law, Third Edition
Russell L. Weaver, Edward C. Martin, Andrew R. Klein, Paul J. Zwier, II, John H. Bauman

Mastering Trademark and Unfair Competition Law, Second Edition
Lars S. Smith, Llewellyn Joseph Gibbons

Mastering Trusts and Estates
Gail Levin Richmond, Don Castleman

MASTERING NATIVE AMERICAN LAW

THIRD EDITION

Angelique W. EagleWoman

SISSETON-WAHPETON (DAKOTA) OYATE OF THE
LAKE TRAVERSE RESERVATION
DIRECTOR, NATIVE AMERICAN LAW AND
SOVEREIGNTY INSTITUTE
MITCHELL HAMLINE SCHOOL OF LAW
FIRST INDIGENOUS LAW DEAN IN CANADA

Stacy L. Leeds

CHEROKEE NATION
DEAN, REGENTS PROFESSOR, AND FOUNDATION
PROFESSOR OF LAW AND LEADERSHIP
SANDRA DAY O'CONNOR COLLEGE OF LAW
ARIZONA STATE UNIVERSITY
FIRST INDIGENOUS WOMAN LAW DEAN IN UNITED STATES

CAROLINA ACADEMIC PRESS
Durham, North Carolina

LIBRARY OF CONGRESS CATALOGING-IN-PUBLICATION DATA

Names: EagleWoman, Angelique Wambdi, author. | Leeds, Stacy L., 1971- author.
Title: Mastering Native American law / Angelique Wambdi EagleWoman, Stacy L. Leeds.
Description: Third edition. | Durham, North Carolina : Carolina Academic Press, LLC, 2024. | Series: Carolina Academic Press mastering series | Includes bibliographical references and index.
Identifiers: LCCN 2024013321 | ISBN 9781531026646 (paperback) | ISBN 9781531026653 (ebook)
Subjects: LCSH: Indians of North America—Legal status, laws, etc.
Classification: LCC KIE110 .E15 2024 | DDC 340.5/27308997—dc23
LC record available at https://lccn.loc.gov/2024013321

Carolina Academic Press, LLC
700 Kent Street
Durham, North Carolina 27701
(919) 489-7486
www.cap-press.com

Printed in the United States of America

This book is dedicated to the future generations of Tribal Nations who have been prayed for and planned for over seven generations. We recognize that our children will carry forth our traditions, lifeways, knowledge, languages, ceremonies, and evolve our laws. For these future generations, we offer this book's words of wisdom and discussions of legal principles as a guide to build upon and as a foundation to grow the knowledge necessary to continue to protect and enjoy Tribal worldviews and ways of living.

With the high rates of foster care and adoption of Native children, Tribal Nations are strengthening Tribal courts and Tribal laws to ensure Native children are protected by Tribal legal systems and placed in homes connecting them to their Tribal families and communities. This generation of Tribal leaders, advocates, lawyers, and judges are devoting efforts to safeguard the futures of their children and grandchildren. We know the profound importance of supporting families, making spaces to heal intergenerational trauma, and the centrality of self-determination for a better and increasingly hopeful future.

CONTENTS

SERIES EDITOR'S FOREWORD

The Carolina Academic Press Mastering Series is designed to provide you with a tool that will enable you to easily and efficiently "master" the substance and content of law school courses. Throughout the series, the focus is on quality writing that makes legal concepts understandable. As a result, the series is designed to be easy to read and is not unduly cluttered with footnotes or cites to secondary sources.

In order to facilitate student mastery of topics, the Mastering Series includes a number of pedagogical features designed to improve learning and retention. At the beginning of each chapter, you will find a "Roadmap" that tells you about the chapter and provides you with a sense of the material that you will cover. "Checkpoints" at the end of each chapter encourages you to stop and review the key concepts, reiterating what you have learned. Throughout the book, key terms are explained and emphasized. Finally, a "Master Checklist" at the end of each book reinforces what you have learned and helps you identify any areas that need review or further study.

We hope that you will enjoy studying with, and learning from, the Mastering Series.

Russell L. Weaver
PROFESSOR OF LAW &
DISTINGUISHED UNIVERSITY SCHOLAR
UNIVERSITY OF LOUISVILLE,
LOUIS D. BRANDEIS SCHOOL OF LAW

ABOUT THE AUTHORS

Angelique EagleWoman (Wambdi A. Was'teWinyan), citizen of the Sisseton-Wahpeton Oyate of the Lake Traverse Reservation, is a law professor, legal scholar, Chief Justice on the Sisseton-Wahpeton Oyate Supreme Court, and serves as an appellate justice in other Tribal Court systems. She has taught in the areas of Indigenous Legal Traditions, Tribal Nation Economics & Law, Native American Law, Native American Natural Resources Law, Contracts, The Business of Law, and Civil Procedure. She presents and publishes on topics involving Tribal-based economics, Indigenous sovereignty, international Indigenous principles, and the quality of life for Indigenous peoples. She has received numerous awards in legal academia and has been a frequent speaker on issues of diversity, inclusion, and professionalism. At the University of Idaho College of Law, she established the Native American Law Emphasis program. She also served as the first Indigenous law dean in Canada. Currently, she is director of the Native American Law and Sovereignty Institute at the Mitchell Hamline School of Law in St. Paul, Minnesota.

Stacy L. Leeds, citizen of the Cherokee Nation, is the Willard H. Pedrick Dean, Regents Professor and Foundation Professor of Law and Leadership at the Sandra Day O'Connor College of Law at Arizona State University. She was the first woman to serve as a Justice on the Cherokee Nation Supreme Court and has also served as a trial and appellate court judge in many other Tribal judiciaries. She was the first Indigenous woman to serve as a law dean in the United States when she was named Dean and Professor of Law at University of Arkansas in 2011. She has taught Property, Native American Law, Energy and Natural Resources, Agricultural Law, Professional Responsibility, Remedies, Business and Economic Development and Cherokee Legal History courses. She was a William H. Hastie Fellow at University of Wisconsin School of Law and directed the Indian Law programs at University of North Dakota and University of Kansas. She presents and publishes on topics involving Indigenous Law and Policy, including nation-(re)building, tribal judiciaries, land restoration and property solutions, Indigenous health and wellness and Indigenous futures.

MASTERING NATIVE AMERICAN LAW

CHAPTER 1

Introduction to Native American Law

ROADMAP

- Understand that Native American Law refers to two bodies of law: law created by Tribal Nations and law created by the U.S. government.
- Understand that Tribal Nations are both the governments of American Indians and Alaska Natives, often referred to as Native Americans and Indigenous peoples.
- Know the legal basis for Tribal membership and federal recognition as a citizen of a Tribal Nation.
- Learn that Tribal governance and laws existed for thousands of years prior to and post contact with Europeans.
- Learn the sources of historical and contemporary Tribal law.
- Learn about the body of federal Indian law and the influences of U.S. Indian policy eras on the legal relationships between Tribal governments and the United States.

The term "Native American law" refers to the law from the governments of both American Indian Tribal Nations and Alaska Native Villages or Tribal Nations. Historical law from these governments is often referred to as Indigenous legal principles, customary law, and traditional law. These laws, principles, and traditions have provided the foundation for Tribal societies to form confederacies and alliances across different languages and cultures. A core principle for

Tribal societies is a kinship worldview that includes a sense of responsibility and interdependence to all living beings. From this kinship worldview, the earth is considered a mother or grandmother and provides natural resources to sustain all life. Tribal peoples in relationship with the earth understand the requirement to reciprocate and not deplete the earth and natural resources.

The terminology used throughout this book reflects proper respect for Tribal Nations by capitalizing the terms: Tribes, Tribal Nations, and "Tribal" when it precedes a noun/entity referring to governance. The term "peoples" is used to reflect the understanding of self-determination for peoples as set forth in the United Nations charter; more on this will be provided in Chapter Ten. The term Indigenous is also capitalized as relating to the Indigenous peoples of North America. As Tribal Nations are nationalities, capitalization is proper for the dignity and recognition of governing bodies that pre-existed the formation of the United States of America.

Throughout this book, the terms Indian, Indigenous, Native, and Native Americans are used, along with Alaska Natives to discuss Tribal Nation citizens. The terms non-Indian, non-Native, White, and Euro-Americans will be used interchangeably to designate those who are lacking Tribal Nation citizen status.

Indigenous legal principles include living values of good faith in commerce, engaging in dispute resolution processes with the support of community, forming kinship alliances lasting for generations, and acting with respect by including all voices in consultation when a decision will have shared consequences. While these values have guided Tribal Nations since time immemorial, which is before living memory, disruption through colonization and military control have required deliberate re-engagement with many traditions, legal principles, norms, and customs. As Tribal peoples reclaim, re-engage, and restore foundational principles and traditions, the health and wellbeing of Tribal communities begins to heal from the genocide and targeted assimilation onslaught experienced through European and Euro-American contact.

The immense legal influence of Tribal Nations on British law, and subsequently the law of the United States and Canada, has been suppressed and erroneously attributed within those governments and societies. Native American legal scholars are presently asserting and correcting the historical record on the Tribal legal influences that have influenced and undergirded the spread of democracy worldwide. Great Britain, a monarchy-based government, entered into alliances and legal treaty agreements adopting gifting and oratory traditions of Tribal leaders to enter into commerce in North America. Interacting with the Haudenosaunee Confederacy, the early British colonists adopted the concept of confederated states to form the new United States of America based on the Tribal model. The field of restorative justice was adapted from the traditional practices of dispute resolution employed for thousands of years in the Western Hemisphere by Tribal peoples. The field of environmental law has been heavily influenced by the Tribal stewardship standards developed and implemented by Tribal governance systems. There is a body of rich scholarship growing as Native Americans document and trace their legal histories and share them in publications and presentations.

In the United States, the term "American Indian" or simply "Indian" refers generally to the Indigenous peoples of mid-North America prior to European arrival and has become common due to its use as a term in federal law. The term "Alaska Native" refers generally to the Indigenous peoples of the northwest in what is now known as the state of Alaska, the forty-ninth state, admitted on January 3, 1959, and includes the cultural groups of Aleut, Athabascan, Cup'ik, Iñupiat, Haida, Tlingit, Yup'ik, and others. Alaska Native Villages are Tribal Nations. This book purposefully adopts "Native American" as inclusive of both those labeled "American Indian" and those labeled "Alaska Native" in the United States legal context.

When referring to an individual Indigenous person, the authors strongly encourage the readers to use specific Tribal Nation names. For example, Professor EagleWoman is a Dakota woman. Her nationality is Sisseton-Wahpeton Oyate of the Lake Traverse, one of the Dakota Tribal Nations. Professor Leeds is a Cherokee woman. Her nationality is Cherokee Nation. They both practice and teach Native American law. Legally, they are both dual citizens of their respective Tribal Nations and of the United States. In addition, the Indigenous peoples of Hawai'i are referred to as "Native Hawaiians" and have been included in U.S. legislation to remedy the overthrow of the Hawaiian monarchy and annexation of the islands of Hawai'i as the fiftieth state of the United States on August 21, 1959. Throughout this book, reference will be made to the term employed from the source being discussed in the legal context.

Native American law encompasses four general categories of laws. First, Tribal Nations enact their own laws and have developed extensive legal materials that are the primary source of law in this field. Tribal law is diverse and includes treaties, agreements, constitutions, statutes and ordinances, caselaw, customary law, and regulations, unique to each Tribal Nation. Like other sovereigns, Tribal Nations have modern laws for current governance purposes as well as historic and traditional laws and cultural norms and standards. For those lawyers representing Tribal Nations, their knowledge must encompass the particular Tribal government's legal history, contemporary Tribal law, and the law developed through interaction with the United States.

Second, the United States has developed a field of "federal Indian law" with an entire section of the United States Code dedicated to the federal statutes enacted in the subject area. Title 25 of the United States Code includes provisions for the Bureau of Indian Affairs and a diversity of subject areas from American Indian and Alaska Native education, health and welfare, to the administration of lands and the environment. Title 25 of the Code of Federal Regulations adds specific details to carry out the provisions of the United States Code. Title 18 of the United States Code contains several provisions for the extension of federal criminal laws over the activities on the lands of Tribal Nations. Federal Indian law also includes federal judicial decisions, federal regulations, and administrative decisions that define and restrict federal powers in Indian affairs, including the federal relationships with and asserted power over Tribes and individual Tribal persons. Some provisions of federal Indian law continue to be in effect from the early laws enacted in the 1790s and throughout the 1800s with lasting repercussions for Tribal governments.

Third, the states within the federal union sometimes enact laws that apply to Indians and Alaska Natives or to the activity of Tribal Nations, but these circumstances are limited and subordinate to federal laws. The federal government, and not the states, is the primary actor in Indian affairs. State powers are commonly invoked only by federal delegation or federal acquiescence. The term "Indian Country" is a legal term codified in the federal criminal statutes in 18 U.S.C. § 1151 since 1948.

Fourth, the international character of the interaction between Tribal Nations and the United States and the European powers precedent to the United States have ongoing relevance to Native American law through the application of international Indigenous legal principles. International legal norms are seeing a resurgence as evidenced from the 2007 adoption of the United Nations Declaration on the Rights of Indigenous Peoples. Once considered an exclusive matter of United States domestic law, modern Tribal Nation advocates have sought relief in international forums and continue to explore international law remedies to challenge the authority of the United States in limiting the exercise of Tribal governance or asserting control over Tribal lands.

In *Mastering Native American Law,* you will be introduced to the primary principles formed from Tribal governance and Tribal interaction prior to and with the United States. With more than 570 federally recognized Tribes, the laws of Tribal Nations will be discussed in summary form and specifics given to highlight certain important characteristics where appropriate. Almost half of the 570 federally recognized Tribal Nations are Alaska Native Tribes. This introductory chapter will introduce you to the U.S. Indian policy eras that provide a structure for comprehending the oscillating policies of federal laws in this field. Use this book as a broad comprehensive resource with the understanding that the law is constantly changing as new laws are adopted, cases are ruled upon by courts, and new agreements are reached refining the relationships between Tribal Nations and other governments.

Introductory Note: Determining Who Is an "Indian" or "Alaska Native" under the Law

In many areas of federal Indian law, the federal courts have distinguished between American Indians and Alaska Natives and non-Indians or non-Natives. There are also distinctions noted between Tribal citizens or members and non-Tribal citizens or members in judicial decisions. One of the characteristics of federal Indian law is that federal court decisions and federal laws often extend the applicability of rulings to all Tribal Nations, even though the legal issues presented in a case are specific to one Tribe. As a result, one court decision can change the law on the subject area (e.g., taxation of goods sold to non-Indians) for all Tribes.

All federally recognized Tribes have Tribal enrollment procedures and criteria for Tribal citizenship. Tribal citizenship, sometimes referred to as Tribal membership, indicates Tribal recognition of the individual by the Tribal Nation. Early interaction between Tribal Nations and U.S. federal officials included the development of Tribal rolls or census by federal officials to establish a federally recognized list of Tribal citizens/members, usually for treaty-guaranteed food rations or for future land allotment under a federal statute or for other federal purposes. The sovereign right of Tribal Nations to determine Tribal citizenship requirements is well-recognized, with the United States Supreme Court opinion of *Santa Clara Pueblo v. Martinez,* 436 U.S. 49 (1978), being the most notable case. Today, Tribal Nations often rely on the early federal rolls to determine ancestry for citizenship applicants and at times to calculate blood quantum based upon such ancestry. The United States government has heavily influenced Tribal identification through these federal documents.

The largest Tribal Nation by population in the United States, the Cherokee Nation, does not require a threshold percentage of Cherokee blood ancestry but does require lineal descendancy from a Cherokee Nation citizen listed on one of the official federal rolls created in the early 1900s. At several times in the 1800s, pursuant to Cherokee legislation, the Cherokee Nation conducted a census of its citizens, and the subsequent federal rolls are informed by but do not mirror, the prior Tribal citizenship census.

Many Tribes have adopted laws and guidelines based on minimum blood quantum such as one-fourth or one-eighth or may calculate all of a person's American Indian or Alaska Native ancestry from various Tribes for Tribal citizenship enrollment purposes. Every Tribal Nation has established specific citizenship criteria under Tribal law. Although some Tribes allow or acquiesce to concurrent citizenship in other Tribes, many Tribal Nations have also followed prior federal guidelines disallowing concurrent citizenship in more than one Tribe. Still other Tribal Nations have established a subset of members through descendant rolls allowing for certain benefits, such as health care with proven descendancy status, usually requiring one biological parent as enrolled or eligible for enrollment. Without Tribal citizenship or membership, a person is not generally recognized as an "Indian" for federal or Tribal purposes.

United States federal Indian law provides recognition of a person as an "Indian" if the person is a Tribal citizen or member. For limited federal purposes such as access to some federal benefits, a person is considered "Indian" or "Alaska Native" by a blood quantum standard of one-fourth degree or more of Indian blood as calculated by federal rolls. For example, the Code of Federal Regulations includes this standard in the following regulations: 25 C.F.R. §§ 26.1, 36.3, and 39.2. This federal criterion applies for some services, such as higher education grants under the U.S. Department of Interior's Bureau of Indian Education. In addition, the Bureau of Indian Affairs, upon request by an American Indian or Alaska Native, may issue a certificate of degree of Indian blood (CDIB) as federal documentation. American Indians and Alaska Natives are the only people in the United States who are federally required to prove identity in such a manner. The best practice is to rely on the Tribal Nation to determine whether a person is eligible for Tribal citizenship or membership. It is common for Tribal constitutions and statutes to provide the eligibility for membership for each Tribal Nation.

Grand Portage Pow Wow. Photo credit: Angelique EagleWoman.

Based on the government-to-government relationship between the Tribal Nations and the United States, Tribal citizens have a political status in U.S. law. For example, the U.S. federal agencies on civil rights in employment exempts the federal "Indian preference" standard implemented in the federal Bureau of Indian Affairs, 25 U.S.C. §§ 5116 and 5117, and required by private employers in close proximity to Tribal reservations or communities. The federal policies of supporting Tribal economic development, Tribal education, and healthcare are formed through the treaty relationship and extend to all Tribal Nations and Tribal citizens.

As in other areas of federal Indian law, there exist contradictions in policies with the U.S. census and other federal agencies including "American Indian/

Alaska Native" as a racial classification and not requiring identification of Tribal citizenship as a political status. This blurring of the Tribal Nation sovereign determination of Tribal membership by various federal and state actors has caused confusion and uneven application of the political relationship between Tribal citizens and the United States and its component state governments. This ongoing issue of asserting the political relationship requires Tribal governments and Tribal citizens to shoulder the burden of educating and enforcing some federal laws and elements of the political status of Tribal citizens. Often American Indians and Alaska Natives are lumped into racial categories by mainstream media and institutions in the United States that are contrary to the actual political and national status of such persons. There is harm from being considered as within a racial category as this type of classification undermines the treaty/political relationship of Tribal Nations with the U.S.

A. Tribal Law

For Tribal Nations, laws have been in place since time immemorial to govern internal Tribal relations, external relations, commercial activities, and all spheres of interaction between Tribal citizens and the world at large. Many of these legal systems include moral obligations and a sense of community balance through dispute resolution principles. Tribal laws, for the most part, were transmitted through oral narratives and the use of symbols to demonstrate complex societal relationships and guidelines. Segments of Tribal society served as the law enforcers in Tribal communities via clan systems. Leadership required dedication to the Tribal laws and many Tribes also embraced a spiritual set of laws known as "natural law." These Indigenous legal traditions are being revitalized in many Tribal Nations as more Native American lawyers engage in the revision and updating of Tribal codes or serve in the capacity of Tribal judges. In Tribal communities, Native American law is the law created through Tribal statutes, regulations, judicial decisions, agency determinations, and traditional customs by the Tribes themselves.

In contemporary times, Tribes generally have prioritized written laws, constitutional governmental forms, and judicial systems partially modeled after the United States. The transition to a hybrid U.S. governmental model largely resulted from U.S. Indian policy in the late 1930s intended to reorganize Tribal governments. Many communities see adaptation as a means of obtaining external recognition of Tribal sovereignty. Size, location, and resources of Tribes have informed the type of governmental structure implemented, along with the methods of law creation, implementation, enforcement, and judicial determinations about Tribal law. For example, smaller Tribes may have fewer formal processes and forums in place. A centralized forum to handle a multiplicity of legal issues would be all that is required in that instance. Larger Tribes may have extensive judicial and administrative adjudicative forums providing specialized attention to categories of legal issues. Tribal governments run the spectrum from traditional clan-based systems dating back thousands of years to adapted constitutional-based governments similar to the three-branch U.S. structure with executive, legislative, and judicial branches.

In whatever fashion Tribal governments are structured, all have written laws and dispute resolution mechanisms. The Tribal governance side of Native American law takes the form comparable to other common law jurisdictions where written laws are interpreted by those performing judicial decision-making functions. Every society has a general sense of moral obligations, social behavior, and commercial interactions that influence and reside in the laws of the citizenry. Tribal governments have the ability to draw upon millennium-old lifeways handed down through oral traditions and symbol knowledge to enhance written Tribal laws. Codification of Tribal laws often developed through careful consideration of neighboring Tribes' general laws. In certain regions of the country, Tribal written laws may bear heavy resemblances amongst neighboring Tribes. As a general rule, each Tribe has its own specific laws and judicial opinions that require research for competent representation involving a Tribal legal matter.

Tribal codified laws also reflect an interaction with federal Indian law. As new federal policies are implemented nationally, particular provisions may relate to Tribes. In response, Tribal leadership often codifies new laws to meet the new national policy. Thus, Tribal law is fluid and part of the ongoing relationship with the United States of America. With the growing body of international Indigenous law, some Tribal Nations are also embedding collective human rights and other legal standards into their domestic laws. Tribal law is also responsive to regional and local Tribal societal initiatives and concerns. For example, in recent years, many Tribal legislatures have passed legislation implementing domestic violence and elder abuse codes to address such issues arising in Tribal communities. Another recent area of codifying Tribal law is recognition of same-sex marriage as a societal tradition and contemporary legal relationship. Also, as commercial activity becomes more complex in

Tribal communities, Tribal legislatures have enacted laws to structure business entities and handle commercial disputes.

Similarly, Tribal judicial opinions originate within an existing body of law and are influenced by the decisions in other jurisdictions. In common law practice, prior court opinions have substantial bearing on the resolution of present disputes. In most Tribal court systems, the order of precedential value given to prior decisions generally follows this hierarchy: (1) prior decisions of the same Tribal court and the related Tribal appellate courts, (2) decisions from other Tribal court systems, (3) decisions from the U.S. federal court systems, and (4) decisions from U.S. state courts. This order may vary depending upon the substantive matter before the court, particularly in legal matters where Tribal and state laws are very similar. For example, some Tribes have adopted the same provisions of the Uniform Commercial Code (UCC) as the surrounding state and refer to state law decisions for Tribal court dispute resolution involving UCC issues to provide certainty for business activities.

Tribal administrative law is derived from the processes for regulation under specific Tribal agencies. There are a wide-ranging number of administrative agencies that may exist within any one Tribal government. A non-exclusive list of administrative agency dispute resolution processes at the Tribal level may include: personnel action review boards, gaming commission hearings, tax commission review hearings, zoning commission review boards, election commission hearings, enrollment review boards, and others. Specific Tribal agency regulations and Tribal laws dictate whether administrative agency decisions are reviewable in the Tribal judicial system.

In general, Tribal law stems from three primary sources: (1) Tribal statutes, (2) Tribal judicial opinions, and (3) Tribal agency determinations. A fourth category of Tribal custom and tradition may exist in legal matters pertaining to families and domestic concerns and other internal matters relating to areas of life formerly governed by Indigenous legal traditions. This fourth category may require practitioners to become familiar with elders and expert witnesses knowledgeable in the forum's region on such traditional principles and matters. The primary sources of Tribal law inform the majority of Tribal litigation in judicial and administrative forums. Due to the close relationship between U.S. Indian policy and Tribal governments, the majority of Tribes are heavily influenced by the U.S. example of statutory, administrative, and judicial lawmaking.

B. U.S. Federal Indian Law

As European nations established trade relations in North America, the British established permanent settlements as colonies along the eastern seaboard. The colonies declared their independence from Britain and formed the United States of America in 1776. The field of federal Indian law traces its roots to the trading relations Tribes developed with Great Britain and then to the new nation, the United States. As mentioned previously, the framers of the United States government were heavily influenced by the confederacy model of Tribal governments along the eastern seaboard. The democratic and consensus-building norms of Tribal governance along with the concept of the servant leader chosen by and for the people were adapted by the British colonists in forming their new governance structure.

With the formation of the U.S. as a constitution-based government, the U.S. Congress was designated as the authority to manage Indian affairs for the new republic. This was an area of concern as land speculation by the Euro-Americans was rampant and the formation of other new governments was a threat as well as individual states seeking relations with Tribal Nations. In article 1, section eight, clause three of the U.S. Constitution, the U.S. Congress was granted the authority "To regulate Commerce with foreign Nations, and among the several States, and with the Indian Tribes." In the field of federal Indian law, this section of the Constitution is commonly referred to as the "Indian Commerce Clause." The U.S. Constitution adopted in 1787 also included a brief reference to "Indians not taxed" for apportionment purposes, noting that Indians were citizens of their Tribal Nations and were not to be counted as persons within the body politic of the surrounding state. Throughout the history of the United States, distinct policy eras in Indian affairs have provided context for federal statutes and judicial decision-making.

1. U.S. Indian Policy Eras

United States Indian policy has been described as resembling a "wave machine" and a "pendulum," as the policy goals appear to swing between two opposite policy stances. In the early phase of the United States federal government, the foreign policy of Great Britain toward Tribal Nations was followed through treaty-making with neighboring Tribes to gain military and trade alliances and access to Tribal territories. The Royal Proclamation of 1763 and the Treaty of Niagara in 1764 are examples of British policies and promises to stop encroachment on Tribal lands and recognition of alliance with Tribal Nations. From this foundation of interaction with Tribal Nations, seven major policy eras have formed federal Indian law since the establishment of the United States.

These United States policy eras can be summarized historically as: (1) sovereign-to-sovereign relationships (1778 to mid-1800s); (2) removal era (1800s); (3) reservation era (overlaps partially with removal era, 1800s); (4) allotment/assimilation era (late 1800s to early 1900s); (5) Indian self-government (1930s to 1940s); (6) termination era (1940s to 1960s); and (7) Indian self-determination (late-1960s to present). Using the policy eras as the context for understanding the (at times contradictory) laws and court opinions in federal Indian law provides a key to studying this field of law. The pendulum swing from acknowledging or supporting Tribal governance is evident in the following policy eras: sovereign-to-sovereign relationships; reservation era; Indian self-government era; and Indian self-determination/present policy. The federal laws and court cases during these policy eras tend to acknowledge and, at times, actively support Tribal governance, including the recognition of Tribal sovereignty and appreciation of local governance as the effective and preferred approach. There were outlying instances in every policy era. The opposing pendulum swing to the detriment of Tribal government is apparent in the remaining policy eras: removal era; allotment/assimilation era; and termination era. These policy eras are shaped by some of the most detrimental federal laws and court decisions continuing to impact Tribal peoples in the United States. It is upon this changing landscape that the permutations of federal Indian law have developed over time.

It is important to note that, in recent years, scholars and advocates for Tribal sovereignty are increasingly critical of the role of the federal courts, particularly the United States Supreme Court, for a trend in judicial decisions that narrow the scope of recognized Tribal jurisdiction. In response to judicial decisions, the U.S. Congress has stepped in several times to restore the prior definitions of recognized Tribal governmental power. This illustrates that U.S. policy periods are fluid and represent generalized trends, but that not all three branches of the United States government subscribe to similar policies at the same time. In other periods, the U.S. Congress and the Executive branches have tried to curtail Tribal rights while the federal courts contemporaneously upheld inherent Tribal rights. The onus is often on Tribal Nations to hold the United States and all of its components to the legal standards of a treaty partner and trustee exercising good faith.

a. Sovereign-to-Sovereign Relationships (1778 to mid-1800s)

As mentioned previously, United States Indian policy traces its roots to Great Britain and the international practice of treaty-making between Europeans and Tribal Nations in North America. Great Britain entered into several treaties with Tribal Nations prior to the Revolutionary War. The first treaty concluded by the United States was with the Delaware Nation in 1778, which guaranteed perpetual peace and friendship and representation in the U.S. Congress. Subsequently, these provisions were violated by the U.S. with the seizure of Delaware Nation lands and forced removal of the Tribe to what became the state of Oklahoma. This example was all too common for Tribal Nations responding to the requests of U.S. officials to enter into legal treaty agreements of alliance and sharing of Tribal lands. The total number of treaties entered into with Tribal Nations exceeds the 400 mark. One of the most comprehensive online digital collections of Tribal Nation treaties is *Indian Affairs: Laws and Treaties,* compiled and edited by Charles J. Kappler (Washington: Government Printing Office, 1904, hosted by the Oklahoma State University Library Electronic Publishing Center).

Within the U.S. Constitution, articles I and II grant the U.S. President and the Congress authority to declare war and enter into treaties. The Supremacy Clause contained in article VI, clause two, states that treaties are part of the supreme law of the land. The sovereign-to-sovereign policy era provides context for the frequent treaty-making occurring between the United States and Tribal Nations up until 1871. In that year, the U.S. House of Representatives passed a rider on an appropriations bill meant to curtail the authority of the Senate to approve further treaty-making with Tribes. The U.S. Congress did not have the authority to revise the constitutional power of treaty-making but did signal that future funding for treaties with Tribal Nations would face opposition. From 1871 forward, the federal government continued to negotiate with Tribes through executive orders and formal agreements, but no longer labeled them as "treaties." The United States continued the practice of negotiating legal agreements with Tribal Nations in the same manner as they had previously negotiated treaties well into the 1900s, but the treaties on return to Washington D.C. were then presented to the House and Senate and produced "legislation" rather than "ratified treaties." During the legislative process, the terms of the treaties/agreements were often altered without the consent of the Tribe and the Tribes had no legal remedy to challenge the change. It was during this time that the federal courts first upheld the right of the U.S. Congress to unilaterally violate the terms of express prior treaty provisions.

The more than one-hundred-year practice of entry into treaties between Tribal Nations and the United States involved separate governmental objectives on each side of the treaty. Interpretation of treaties requires discerning the mutual understanding reached within the concluded document. United States representatives in regional areas often formulated template treaty documents for land purchases, referred to as "land cessions," and then added specific language depending on the negotiations with the local Tribal leaders.

A primary motivation for the United States was to secure land cessions from the Tribal Nations to build a permanent presence in North America to the exclusion of other governments from Europe. Tribal leadership commonly negotiated treaty agreements from a kinship perspective by granting territorial rights to allow for nearby United States settlement while maintaining homeland guarantees and access to resources for Tribal peoples. The kinship perspective embodied a belief in taking the United States citizens as relatives and employing familial terms to the negotiation process in furtherance of alliance building. These two divergent perspectives continue to impact the significance of treaty documents between Tribal Nations and the United States.

Much has been written on the uneven balance of power through these treaty negotiations due to the template format, the documents written in the English language using legal terminology, the false promises made to obtain signatures, or the failure to obtain valid consent from legitimate Tribal leadership. In addition, many treaties sent to the U.S. Senate for approval were unilaterally modified without the knowledge of the Tribal leadership and approved contrary to the terms consented to. These circumstances surrounding the treaty documents have resulted in special interpretive tools applied by the U.S. judiciary for construing treaty terms. The federal Indian law "canons of construction" apply to treaty documents and require the following: (1) treaties are to be construed as the Indians would have understood them, (2) any ambiguities are to be construed in favor of the Indian understanding of the treaty document, and (3) all powers and rights are reserved to a Tribe unless expressly relinquished in a treaty document. These interpretative tools have been expanded to also apply to federal statutes and regulations enacted on specifically Native American matters.

The reserved lands of a Tribe are commonly referred to as the Tribal reservation. Reservations were formally acknowledged in U.S. law through treaties, executive orders, or formal agreements. Tribal territories are often much larger than the current size of the boundaries forming the Tribal reservations. Many Tribal Nations reserved off-reservation access to customary fishing locations, hunting territories, and harvesting places that remain in force today. The totality of Tribal land holdings and territorial boundaries are referred to as "Indian Country," a legal term of art. A more extensive discussion of Tribal property is provided in Chapter Two: "Native American Property Law."

In conclusion, the treaty negotiation was the basis of interaction founding the current relationships between Tribal Nations and the United States. In the treaty negotiation process, the U.S. representatives sought out Tribal Nation leadership and engaged in Tribal customs of gift giving and concluding the exchange of promises with ceremonial acknowledgment. Upon this foundation have been added hundreds of additional agreements between Tribes and the United States, a variety of federal laws, and many federal regulations involving these relationships. A common feature of the treaty-making foundation is the pledge of alliance and protection from both Tribal and federal leadership.

Treaties, formal agreements, compacts, and contracts continue to have vitality in the field of federal Indian law and Tribal Nation law. These are the primary sources for resolving legal issues between Tribal Nations and the United States. The first step in analyzing a cross-governmental issue involving a Tribal Nation and the U.S. federal or state governments is to review relevant treaties, agreements, or other negotiated instruments.

b. Removal Era (1800s)

Following the treaty-making of the sovereign-to-sovereign era, White/ Euro-American settlers began encroaching into tribally reserved territories and homelands. U.S. political voices of the time called for removal of all Tribal Nations from the eastern seaboard to beyond the Appalachian mountain range into lands west of the Mississippi River. Under the administration of U.S. President Andrew Jackson, the official policy of the United States government was to remove all Tribes to the West. This policy was memorialized by Congress in the Indian Removal Act of May 28, 1830, 4 Stat. 411. While this Act was merely a policy statement and had no self-executing power, the law outlined a voluntary removal policy for Tribes that would exchange their homelands for western lands. As pressure mounted, the policy was ultimately implemented by the United States military with forced removal marches of men, women, and children where thousands died as they were marched hundreds of miles without adequate food, water, or protection from the elements to new territories.

The Cherokee Nation removal story is well-known as most Tribes endured forced or coerced removal and relocation, and some Tribes experienced this more than once. The Cherokee Nation resisted local, state, and federal government actions seeking their removal from homelands by strengthening their own institutions and seeking remedies in the federal courts. In the 1835 Treaty of New Echota, the federal government obtained signatures from a delegation of Cherokee persons, although not the duly-elected Cherokee officials, exchanging the Cherokee homelands for a new territory and a promise of perpetual recognition of self-governance within the new Cherokee Nation in Indian Territory, now present-day Oklahoma. Although this proposal was rejected by the elected Cherokee Nation leadership, the treaty was enforced by United States military pressure. The Cherokee leadership ultimately obtained federal agreement that the Cherokee Nation would oversee their own removal in 1838 and 1839 as a means of mitigating the death toll. Still, it is estimated that one-quarter of the 16,000 removed Cherokee persons died on the removal known as the Cherokee Trail of Tears. Several other Tribal Nations in the South endured a forced military march, including the Seminole, Muscogee (Creek), Chickasaw, and Choctaw Nations.

Numerous Tribal Nations were impacted by the removal policy from the northern Tribal Nations, such as the Seneca, Onondaga, Tuscarora, Cayuga, Mohawk, Oneida, Potawatomi, Shawnee, and many others. The Potawatomi removal has become known as the Trail of Death along the route from present-day Indiana and Illinois to reservations in present-day Kansas and Oklahoma. The removal routes are recalled in oral and written Tribal histories. A single Tribal Nation may have splintered into several different governments with the federal government dictating and effectuating the separations. From these histories, a series of Tribal governments have formed for certain formerly consolidated Tribal Nations. For almost every forced Tribal removal, a group remained behind in the homelands and some eventually did receive formal federal recognition as independent Tribal Nations.

Wars of resistance to removal efforts were fought during the 1800s by many Tribal Nations, often lacking the metal weapons and numbers of the U.S. military forces they faced. Between 1866 and 1891, more than 1,000 battles were fought between Tribal Nations and the United States military. When the U.S. military attacked peaceful settlements of unarmed men, women, and children, the resulting mass killings have been labeled massacres by historians. Examples of such massacres, include the Whitestone Hill Massacre on September 5, 1863, where an estimated 300–400 Dakota and Lakota (referred to by the U.S. as "Sioux") men, women, and children were killed after surrendering under a white flour sack and the military proceeding to burn 300 tipis and the winter supply of buffalo meat estimated at 400,000 pounds near present-day Kulm,

North Dakota; the Sand Creek Massacre where Cheyenne and Arapaho men, women, and children were slaughtered under a flag of truce on November 29, 1864; and the Wounded Knee Massacre of December 29, 1890, where more than 300 unarmed men, women, and children on their way to the Pine Ridge Reservation to seek protection were gunned down by the U.S. cavalry and later heaped into a mass grave. A leading historical text on many of the U.S. military campaigns and wars of Tribal resistance is Dee Brown's *Bury My Heart at Wounded Knee: An Indian History of the American West* (Henry Holt and Company 1970).

c. Reservation Era (1800s)

Overlapping with the Removal Era was the Reservation Era of U.S. Indian policy. The Reservation Era is treated as a separate policy era due to the extensive redefining of Tribal property boundaries and relationships with the Euro-Americans. During this era, the Bureau of Indian Affairs (BIA) was created in 1824 in the Department of War to administer the 1819 Indian Civilization Fund Act targeting Tribal children and acting to force Tribal leadership to agree to removal, sell of, and allotment of Tribal homelands. In 1849, the BIA was relocated from the Department of War to the Department of the Interior. The BIA, following federal policy, sought to impose control over Native Americans through federal Indian agents located within Tribal territories. The lands reserved under treaty and formal agreements known as reservations for Tribal peoples had exact boundaries established during this era. From the U.S. policy perspective, separation between Native and White communities was accomplished through the reservation policy. From the Tribal Nations' perspectives, stability and re-structuring opportunities were viewed as the benefits of the reservation era, sometimes after removal and/or wars of resistance had been fought with the United States. The choices facing Tribal leaders during the 1800s were often difficult in seeking peaceful lives for Tribal citizens.

Many Tribal Nations, when relocated to completely new geographical locations, became immediately dependent on treaty-guaranteed food and equipment provisions. The BIA was the federal agency charged with carrying out the treaty responsibilities of the U.S. government, such as providing the food rations, farming implements, cloth, and other goods agreed upon in the exchanges between Tribes and federal officials. During this time period, the leadership in the BIA began forming a comprehensive agenda to control and re-orient Native Americans into Euro-American norms. Supported by Euro-American theories of superiority and civilization, federal policy started to shift from the idea of neighboring communities to fundamental resocialization of Native people, particularly aimed at Native children as young as four or five years old.

d. Allotment/Assimilation Era (late 1800s to early 1900s)

The devastation and trauma to Tribal communities during the Allotment/Assimilation Era cannot be overstated. Through corresponding goals of breaking up Tribal land bases and re-socializing Tribal citizens to follow Euro-American Christian norms as farmers, the U.S. implemented policies in violation of treaties, formal agreements, and promises made to Tribal leaders. In fact, these policies are more properly characterized as genocidal and human rights violations, especially in regard to the abuse of Tribal children that occurred under the supervision of the U.S. government. With Indian agents on reservations dictating food rations and controlling monetary payments under treaties and agreements, the BIA began to implement a policy of social experimentation to convert Native people into the mold of White Christian farmers. This policy era would be characterized in contemporary terms as intergenerational trauma through the experience in Tribal communities of egregious human rights violations and genocidal actions aimed at destroying the very existence of Tribal Nations and Tribal lifeways, spirituality, language, and family.

In 1883, the federal Indian Commissioner established the Courts of Indian Offenses as mechanisms that served, at best, for peace and order in Tribal territories and at worst, as means to punish the expression of Tribal practices and customs or resistance to the taking of Tribal children by their parents. In *U.S. v. Clapox,* 35 F. 575 (1888), the federal district court in Oregon held that those who had rescued a fellow Tribal member, Minnie, from the jails of the local Indian agent had violated federal law. Although Minnie was being held on a charge of adultery not listed as any offense under federal statute or the regulations for the Court of Indian Offenses, the federal judge broadly read the treaty with the Umatilla Tribe to allow for the U.S. to punish any behavior categorized as a crime on the reservation. 35 F. at 576–77. Further, the federal judge distinguished the Courts of Indian Offenses from the U.S. courts established under the authority of the U.S. Constitution in article III, section 1. Rather, the court's opinion characterized the Courts of Indian Offenses as: "mere educational and disciplinary instrumentalities, by which the government of the United States is endeavoring to improve and elevate the condition of these dependent tribes to whom it sustains the relation of guardian. In fact, the reservation itself is in the nature of a school, and the Indians are gathered there, under the charge of an agent, for the purpose of acquiring the habits, ideas, and aspirations that distinguish the civilized from the uncivilized man." 35 F. at 577. With no limitations on the discretionary authority of U.S. Indian agents, Native American adults were punished for all manner of Tribal activities from participating in spiritual ceremonies to wearing their hair long as a cultural practice to refusing to allow their children to be taken to the government-endorsed boarding schools known for child abuse.

In the late 1800s, the official agenda of BIA leadership was to assimilate Native people into "White civilization." The quickest path to re-socialization of Native Americans was determined to be the mass kidnapping of Native children and forced attendance in military-style governmental and religious boarding schools. There have been many accounts of heartbroken parents having their crying children, usually four- to eight-year-olds, seized from their homes and sent long distances to experience often physically, mentally, emotionally, and sexually abusive conditions. Other accounts include parental consent to send children to boarding schools on the hopelessness and resignation that this choice would be the only way that children would survive with adequate food or make a good life for themselves.

In many Tribal communities, at least four generations of children grew up under the brutal conditions of mandatory boarding school education where they were punished for speaking their languages, for failing to immediately respond to English commands, and for trying to assist other younger children being punished and/or abused at the hands of governmental officials, nuns, priests, and other religious leaders. Members of this generation have described the ultimate consequences of the government-endorsed boarding schools as: disruption of family structures, loss of language, an epidemic of alcoholism and drug abuse in Indian Country, intergenerational abuse toward children, and a sense of isolation from both Native and White communities that led in many instances to high rates of suicide. Unfortunately, some states, like South Dakota, have passed legislation imposing a statute of limitations on child abuse court filings to prohibit the survivors of the Indian boarding schools from bringing lawsuits to provide some remedial measures for the abuse suffered at these so-called educational institutions.

In addition to the social experimentation on Native American peoples individually, formal U.S. Indian policy increasingly focused on breaking up the Tribal land base. The United States deemed preserving the Tribal land base as unworkable, citing communal ownership and the application of Tribal property law concepts as an impediment to the goal of "civilizing" Tribal Nations. A catalyst to these federal policies was Henry Dawes from Massachusetts. As a member of Congress, Dawes introduced a rider on a federal appropriations bill in 1871 to end the funding of any further treaty-making with Tribal Nations. After that date, the U.S. continued to enter into formal agreements and recognize reservations through federal legislation and the executive authority of the U.S. president. As a Senator, Henry Dawes secured a position on the Senate Indian Affairs Committee and sponsored federal legislation to parcel out the communal Tribal land bases to individual Tribal citizens and return the "surplus" lands to the public domain, thereby "freeing up" Tribal lands for continued White settlement. In this process, Tribal Nations have not been compensated for the removal of collective lands into individual allotments. This legislation was formerly titled the General Allotment Act of 1887, 25 U.S.C. § 331 subsequently repealed in 1934, and is commonly referred to as the Dawes Act.

One of the processes established through implementation of the Dawes Act was the drawing up by federal officials of formal Tribal rolls to determine who would be entitled to a parcel of land—an allotment. The U.S. government asserted the authority of trustee over allotments and Tribal lands during this time period. The federally created Tribal rolls would have a lasting impact on designating those who were counted as citizens of a Tribal Nation. Mistakes made in the process were memorialized in the federal rolls and would impact all descendants of that Tribal member, family, or group. Anecdotal accounts of U.S. Indian agents purposefully excluding "troublesome" Tribal citizens from the rolls exists. In contrast, there was significant Tribal opposition to allotment and times when resisters refused to present themselves for "enrollment" to accept an allotment, some resisters were jailed, and their names were added to the rolls without their consent to the process. Tribal peoples were also renamed by U.S. Indian agents with either English interpretations of their names or wholly renamed in the process by federal officials. In the next time period, the federal Tribal membership rolls became further solidified as the starting point for Tribal citizenship when written into Tribal constitutions.

Another extension of federal authority over Tribal citizens was embodied in the Indian Citizenship Act of 1924, 43 Stat. 253, Act of June 2, 1924, where U.S. citizenship was extended over all Tribal peoples that had not already been defined as United States citizens in treaties or other agreements, whether consent to United States citizenship was obtained or not. Some Tribal allotment processes combined U.S. citizenship with the acceptance of the allotment. The newly created U.S. citizenship did not stamp out preexisting Tribal citizenship, but merely gave rise to dual citizenship in the United States and specific Tribal Nations. Some Tribes and individuals continue to reject the concept of unilateral imposition of U.S. citizenship as lacking the requisite consent to be governed. Through this federal law, American Indians and Alaska Natives born in the United States have U.S. citizenship by birth but must apply for Tribal Nation citizenship and meet the criteria approved under Tribal and federal law.

With completion of the Tribal rolls, the process of allotment differed among Tribal Nations. In some cases, U.S. Indian agents either selected an allotment within the reservation boundaries or requested the Tribal member select an allotment. For example, a Tribal member may have selected an allotment where family members had been laid to rest to prevent the family cemetery land from leaving the family. As the family cemetery area, the Tribal member would then flout the wishes of the agent by refusing to till the land for farming purposes. Accounts exist of the best farming lands being excluded from the available areas Tribal members were allowed to pick from. The practical results of the allotment policy were the allotment of the Tribal lands to private ownership without regard to prior property laws or norms; the transfer of the unallotted lands, labeled "surplus" lands by the U.S. Indian agent, to the U.S. government at a price it set; destruction of the seasonal harvesting and rotation within the Tribal territory due to the private property boundaries from allotments; influx of White settlers into the Tribal territory through purchasing title from the U.S. government; and the loss of more than 27 million acres.

Between 1887 and 1934, the Tribal lands of 118 reservations were allotted, although many reservations, particularly in the Southwest, escaped allotment due to tribally specific circumstances. From 1887 to 1900, the U.S. government approved 53,168 allotments, totaling nearly 5 million acres, and almost 36 million acres were allotted by 1920. By 1934, approximately 27 million acres, or two-thirds of all the land allotted to Tribal members, had passed by sale or involuntary transfer from the American Indian fee owner into non-Indian ownership. See *Cohen's Handbook of Federal Indian Law*, 16.03[2][b] (Lexis Nexis 2012 edition). Further, the 1906 Burke Act provided the means for the local U.S. Indian agent to determine the allottee owner "competent" resulting in the removal of tax exemption or limitation on sale of the land that resulted in the loss of almost 60 million additional Tribal lands. In sum, an estimated 90 million acres of Tribal land were lost in the allotment scheme created by U.S. legislation.

Without the Tribal territory as a resource for harvesting, fishing, and hunting, some Tribal Nations became impoverished in a short amount of time and completely dependent on federal food rations for survival. Furthermore, the loss of lands within reservation borders and Tribal territories has significantly altered recognized Tribal jurisdiction and Tribal management of the homelands reserved by Tribal Nations for the continued livelihood of Tribal citizens. Often, sacred sites, cemeteries, and spiritual locations were taken from Tribal stewardship under allotment policies. The allotment process did not provide for a long-term sustainable homeland for Tribes. To the contrary, proponents of the allotment policy asserted their intentions were to facilitate the end for Tribal Nations with Tribal citizens eventually becoming assimilated U.S. citizens with no distinct sovereignty or distinct territory over which to exercise Tribal government powers. The survival of Tribal peoples has been characterized by the traits of resilience, fortitude, and grit in the face of these U.S. policies and actions.

The dire poverty experienced by the majority of Tribes during this period gained federal attention by the 1920s. In response to the conditions on Indian reservations, Secretary of the Interior Hubert Work requested that Lewis Meriam preside over a committee to report on the conditions in Indian Country. Commonly known as the Meriam Report, the findings submitted to Secretary Work on Feb. 21, 1928, described a depressing state of impoverishment for Native Americans. In Chapter One of the report, the first sentence stated: "An overwhelming majority of the Indians are poor, even extremely poor, and they are not adjusted to the economic and social system of the dominant white civilization." The Meriam Report also identified the federal government's past policies toward Tribal peoples as largely creating the poverty conditions described.

e. Indian Self-Government Era (1930s to 1940s)

Following the Meriam Report, federal Indian policy again shifted with key federal officials in the Department of the Interior seeking to include Native Americans into the New Deal policies of the 1930s. With Indian Commissioner John Collier advocating for federal legislation to halt the allotment process and provide for re-structuring of Tribal governments, the new policy era of Indian self-government was embodied in the Indian Reorganization Act (IRA) of 1934, 25 U.S.C. §§ 5101–5125, 5129, recodified in 1990 from former 25 U.S.C. §§ 461–479. The details of Collier's legislative proposal and the eventual enactment of the compromise IRA by Congress are carefully set forth in Vine Deloria, Jr. and Clifford M. Lytle's book, *The Nations Within: The Past and Future of American Indian Sovereignty* (University of Texas Press 1998).

Several significant features of the IRA changed the political and economic landscape for Tribal Nations. The first provision of the IRA ended the policy of allotment for American Indian lands. 25 U.S.C. § 5101. The second provision indefinitely extended the trust status of Tribal Nation and individual Tribal member lands held by the U.S. government as trustee. 25 U.S.C. § 5102. With the trust status extended and allotment halted, the IRA also provided for the restoration of lands to Tribal ownership and purchase by the Secretary of lands for the benefit of Indians. 25 U.S.C. §§ 5103, 5104. Under the IRA, the Secretary of the Interior was granted the authority to establish new Indian reservations and to add lands to existing reservations. 25 U.S.C.§ 5110.

Other key provisions focused on the reorganization of Tribal government loosely modeled on the U.S. three-branch system under a constitution. The IRA provided that Tribes were allowed to organize under a Tribal constitution as approved by the Secretary of the Interior. 25 U.S.C. § 5123(a). The U.S. Indian agents circulated templates of Tribal constitutions for adoption by Tribal citizens. The boilerplate constitutions enshrined the standard of Tribal membership as based upon the federal Tribal rolls with blood quantum requirements for all future members. Often these constitutions contained limits on Tribal governmental authority by requiring the U.S. Secretary of the Interior to approve of Tribal laws or constitutional amendments before funding would be released from the U.S. Treasury accounts of the Tribes. On the positive side, the Tribal constitutions authorized tribally elected officials to oversee local Tribal affairs and resources of the Tribal Nations, reducing the power of the U.S. Indian agents over Tribal resources and returning some decision-making back to elected Tribal leaders.

With federal recognition of Tribal government authority, the Tribal Nations were also empowered under the IRA to establish corporate charters under federal law to manage Tribal economic operations. 25 U.S.C. § 5124. This shift in federal Indian policy signaled a return to the commercial interaction of historic times between Tribal Nations and the United States. To further the economic rebuilding of Tribal commerce, the IRA instituted a Tribal revolving loan fund for Indian chartered corporations. 25 U.S.C. § 5112. However, at this point in history, the United States had established itself as the trustee over Tribal resources, and thereby limited the negotiating, contracting, or maximizing of Tribal commercial activity.

In spite of the intergenerational poverty of Tribal communities, hundreds of Tribal Nations reorganized under federally approved Tribal constitutions. Those who rejected the IRA constitutions also benefited from the federal policy shift in reestablishing economic activity and greater control over the future of Tribal communities. As the tides turned and Tribal governments regained some of their former strength, moderate economic activity began to return on a foundational level for a significant number of Tribal communities. Native law scholars have opined that as Tribal Nations re-establish economic strength and exercise sovereignty a backlash from political opponents has led to a negative pendulum swing in the U.S. to undermine Tribal governance and authority.

f. Termination of Federal Status Era (1940s to 1960s)

As Tribal communities began to pursue economic development under the IRA incentives, anti-Tribal forces sought to prevent and hinder the progress of Tribal governmental authority; end the separate landholdings of Tribal government and citizens; and assert state jurisdiction over Tribal territories. Representing state interests in the federal government, U.S. Congress members responded to these political forces by stating the official federal Indian policy as terminating federal recognition of certain Tribal Nations and placing Tribal citizens exclusively under the laws of the United States with House Resolution No. 108, 83rd Congress (August 1, 1953). Under the termination policy, approximately 120 Tribal Nations were terminated from federal recognition. Tribal lands were auctioned off or parceled out, losing their Tribal character under federal law. Resources and assets were sold with payments divided between those on the Tribal rolls. Termination of federal recognition disqualified Tribal citizens from receiving treaty-guaranteed services in health, education, or training programs.

This policy era galvanized Tribal leadership nationally to establish formal associations to address federal policymakers and voice Tribal perspectives on legislation directed their way. The National Congress of American Indians (NCAI) was founded in 1944 and regional Tribal leadership organizations emerged across the country. The termination era was diametrically opposed to the prior era of Indian self-government. Instead of negotiating with Tribal Nations under federal Indian policy, the U.S. policy had switched to refusing to recognize the existence of specific Tribal Nations as governments with citizens and authority over territories.

Programs implemented to hasten the termination policy included the urban relocation program and the delegation of federal criminal jurisdiction to states in Indian Country. The 1952 Urban Indian Relocation Program brought hundreds of Native Americans from rural reservation communities to heavily populated, industrialized major cities in the United States. The program initially promised relocatees temporary housing, guidance, and job counseling by the BIA in seven cities: Chicago, Denver, Los Angeles, San Francisco, San Jose, St. Louis, Cincinnati, Cleveland, and Dallas. In metropolitan areas, like Minneapolis, Minnesota, American Indians faced severe job discrimination and eventually formed urban communities in economically depressed sections of the cities. An estimated 750,000 Tribal citizens relocated during this time to urban areas, but some did return to Tribal communities after the promises of the BIA went unfulfilled and a sense of alienation set in at the new urban locations. As Tribal peoples, those raised in urban locations continued to maintain familial and cultural connections to their homelands and Tribal communities.

A second thrust of the termination era was the enactment of Public Law 280, codified at 18 U.S.C. § 1162, providing a delegation of federal criminal jurisdiction to states and an opening for state courts to hear civil matters that were previously outside state jurisdiction, codified at 28 U.S.C. § 1360. This extension of state criminal jurisdiction over Tribal communities did not require Tribal consent until 1968. Due to the often-strained relationships between state government and Tribal governments, the federal delegation to state authority was unwelcome from the Tribal perspective. An extension of some state criminal jurisdiction was authorized in the *Oklahoma v. Castro-Huerta* decision as recently as 2022 over non-Indians committing crimes within Tribal jurisdictions without the federal delegation process set out in Public Law 280, which has been a source of further confusion in the area of criminal law jurisdiction. Public Law 280, its implications, and relevant U.S. Supreme Court decisions will be more fully explored in Chapter Three: "Criminal Jurisdiction in Indian Country."

In sum, the termination era was a reversal of the prior U.S. Indian policy era empowering Tribal governments to rebuild economically and politically. To many, the federal Indian policy of termination was viewed as an injustice to Native Americans. Through the urban relocation program, many Tribal citizens became familiar with political movements emerging in the 1960s. In the late 1960s, new Tribal voices emerged from reservations and urban areas in opposition to the termination policy and past U.S. policies negatively impacting Tribes.

g. Indian Self-Determination Era (late 1960s to present)

With the U.S. nationally focused on the civil rights movement in the 1960s, urban Native Americans were inspired to arrange protest activities against the imposition of federal control over Tribal communities and the termination policy. In response to the national attention being garnered by Native Americans in protest of the termination policy, U.S. President Richard Nixon delivered a Special Message on Indian Affairs to the U.S. Congress on July 8, 1970. President Nixon called the forced termination policy wrong in his message and called upon the U.S. Congress to encourage "Indian self-determination." One of the pivotal pieces of legislation enacted heralding in the new federal Indian policy was the Indian Self-Determination and Education Assistance Act of 1975, 25 U.S.C. §5301–5423 recodified from §450 et seq. This statute and others enacted since have encouraged Tribal Nation administration of services to Tribal citizens with the intention of lessening BIA control. The current era of U.S. Indian policy remains the Indian self-determination era and will be more fully discussed in later chapters.

2. Federal Statutes, Federal Agencies, and Federal Regulations in Federal Indian Law

By virtue of the Indian Commerce Clause, the U.S. Congress is empowered within the federal government to regulate Indian affairs. The confines of Indian affairs originally related to the acquisition of Tribal land and the regulation of trade with Tribal Nations, but that definition and the accompanying power has expanded in scope over the years. Federal courts have long since recognized congressional power to enact laws well beyond trade and commerce, including laws that govern otherwise internal Tribal law and policy issues. In the recent U.S. Supreme Court decision, *Haaland v. Brackeen*, 599 U.S. 255 (2023), the Court identified the following sources of power for federal legislation involving Tribal Nations and members: in the U.S. Constitution, the Indian Commerce Clause, art. I, sect. 8, cl. 3, and the Treaty Clause art. II., sect. 2, cl. 2. The Court also identified preconstitutional powers inherent in the federal government as necessary to nationality permitting the U.S. Congress to legislate regarding Tribal Nations and members. Furthermore, the federal trust relationship towards Tribal Nations and Tribal members is a source of authority recognized by the Court for federal legislation. "In sum, Congress's power to legislate with respect to Indians is well established and broad. Consistent with that breadth, we have not doubted Congress's ability to legislate across a wide range of areas, including criminal law, domestic violence, employment, property, tax, and trade." 599 U.S. at 275.

The impact of federal legislation on the lives of Tribal citizens cannot be overstated. Federal Indian laws and policies have redefined and often ignored and replaced Tribal laws on property rights, education, health services, law enforcement, trade, Tribal civil and criminal jurisdiction, and many other aspects of Tribal society and governance. As the U.S. judiciary broadly defined congressional authority over Tribes as "plenary" authority stemming from political relationships and based on the Indian Commerce Clause and the special nature of Indian affairs, the U.S. Congress has passed legislation touching nearly every facet of Tribal life. Federal statutes form a large portion of federal Indian law and will be extensively discussed throughout this text. Title 25 of the United States Code is entirely composed of federal laws regarding American Indian and Alaska Native governments and peoples, with some federal laws also including Native Hawaiians.

Under the U.S. executive power are the federal administrative agencies that implement federal legislation and policy. In 1824, the U.S. Bureau of Indian Affairs (BIA) was established within the Department of War and in 1849 was transferred to the Department of the Interior. The BIA has primary responsibility to implement federal Indian law and policy; to deliver treaty-guaranteed services; and to administer the daily trust management functions of the federal government to Tribal Nations and Tribal citizens. The BIA has its headquarters in Washington, D.C., operates 12 regional offices, and various area offices located directly in Indian Country. A wide range of Tribal programs are overseen and administered through the BIA, including: child protection, education, economic development, healthcare, housing, law enforcement, and court services of Tribal Nations. Federal funding for Tribal services flow through the BIA to Tribal Nations for these programs based upon treaty entitlements, self-determination contracts, and self-governance contracts in the interest of restoring the quality of life to Tribal citizenry after the devastating federal Indian policies of the 1800s.

Supplementing the BIA provision of federal services are other federal agencies interacting with Tribal Nations. The Indian Health Service (IHS), originally within the Department of the Interior, operates from the Department of Health and Human Services (DHHS) to provide healthcare to American

Indians and Alaska Natives. Another specialized agency is the Office of Special Trustee (OST) created in 1994 under the American Indian Trust Fund Management and Reform Act within the Department of the Interior. The OST implements the fiduciary responsibilities for Tribal beneficiaries owning Tribal lands in federal trust status. The U.S. Department of Agriculture (USDA) administers programs specifically impacting Tribal farming, cultural site protection, and food supplies.

Other federal agencies, such as the Bureau of Land Management (BLM) and the Department of Housing and Urban Development (HUD), may administer specific federal programs intended for Tribal governments and Tribal citizens within their overall responsibilities. By Presidential Executive Order No. 13175 Consultation and Coordination with Tribal Governments (November 6, 2000) and Presidential Memorandum, Tribal Consultation (November 5, 2009), federal agencies have been directed to provide meaningful consultation and collaboration with Tribal governments prior to taking action that will significantly implicate Tribal interests. The directive to consult with Tribal governments to federal agencies has led to more Tribal leadership input into the federal decision-making process where Tribal Nation interests are affected but remains a challenging process depending on which federal agency is at issue.

Due to the broad involvement of federal agencies in relationship with Tribal Nations, regulations promulgated by such federal agencies are important in federal Indian law. Administrative law principles are applicable when federal regulations involving federal Indian law are being construed. In addition, the aforementioned Indian canons of construction apply with equal force to federal statutes and federal regulations involving Tribal interests. Thus, ambiguities in federal Indian laws and regulations are to be interpreted in favor of American Indian and Alaska Native governmental interests.

3. Federal Court Decisions: Key Role in Federal Indian Law

The U.S. Supreme Court has taken a leading role in the development of federal Indian law since the beginning of the federal judiciary. Most scholars view the foundation of federal Indian law as defined by three U.S. Supreme Court opinions penned by Chief Justice John Marshall in the early 1800s, known as the Marshall Trilogy. A note of caution on the language in the Marshall Trilogy is warranted as dehumanizing and racist language is employed to characterize Native Americans in a derogatory manner to assert U.S. control over Tribal lands and Tribal peoples. The first of the three decisions, *Johnson v. McIntosh* (21 U.S. (8 Wheat.) 543, 1823), set forth a limitation on the scope of Tribal property rights based on the papal bulls and Christian "doctrine of discovery," which influenced the development of international law to the detriment of Indigenous peoples worldwide. With no Tribal Nation or citizen as a party to the lawsuit, the U.S. Supreme Court defined all Tribal property rights as akin to a right of occupancy in Tribal lands rather than full ownership, known as fee title. Under this doctrine, only the "discovering" European nation holds the authority to acquire Tribal lands and subsequently holds a superior title to those same lands. If individual subjects of the crown entered into land deals with Tribes, the subjects only acquired the Tribal interest subject to the overriding power of the European sovereign. The United States, as the opinion reads, became the successor in interest to Great Britain, according to the Court's decision, and had thus obtained the exclusive right among sovereigns to acquire and then hold superior title to Tribal lands within the newly imposed borders of mid-North America. The doctrine of discovery was stated to be held only by European nations, so the claim by the United States to application of the doctrine remains suspect according to some Native legal scholars. The U.S. Supreme Court went on to hold that the ability of Tribal Nations to freely sell or exchange ownership in lands to any purchaser except the United States, or to have Tribal law govern the property law conveyances of Tribal lands, was limited by the constraints set out in this decision. In March of 2023, the Vatican repudiated the "doctrine of discovery" as a colonizing principle that deprived Indigenous peoples of basic human rights, but failed to take responsibility or offer redress for the harm that has reverberated through the centuries.

The second and third cases in the Marshall Trilogy involved the resistance of the Cherokee Nation to the adverse actions of the state of Georgia. In *Cherokee Nation v. Georgia* (30 U.S. (5 Pet.) 1, 1831), the Cherokee Nation sought an injunction to stop Georgia from extending state laws and governmental authority into the Cherokee Nation based on the principles that Tribal sovereignty and treaties with the United States barred state power. The U.S. Supreme Court ruled that the Cherokee Nation lacked standing to be a litigant because the Nation was not to be considered a foreign nation under article III, section two of the U.S. Constitution. Rather, the Court found that the Cherokee Nation's political status was as a "domestic dependent nation" rather than as a foreign nation, although the United States entered into treaties with the Cherokee Nation. "Domestic dependent" nationhood became a new political term created by the Court, which in this instance foreclosed the Cherokee Nation's ability to sue in federal court. The Court also stated that a ward/guardian relationship existed between the Cherokee Nation and the United States, a relationship that would be the basis of the United States' extension of power over Tribal Nations in the years that followed. Some Native law scholars have opined that this decision is the foundation of the trust relationship by the United States towards Tribal Nations.

The third case mirrored the underlying issues of *Cherokee Nation v. Georgia*, but with a plaintiff that could seek a remedy in the United States Supreme Court where the Cherokee Nation could not—a White Christian missionary under protection of federal law, Samuel Worcester. Worcester was a citizen of another state within the union but was arrested and incarcerated by Georgia officials for entering and residing inside the Cherokee Nation in violation of Georgia state law. In *Worcester v. Georgia* (31 U.S. (6 Pet.) 515, 1832), Chief Justice John Marshall reached the merits of the underlying controversy and provided a detailed account of the relationships between the United States and Tribal Nations based upon the sovereign-to-sovereign era. The Court held that federal law preempted state law in Indian affairs, upholding the treaty relationship between the United States and the Cherokee Nation and voiding the Georgia laws in contravention of treaty provisions. Thus, the Marshall Trilogy has served as a foundation for federal Indian law in imposing limits on Tribal property rights, redefining Tribal governments as "domestic dependent nations" in a "ward/guardian" relationship with the United States, and establishing federal preemption over state power in Indian affairs.

U.S. Supreme Court decisions have been crucial in controversies involving Tribal Nation treaty rights, Tribal jurisdiction, Tribal land rights, and many other major aspects of Tribal concern. The U.S. federal judicial system is composed of 12 regional circuits, each with district and appellate level courts, and one specifically federal circuit for a total of thirteen. Federal courts regularly decide important issues on Tribal Nation and Tribal citizen interests. Legal doctrines developed through federal judicial decisions have solidified into federal Indian law principles with significance for Tribal Nation litigants. In many instances, cases that have significant impact on Tribal rights have advanced in controversies between non-Indian parties where the Tribes were never permitted to make arguments in the Courts or otherwise have their perspectives considered. Many Native American law scholars have criticized the broad authority of the federal judiciary to pronounce new legal doctrines in federal Indian law that lack textual support in the U.S. Constitution or other written sources of federal law. The federal judiciary has played and continues to play a key role in the formation of federal Indian law.

CHECKPOINTS

- Tribal law is formed from Indigenous legal traditions, codified statutes, regulations, and judicial opinions. Tribal Nations have legal histories that extend for thousands of years and continue to exercise their own law. American Indian and Alaska Native Tribal governments compose the over 570 Tribal Nations in mid-North America.
- Together Tribal law and federal Indian law form Native American law. Federal Indian law in the United States is derived from concepts developed through European Christian doctrines and early international law. The interaction between Tribal Nations and the United States developed through the treaty-making process.
- There is an active interaction between Tribal Nation law and the law of the United States. Tribal law has influenced the formation of the United States and concepts such as democracy, dispute resolution principles, and environmental stewardship enacted into law.
- There are more than 570 federally recognized Tribal Nations in the United States. Each Tribe has its own governance structure and set of Tribal laws. Almost half of the 570 federally recognized Tribal Nations are Alaska Native Tribes.
- Federal Indian law is applied generally to all Tribes whether enacted by federal legislation or through a federal judicial opinion. Title 25 of the U.S. Code contains the set of federal laws dealing with American Indians and Alaska Native governments and peoples, with some federal laws including Native Hawaiians. Federal agencies implement many of the federal Indian law provisions. The Bureau of Indian Affairs has a primary role in implementing federal Indian law and policy.
- The Marshall Trilogy of cases serves as the U.S. interpretation of the foundation of the relationship between Tribal Nations and the United

States. Key concepts from the cases include: Tribal Nations characterized as domestic dependent nations, the United States as the successor to the discovery doctrine from the European nation known as Great Britain, the beginning of the federal trust relationship from the announcement of the ward/guardian status, and federal preemption of state law in Native American affairs.

CHAPTER 2

Native American Property Law

ROADMAP

- Understand that Native American property systems were and are diverse and existed prior to European contact and were based on family, clan, and individual ownership and land use concepts, depending on the community.
- Learn that the international "doctrine of discovery" was employed by the U.S. Supreme Court to transform and redefine Tribal property rights into limited Tribal rights of occupancy.
- Know that to acquire Native American property, U.S. federal Indian law requires Tribal lands be purchased with the permission of the U.S. government or taken by conquest by the U.S. government.
- Understand that Tribal property rights were fundamentally changed by federal law through the General Allotment Act of 1887 and other tribally specific allotment legislation. These federal laws dramatically reduced the reserved Tribal land base and provided the means for federal agents to allot reserved Tribal lands into small parcels in individual Tribal ownership, with or without the consent of the impacted Tribes. These allotments are generally held in trust status by the United States for the benefit of the Native allottees.
- Learn that the status of Tribal land as either held in trust by the U.S. government or as owned in fee simple title has legal implications on whether the Tribal or the state government is viewed as the primary regulatory authority.

- Learn about the Tribal title history for Alaska Native Villages and the compromise legislation known as the Alaska Native Claims Settlement Act of 1971 that restructured land management under regional and village corporations with state and federal requirements. The Alaska Native Villages as Tribal Nations have the ability to use the fee-to-trust federal process to increase Tribal land holdings.
- Know that after the loss of millions of acres of land through dealings with the U.S. government, Tribal governments and Tribal citizens continue to own over 55 million acres of land. There is a contemporary movement known as "Land Back" to recover lands taken from Tribal Nations by unlawful or coercive methods.

This chapter will provide an overview of the historical and contemporary property and land tenure systems of American Indian and Alaska Native Tribal Nations. As almost every other aspect of Native American law, from criminal jurisdiction to taxation to business transactions, will turn on the status of the land where a particular activity occurred, it is particularly important to have an understanding of the different forms of property ownership that exist inside Indian Country.

A. Historical Context

1. Tribal Property Rights Prior to Colonization

Prior to European contact, Natives had systems of law for recognizing and enforcing property rights. Property rights and dominion over lands existed in varying contexts and Tribal communities regulated land use by laws, custom and norms. Tribal Nations understood protocols for entering the territory of another Tribal Nation, often through lighting a fire and waiting on a boundary to seek permission to enter the territory. Shared territories were co-managed by two or more Tribal Nations for specific resources or purposes in recognition of common stewardship principles. Beliefs on the spiritual nature of the earth and respect for her resources guided sustainable practices and responsibilities to all living beings dependent on particular lands, waters, airs, and other resources.

Mainstream history texts often over-generalize and stereotype the nature of Tribal property ownership and rights by suggesting that Tribal Nations did not understand or appreciate the concept or value of property or ownership of property. In these texts, if Tribal property ownership is acknowledged at all, it is described as a monolithic Tribal worldview that limits all Tribal "ownership" to one form. The presumed form of ownership that is described is "common use:" a pure common property system where every individual or family within a Tribe was free to use lands and natural resources, that such land use was temporary in nature, but no one Tribe or individual "owns" anything.

It is doubtful that many Tribes actually practiced a simplistic form of common ownership as the mainstream history texts describe. The historical record of Tribal communities departs significantly from the accepted narrative of the mainstream. Tribal communities, particularly those that lived within the same territories for generations, would not have escaped the tragedy of the commons that led to property laws and controls elsewhere throughout the globe without regulatory systems and recognition of rights, including the right to exclude. Whether those rights lived in families, individuals, community governance, or some combination thereof would differ given the diversity of Tribal cultures, Tribal Nations exerted ownership or property rights in their lands and territories.

There is evidence that many Tribes exercised regulatory control over land, and in many instances, Tribal Nations had elaborate land tenure structures. For example, the Pueblos of the Southwest, the Tribes of the southeastern United States, and the Iroquois are very well-documented as having elaborate property schemes and land tenure around agriculture.

It is also well-documented that some Tribal property systems provided government protection to individual property rights that could pass during life and at death. In the Cherokee Nation land tenure system, as consistent with nations around the globe today, individuals could freely acquire and transfer surface rights, including the improvements thereon, but the underlying estates were held by the sovereign, which possessed reversionary interest should private property rights cease by operation of law. These traditional legal principles are being reinfused into contemporary Tribal laws.

2. Early European/International Law

When Europeans arrived in North America, they engaged with the Native Americans as the pre-existing property owner. Terminology to disconnect Native peoples from the continent was used by employing the term "American Indians" in contradiction to the actual state of things. Although these Europeans marginalized the nature of Tribal ownership and dominion over lands, international law recognized that Natives had property rights that could not simply be ignored by the colonizing country. International law's "doctrine of discovery" governed the relationships between the various European powers and governed how European powers would interact with one another as they sought to acquire ownership in Tribal Nation lands. From the European perspective, Tribal Nation lands could either be purchased or taken as the spoils of a "just war."

European sovereigns could not simply declare and gain absolute ownership over Tribal lands without the consent or knowledge of the Tribe in possession of those lands. An affirmative extinguishment of Tribal Nation ownership and title in property rights was first necessary in order to clear title for future ownership by a non-Tribal sovereign or individual. Under international law and subsequent domestic U.S. federal law, "discovery" merely gave the colonizing country a superior right, as to other sovereigns and their subjects, to acquire lands from the Tribal Nations at a future point in time. Through the so-called "discovery" of lands already in the possession of Tribal Nations, European officials claimed some form of ownership by planting a flag and stating words aloud in a language foreign to the Tribal Nations of the continent.

The early treaties between European powers and Tribal Nations reflect the understanding that Tribes exercised ownership and dominion over lands and that European powers lacked the same powers over land. The fact that Europeans sought treaty permission from Tribal Nations to cross Tribal territory is consistent with Tribal Nations being the recognized owners of Tribal property that formed North America.

Tribes did not receive land grants from other sovereigns. European powers were the grantees who acquired their property interest through treaty conveyances from the Tribes. The very terms of these early treaties recognize that the Tribal Nations, as the grantor, were the party with the power to cede, transfer or convey lands to others.

When one European power became the successor in interest to the previous European powers, as the United States claimed to be after the American

Revolution, title or ownership to all lands within the newly claimed boundaries did not automatically pass to the new sovereign. The new sovereign simply stepped into the shoes of the old sovereign and acquired the exclusive right among European powers to acquire through purchase Tribal lands at a later date.

3. Early U.S. Law and Tribal Lands

The newly independent United States of America acknowledged Tribal Nation dominion over lands in its first Tribal property legislation—the Trade and Intercourse Act of 1790—and in numerous treaties whereby Tribes gave permission to federal troops to cross Tribal lands. It should be noted that the early U.S. government to the present often employs the misnomer terms: "American Indians" and "Indians" in its law. Other treaties involved the outright purchase of lands from the Tribes via deeds, land grants and treaties.

In passing the first federal legislation dealing with Tribal Nation property, the United States did not assert title to all Native lands but instead, the Trade and Intercourse Act made it unlawful for non-Native individuals or the states to acquire lands directly from Tribes. Rather, it preserved the exclusive right of the United States to approach Tribal Nations for land conveyances, cession, rights of ways or other property transfers. Although the early United States leaders marginalized the nature and extent of Tribal Nation property ownership, the body of legislation that followed institutionalized the notion that the United States needed to acquire land from Tribes or formally extinguish Tribal property rights before the United States could "own" land. Without this formal step, Tribal property rights would remain a cloud on the title.

As a practical reality, prior and after the passage of these Non-Intercourse acts, individual colonists and landed colonies had frequently purchased lands directly from Tribes or individual Natives. This created a series of conflicts over competing chains of title where Tribal Nations were the original grantors of lands and several grantees later claimed that their competing claims to property originated from different conveyances from the Tribes. The United States Supreme Court's decision in *Johnson v. M'Intosh,* 21 U.S. (8 Wheat) 543 (1823), is a foundational federal Indian law case where the parties sought a judicial determination of property rights. One party produced a chain of title originating directly with a Tribal Nation where the successor in interest from the Tribe was a private individual. One party produced a chain of title originating directly with a Tribal Nation where the successor in interest was the United States of America. The United States acquired lands from the same Tribal Nation via an armistice treaty after the Tribe had purportedly transferred some parcels of the total land base to a private individual. In reaching the decision that the chain of title involving the United States was superior, the United States Supreme Court set a precedent that diminished the relative property interests of all Tribal Nations. No Tribal Nation participated in the lawsuit but the legal claims to subsequent property rights originated in documents executed by the particular Tribe. In the context of the United States claims, the Tribal leaders signed a treaty that ceded land to the United States. In the context of the private parties, the Tribal leaders signed a deed transferring the property to the private parties in exchange for the purchase price paid for the land. It should be remembered that these documents were written in the English language, utilizing English legal terminology, and purported signatures by Tribal leaders were often "x" marks.

Rather than recognizing that Tribal Nations, as the original landholders, held fee simple ownership in their lands, the U.S. Supreme Court defined the original Tribal Nation property interest as similar to a right of occupancy. And, although the Tribes necessarily retained the power to convey that limited property interest to others, only Tribal Nation conveyances to the United States would be recognized and enforced under federal law. In other words, only the United States has the power to acquire or extinguish "Indian title." Individuals that acquire lands from Tribal Nations do so at their peril because those purchases will not be recognized as absolute purchases in the courts of the United States.

The U.S. Supreme Court's decision is justified, in part, on the previously mentioned narratives and racial stereotypes of Native Americans, as an ethnic group that did not use the land as efficiently as Europeans and as entities incapable of or unwilling to consider property ownerships to the same extent as their European counterparts. U.S. Supreme Court Justice John Marshall wrote:

> We will not enter into the controversy, whether agriculturists, merchants, and manufacturers, have a right, on abstract principles, to expel hunters from the territory they possess, or to contract their limits.
>
> But the tribes of Indians inhabiting this country were fierce savages ... whose subsistence was chiefly drawn from the forest. To leave them in possession of their country, was to leave the country a wilderness....

21 U.S. at 588, 590.

Whether disingenuous or not, two narratives in the Court's opinion served as justification to pave the way for westward expansion and made it easier for the federal government to quickly acquire Tribal Nation lands for future redistribution to non-Native settlers. First, Native American property rights were inferior to non-Native property rights. Second, Tribal Nation land uses were less efficient, and therefore inferior to, non-Native land uses. These misguided assumptions and stereotypes would have far-reaching detrimental consequences for the lands of Tribal Nations stretching from coast-to-coast.

4. Native American Title or Tribal Title or Aboriginal Title

Property rights of Native Americans were well understood under Tribal legal principles before contact with Europeans. With vast amounts of land hanging in the balance, U.S. officials sought to categorize Native American title, also known as Indian title and aboriginal title, for purchase. The chain of title for most lands within the United States begins with the extinguishment of Tribal title followed by subsequent government redistribution from the U.S. government to a state, an individual or corporate entity, such as railroads. The Trade and Intercourse Acts provided the U.S. government as the only purchaser of Tribal title that would be valid under U.S. law. Although largely a historical footnote, there are modern day claims regarding Tribal Nation lands that were acquired by colonies, states or individuals directly from Tribes

Tipi at Crow Nation Reservation. Photo credit: Angelique EagleWoman.

without federal extinguishment of Tribal title or property interests. For those acquisitions not following federal law, a cloud on the title may remain.

Most of the situations where lands were acquired in violation of the Trade and Intercourse Acts have been addressed through court cases and/or various legislative acts passed for the purposes of settling any outstanding land claims that could prevent the passage of clear title in the current real estate market. It is possible, however, in researching the land transactions for a given tract of land to find unresolved Tribal Nation title issues that may impact the ability to freely alienate lands once held by Tribes.

5. Recognized Title of Tribal Nations and Tribal Citizens

Although original Tribal title was deemed to be limited to an occupancy right or possessory interest in lands, other more complete Tribal Nation property interest followed. Once the United States affirmatively recognizes a Tribal Nation property right in specified lands, the federal government cannot take the property without compensation. The "recognition" of such a property right may be found in a treaty or federal statute, or in a deed and land patent. Where there is no clear evidence that the United States "recognized" Native American title to land, the Tribe may not be entitled to compensation for takings under United States law.

The story of HeSapa or Paha Sapa, the Black Hills of the Great Sioux Nation, highlights the problem, from a Tribal perspective, of a federal system that acknowledges Tribal ownership of lands on one hand, but then empowers a system where Tribes can be dispossessed of those lands without their consent. The Tribal Nations at issue have spent two centuries fighting for the return of their sacred Black Hills after they have been dispossessed from lands that hold not just property rights, but religious, cultural and political significance. The wars of the 1860s were fought by the Lakota Nations, otherwise known as the Sioux Tribes in the English language, to protect the integrity of earlier recognized treaty lands from incursions from non-Native settlers. At the conclusion of those battles, the terms of the Treaty of Fort Laramie constituted recognized title in which the United States acknowledged the future property rights of the Tribal Nations to the exclusion of non-Natives. "Recognized title" included the Black Hills, which were later transferred into non-Native ownership in a series of transactions intended to open the lands for mining purposes.

The U.S. Supreme Court in *United States v. Sioux Nation,* 448 U.S. 371 (1980), ruled that the dispossession of HeSapa or Paha Sapa was an uncompensated taking of Tribal property rights by the United States. The judicial remedy available to the Sioux Nation is limited—the only remedy for the taking of the lands is monetary, based on the value of the land at the time of the taking. The Sioux Tribes are entitled to a money judgment but are not entitled under federal law, to a return of the lands.

Recognized title is superior to Tribal or aboriginal title in the U.S. hierarchy of land ownership structures. As the Sioux Tribes example best describes, it provides inadequate protections when the United States disregards the will of the Tribal Nation as property owner and acts without Tribal leaders' consent, or in this case, over the express objection of the Tribal leadership. The *Sioux Nation* decision affirmed the lower federal court's determination that the Tribal Nations were entitled to a monetary award of at least 17.1 million dollars, as of 1980, with the amount increasing over the decades, which the Tribal Nations have refused to accept on the basis of their principles that there was no consent to ever sell the sacred Black Hills.

That fact that Tribal Nations are awarded compensation through legislation or court decisions does not lessen the impact, from the Tribal perspective, of repeated actions by the federal government to invoke a large scale compulsory purchase system for the purpose of removing Native Americans from lands wanted for non-Native settlement.

The most common story known to the mainstream audience of dispossession of Indian lands is likely the Cherokee Trail of Tears, a forced removal of the Cherokee people from their lands in the southeastern United States to lands within present-day northeastern Oklahoma. Almost every Tribal Nation has endured a similar relocation.

After events such as relocation to other lands or a reduction in territory, new treaties were entered into by Tribal Nations to once again establish recognized Tribal Nation property ownership and often to re-recognize prior self-governance guarantees. Typically, the Tribal Nation was recognized as being the beneficial owner of the land base or territory on behalf of the Tribal peoples. In some circumstances, lands were conveyed to the Tribal Nations in fee simple absolute as a single large contiguous land base due to Tribal leader negotiation points. Some Tribal Nations in the southwest had their land ownership recognized by Spain and/or Mexico in fee title and when the United States border was altered to encompass the Tribal Nations, the fee title continued to be recognized as part of the sovereign-to-sovereign agreement between the United States and Spain and/or Mexico.

During the immediate post-removal period, most Tribes held their lands in common in a contiguous land base and non-Native ownership of lands inside the Tribal territory was prohibited. Early on, this understanding was enforced by the federal government. In fact, it was the preference of the federal government that the Tribal Nation as a whole, and not individual Tribal citizens, hold ownership rights in the land. If any further land cessions were to be acquired from Tribal Nations, it was much easier to have a single transaction with the Tribal government than to recognize, as a matter of federal law, that individual Tribal members had property rights. In fact, where Tribal law unequivocally recognized and protected individual property interests, the federal government ignored those laws to the detriment of the individual Tribal member land owners.

The continued desire for Native American land for non-Native settlement soon ushered in a new federal Indian policy as set forth in the General Allotment Act of 1887, codified at 25 U.S.C. § 331 and later repealed.

B. Allotment Process

The General Allotment Act was not self-executing legislation and did not apply to all Tribes. Some Tribal Nations were successful in avoiding allotment and continue to maintain contiguous land bases where they retain the right to exclude non-Native ownership to this day. The overwhelming majority of Tribal Nations experienced allotment and it is deemed to be the most devasting event for Tribal sovereignty and Tribal property regimes since the forced removals and relocations.

Where allotment occurred, it was the result of tribally-specific treaties/agreements that were advanced by the United States government, generally under duress or a result of unilateral federal action. Lands were allotted over Tribal officials' objection and resistance and when Tribal Nations sought relief in federal court to stop the process the resulting judicial opinions upheld the U.S. law. A primary example is the U.S. Supreme Court decision in *Lone Wolf v. Hitchcock*, 187 U.S. 553 (1903), that solidified the U.S. legal principle of congressional "plenary" power over Indian affairs, including Tribal lands. That power included the right to allot Tribal Nation land over the objection of the Tribal leadership, even if it meant a unilateral abrogation of prior treaty guarantees. The United States Supreme Court in the *Lone Wolf* decision acquiesced to forced allotment of Tribal Nation lands:

> We must presume that Congress acted in perfect good faith in the dealings with the Indians of which complaint is made, and that the legislative branch of the government exercised its best judgment in the premises. In any event, as Congress possessed full power in the matter, the judiciary cannot question or inquire the motives which prompted the enactment of this legislation. If injury was occasioned, which we do not wish to be understood as implying, by the use made by Congress of its power, relief must be sought by an appeal to that body for redress and not to the courts.

187 U.S. at 568.

It is important to note that allotment occurred in different ways, depending on the reservation or territory, and it is critical to research the Tribal Nation specific federal laws that give rise to the modern land tenure system within each Tribe's land base. The federal allotment policy of the late nineteenth century, which converted the Tribal Nation land base into small parcels of individually-owned property, has compromised most Tribal Nation economies and continues to negatively impact land use planning and access to capital. The consequences of the allotment policy continue to limit economic development for both private endeavors of individual Tribal members and sustainability of Tribal Nation economies. The allotment legacy also complicates the jurisdictional landscape as the United States and local state governments continue to point to the practical results of allotment, as a reason to limit Tribal Nation sovereignty to lands the Tribes or Tribal citizens retain land ownership over rather than viewing territorial boundaries as the markers of Tribal jurisdiction, similar to all other modern governments.

As discussed in Chapter One, the allotment and assimilation policy era involved both destruction of the Tribal Nation land base and served as a social experiment designed to assimilate individual Natives into mainstream American society. Through the allotment policy, as an economic and property experiment, individual Tribal citizens were to be transformed into owners of privately held lands subject to the United States property law system, to the exclusion of prior property laws and ongoing Tribal government involvement.

Proponents of allotment convinced Congress that Tribal citizens did not understand or value individual property rights. Allotment would ideally teach Native Americans the importance of individual property rights as a way to better prepare them for future United States citizenship. In fact, for many Tribal Nations, acceptance of an allotment was coupled with immediate U.S. naturalized citizenship of their Tribal members. Prior to allotment, Tribal citizens/members held exclusive citizenship in their Tribal Nation and were not citizens of the United States.

Being born within the boundaries of the United States did not convey United States citizenship to Native Americans because their allegiance and relationship was with their Tribal Nation. Factually and legally, Tribal Nations are both pre-constitutional and extra-constitutional. As such, the 14th Amendment to the United States Constitution extended citizenship to African Americans who could not become citizens of the United States prior to the Civil War, but not to Native Americans as citizens of their own Tribal Nations. After the Civil War, enslaved persons who were once held in bondage pursuant to Cherokee law became Cherokee Nation citizens by virtue of an amendment to the Cherokee Nation Constitution and by virtue of a treaty between the United States and the Cherokee Nation. Like other Cherokee citizens at the time, Cherokee freedmen citizens received allotments of land from the Cherokee Nation land base and at that time, became United States citizens. Because the Cherokee Nation held its land base in fee title pursuant to a prior treaty, all Cherokee Nation allotment deeds are signed and executed by the Cherokee Nation Principal Chief and not by the federal government. This is not to suggest that the Cherokee Nation failed to resist allotment. In fact, the Cherokee Nation electorate approved a 1902 allotment "agreement" with the United States after the United States moved forward with the allotment process. The Cherokee Nation leadership did what they could to control the allotment process, even if the Cherokee Nation leaders could not control the ultimate outcome.

Although a growing number of contemporary scholars have refuted the notion of Tribal Nation communal ownership by providing evidence of extensive private property rights in Tribal law, the federal government simply disregarded the existence of pre-existing Tribal Nation property laws that were in effect at the time of allotment. The federal government also ignored the opposition of Native peoples who were content with Tribal Nation property law regimes. In doing so, the rights of the individual Tribal members that were otherwise protected under Tribal Nation law were ignored to make way for the forced federal allotment of Tribal Nation lands. Sometimes, allotment deeds actually reduced the land holdings of individual Tribal members, as evidenced by the testimony of a Native farmer:

> Under our old Cherokee regime I spent the early days of my life on the farm up here of 300 acres, and arranged to be comfortable in my old age.... When I was assigned to that 60 acres, and I could take no more under the inexorable law of allotment enforced upon us Cherokees, I had to relinquish every inch of my premises outside of that little 60 acres.... What am I going to do with it? For the last few years.... I have gone out there on that farm day after day.... I have exerted all my ability, all industry, all my intelligence ... to make my living out of that 60 acres, and, God be my judge, I have not been able to do it.... I am here to-day [sic], a poor man upon the verge of starvation—my muscular energy gone, hope gone. I have nothing to charge my calamity to but the unwise legislation of Congress in reference to my Cherokee people.

D.W.C. Duncan, *How Allotment Impoverishes the Indians: Testimony Before a Senate Comm. Investigating Conditions in the Indian Territory*, November 1906, in GREAT DOCUMENTS IN AMERICAN INDIAN HISTORY 287–88 (Wayne Moquin with Charles Van Doren eds., 1973).

Once an individual allotment was conveyed to the individual allottee, the land was then governed by Anglo-American property law, most often federal law but in some instances, federal legislation provided for the property law of the surrounding state to control Tribal property in certain transactions, such as probate and heir distribution.

In addition to creating highly fractionated estates where the subsequent Tribal member generations would inherit smaller and smaller interests in a reduced and finite land base, the allotment process resulted in a catastrophic loss of tribally owned land. Estimates suggest that by 1934, the allotment process resulted in the loss of 86 million acres to non-Tribal ownership, either individual private or state/federal public lands. Other estimates suggest that by the end of the allotment era, two-thirds of all the land allotted passed out of Tribal ownership.

The proponents of the allotment policy thought it was in the best interest of the Tribal Nations to abandon all forms of common ownership in favor of individual property rights. It was believed, or at least stated, that common Tribal ownership was stagnating any chance for economic or social development in Indian Country.

The allotment policy was firmly rooted in the notion that farming and other agricultural pursuits were the best use for land. Common lands should be divided into individual parcels so that the individual Tribal member could become a farmer with the incentive to work harder and make the most profit from his land. The policy ignored that many individual Tribal citizens had been farmers for many generations and that those agriculturalists held individual title, under Tribal Nation law, to lands they had already improved. The Tribal governments were never compensated for the loss of Tribal Nation ownership even when the transactions violated express treaty guarantees. The allotment of Tribal lands eventually led to the loss of most of the land that was still under Tribal control at the end of the late nineteenth century. Ninety percent (90%) of the land owned by Native Americans at the time of European contact had already been taken before the allotment process ever began.

The loss of land continued, and in fact rapidly increased, following allotment. One reason for rapid loss of land is that once the lands were parceled out to individual Tribal members, those lands were no longer under the watchful protection of either the federal government or the Tribal Nation. Individual lands were freely alienable and could be acquired by state eminent domain or by adverse possession. The lands became subject to state debtor-creditor laws and forced sales for failure to pay state taxes. Prior to allotment, only the federal government could acquire Tribal lands. After allotment, Tribal lands could be acquired through private transactions like any other piece of land. The land transactions that followed almost always resulted in the land passing, once and for all, to non-Natives.

After allotments were made to those on the Tribal rolls, there were often significant parcels of land remaining. These lands were deemed "surplus" because it was presumed that the Tribal Nation didn't need the land, or implicitly, that the Tribe wouldn't make good use of the lands. If a future Tribal use for the lands could be contemplated, there were other people who could make better uses of the land: the White settlers who the federal government had previously promised to keep away from Tribal land. In fact, states and U.S. citizen homesteaders acquired 60 million acres of Tribal land through this federally sanctioned program. Although Tribes received some compensation for the loss of "surplus" lands, their consent was irrelevant and the legal remedies are limited to cash rather than land repatriation. After Tribal Nation land was acquired by the United States, the "surplus" lands were typically returned to the public domain, making way for homestead deeds to private non-Tribal, usually White landowners.

1. The Impact of Allotment

Today, the allotted lands that remain under Tribal control are typically highly fractionated with multiple co-owners sharing the same parcel of land deeded to a common ancestor. There was no foresight for dealing with these issues, because the allotment policy was designed to end Tribal governance and Tribal community life. This entire process violated the many treaties entered into by the United States of America, often containing provisions of perpetual peace and friendship with the Tribal Nations.

The allotment process was intended by U.S. advocates to prepare Tribal citizens for ultimate United States citizenship and full inclusion into the so-called American melting pot. The tenacity of Native Americans to their identity, languages, cultures, and principles of stewardship for their homelands resulted in the failure of assimilationist policies. When Tribal citizens resisted the melting pot of assimilation, the practical problems with allotment were quickly revealed and those problems have been exacerbated with each passing generation's ability to steward their Tribal lands.

On a positive note, Congress quickly repudiated the federal policy of land allotment when it passed the Indian Reorganization Act of 1934, 25 U.S.C. § 5101. Although the legislation is best known and more often cited for provisions that recognized the rights of Tribes to pass their own constitutions and move toward self-government, the legislation contained property provisions that ended the allotment process. Lands that were still held in trust by the federal government for an allottee in 1934 had the trust periods indefinitely extended so that the lands remained inalienable. 25 U.S.C. § 5102. Although there continue to be considerable problems with land fractionation and trust administration, lands have not passed out of Tribal hands as a result of the Indian Reorganization Act's extension of the trust period.

Much of the problems associated with the administration of trust lands come from the number of co-owners that frequently exist on a single tract of land. When an original allottee dies without proper U.S. legal estate planning, their property interest will pass, in intestate succession, equally to all of their children. With each generation, the number of co-owners increases, yet the Tribal land base can never expand because it is locked into a finite number of parcels. As the number of co-owners increase, the property interest of each co-owner is diminished and the more difficult it becomes to make efficient use of the land.

The U.S. Congress has recognized that highly fractionated allotments preclude any meaningful economic development in Indian Country. The allotment process that was premised on maximizing the efficiency of Tribal land use has rendered most Tribal land useless. There are multiple examples that illustrate the problem of fractionated ownership in Indian Country but the most famous description follows from a tract of land on the Sisseton-Wahpeton Lake Traverse Reservation in South Dakota:

> Tract 1305 is 40 acres and produces $1,080 in income annually. It is valued at $8,000. It has 439 owners, one-third of whom receive less than $.05 in annual rent and two-thirds of whom receive less than $1.... The common denominator used to compute fractional interests in the property is [3 trillion, 394 billion, 923 million, 840 thousand.] The smallest heir receives $.01 every 177 years.... The administrative costs of handling this tract are estimated by the Bureau of Indian Affairs at $17,560 annually.

Hodel v. Irving, 481 U.S. 704, 712–13 (1987).

In an effort to redress this legacy of allotment and reform a broken system, the U.S. Congress has passed a series of legislation in the last few decades attempting to consolidate lands, promote estate planning to relieve an overburdened and inefficient federal probate system for Tribal lands, and other systemic reforms in management of Tribal lands and natural resources. Some of these attempts, with limited success, have included provisions for land to escheat small, fractionated interests to the Tribal Nation or otherwise be consolidated with existing landowners to better manage the number of co-owners. Other legislative fixes have attempted to return some control to the Tribal Nation to administer Tribal Nation and individual Tribal member property. For example, in 1994, the U.S. Congress enacted the American Indian Trust Reform Act, 25 U.S.C. § 161a, § 162a, and § 4001 et seq., which created the Office of the Special Trustee (OST). The OST has primary responsibility to ensure the accountability of the Department of the Interior in managing the trust accounts for Individual Indian Monies (IIM) accounts and for Tribal Nation trust funds.

Other efforts to address fractionation of Tribal ownership include the Indian Land Consolidation Act (ILCA) of 1983, 25 U.S.C. § 2201 et seq., amendments to ILCA in 2000, and the American Indian Probate Reform Act (AIPRA) of 2004. Pursuant to AIPRA, Tribal Nations are encouraged to enact

Tribal probate codes to work in conjunction with the probate of trust lands. 25 U.S.C. § 2205.

Today, throughout Indian Country, multiple co-owners share fractional property interests in single parcels of allotted lands. The lands, if held in trust by the federal government, are inalienable due to federal restrictions. The lands, if held in fee by the Tribal citizen co-tenants, become de facto inalienable because they are largely unmarketable and lack the capacity to be put to efficient economic use. Banks and other investors are cautious about lending money on lands with multiple Tribal citizen co-tenants each owning small fractional property interests, although with federal involvement and guarantees, mortgages and other security interests may be collateralized by long term leasehold interests. Comprehensive land reform is necessary to allow for the beneficial use of the Tribal lands that remain in Tribal ownership.

2. U.S. Supreme Court Decisions Interpreting Allotment Legislation and the Rule of Law

As proponents of the allotment policy anticipated the end of Tribal Nations and reservations, contemporary state officials have engaged in efforts to assert that the allotment agreements stemming from the 1887 General Allotment Act did more than allot parcels within reservation limits. The arguments from state officials have focused on language in the allotment agreements eliminating, diminishing or otherwise changing the status of reservations as inferred by the agreement language enacted into federal law by the U.S. Congress. States like South Dakota, Washington, Utah, and Oklahoma asserted in litigation that reservations, established by treaties that opened up the land to allow these states to be formed, had been severely diminished, disestablished, or disappeared through allotment agreements.

These anti-reservation arguments were summarized into factors that went beyond the plain reading of the text of allotment federal laws and disregarded the Indian canons of construction to find federal laws specifically enacted for Native Americans were to be interpreted in favor of Tribal interests. In *Hagen v. Utah*, 510 U.S. 399 (1994), the U.S. Supreme Court reviewed the Uintah Indian Reservation and the relevant allotment act under a three factor test.

> In determining whether a reservation has been diminished, "[o]ur precedents in the area have established a fairly clean analytical structure,"

> id., at 470, directing us to look to three factors. The most probative evidence of diminishment is, of course, the statutory language used to open the Indian lands. Ibid. We have also considered the historical context surrounding the passage of the surplus land Acts, although we have been careful to distinguish between evidence of the contemporaneous understanding of the particular Act and matters occurring subsequent to the Act's passage. Id., at 471. Finally, "[o]n a more pragmatic level, we have recognized that who actually moved onto opened reservation lands is also relevant to deciding whether a surplus land Act diminished a reservation."

510 U.S. at 411–412.

In addressing the U.S. Solicitor General arguing that a clear statement from the U.S. Congress plus consent from the Tribal Nation was the correct standard, the majority opinion refuted this standard by stating that "[w]e thus decline to abandon our traditional approach to diminishment cases, which requires us to examine all the circumstances surrounding the opening of a reservation." 510 U.S. at 412.

In reviewing the factors that the U.S. Supreme Court employed to find diminishment or disestablishment of reservation status throughout the 1970s through the 1990s, the Court relied on sources from primarily White advocates who sought to overtake the reservation lands in reviewing the "contemporaneous understanding" in the 1880s to early 1900s and "who actually moved onto opened reservation lands." The ability to infer the intent of the U.S. Congress where no express language existed to change the reservation boundaries or status was a hallmark of this line of cases until very recently.

Then, the U.S. Supreme Court issued its decision in *McGirt v. Oklahoma*, 591 U.S. ___, 140 S.Ct. 2452 (2020), in which the state of Oklahoma asserted that the Muscogee (Creek) Nation Reservation, established in the Treaty of 1833 and affirmed in subsequent treaties of 1856 and 1866 and other federal laws, did not survive an allotment act of 1901. The U.S. Supreme Court referred to the Indian Country statute of 1948, 18 U.S.C. § 1151, which included language that a reservation includes patents issued or rights of ways running through it. Further, the decision clarified that the factors previously relied on were not the rule of law for common statutory interpretation or Tribal land issues in the United States. Rather, the Court held: "[a]nd, as we have said time and again, once a reservation is established, it retains that status 'until Congress explicitly indicates otherwise.' *Solem*, 465 U.S., at 470, 104 S.Ct. 1161 (citing *Celestine*, 215 U.S., at 285, 30 S.Ct. 93); see also *Yankton Sioux*, 522 U.S., at 343, 118 S.Ct. 789 ('[O]nly Congress can alter the terms of an Indian treaty by diminishing a reservation, and its intent to do so must be clear and plain')." 140 S.Ct. at 2469. This decision was welcomed as the rule of law properly applied after forty years of U.S. Supreme Court decisions searching allotment acts, newspaper articles, and other non-Native sources to diminish, disestablish, or otherwise alter the boundaries of reservations solemnly negotiated in treaties with the United States.

C. Modern Tribal Territorial Boundaries and Indian Country

Tribal lands include all real property inside the exterior boundaries of a recognized Tribal reservation or within the territorial jurisdiction of a Tribal Nation. The exterior boundaries of a Tribe's territory are generally defined by treaty language, executive order provisions, federal statute or in a property description of a land patent or deed to a large tract of land. These lands include multiple land tenure patterns and include lands owned by Tribal Nations, Tribal businesses, Tribal members, and non-Native persons, including lands owned by individuals and lands held in various co-ownership arrangements. The existence of non-Native owned lands inside a Tribal Nation territory does not necessarily defeat the Indian Country or Tribal status of a tract of land.

In 1948, the U.S. Congress codified the definition of Indian Country in the U.S. criminal code and was influenced by decisions of the U.S. Supreme Court. The Indian Country statute is provided as follows:

> Except as otherwise provided in sections 1154 and 1156 of this title, the term "Indian country", as used in this chapter, means (a) all land within the limits of any Indian reservation under the jurisdiction of the United States Government, notwithstanding the issuance of any patent, and, including rights-of-way running through the reservation, (b) all dependent Indian communities within the borders of the United States whether within the original or subsequently acquired territory thereof, and whether within or without the limits of a state, and (c) all Indian allotments, the Indian titles to which have not been extinguished, including rights-of-way running through the same.

It is important to note that the first category of "Indian reservation" includes all lands "notwithstanding the issuance of any patent," meaning regardless of whether non-Natives own parcels under a deed or patent from the U.S., within the reservation limits. This is an important provision relating to the jurisdiction of a Tribal Nation within the limits of the Tribe's reservation. The same provision includes that the limits of the reservation are not impacted by "rights-of-way running through the reservation" and so remain within the Tribal Nation's reservation and jurisdiction. The U.S. Supreme Court has not faithfully interpreted this language as will be further discussed in subsequent chapters.

The Tribal Nation understanding of reservations is the reserving of permanent homelands through a negotiation process with the United States, which sought to dispossess or contain Tribal Nations to certain land areas. This chapter has detailed the aggressive actions of the U.S. government to remove Tribal Nations from their homelands, to force Tribal Nations to engage in new agreements to secure permanent homelands, and to coerce Tribal Nations to agree to allow non-Native settlement through the allotment policy, which jeopardized economic development, natural resource stewardship, cultural site protection, and water management within the reservation limits.

1. Current Types of Property Ownership in Indian Country

a. Reservation and Trust Lands

A significant percentage of Tribal land holdings are held in trust status with the U.S. government as the trustee and are commonly referred to as "trust lands." In this arrangement, the United States holds the legal title to property and the individual Tribal member(s) or Tribal Nation holds the beneficial interest. The over 55 million acres of lands that are held in trust by the United States are subject to an overarching restraint on alienation, in that the lands cannot be sold, leased, mortgaged, or taken by eminent domain or otherwise encumbered without the consent and approval of the United States. Trust lands cannot be taxed by state or local entities but are generally treated as "federal lands" subject to substantial federal statutory and regulatory schemes. Tribal trust lands exist within the limits of reservations, the reserved permanent homelands of Tribal Nations.

Individually owned trust land parcels are generally the outgrowth of the allotment process. Current Tribal property interest holders are usually the descendants and/or the successors in interest to an original allottee that received property during the allotment process. Most individually owned trust lands have multiple co-owners, and the general administration of the land involves the United States Department of Interior as trustee, responsible for approving land transactions and accepting income derived from lands on behalf of the beneficiary. Probate and other legal matters involving trust lands come under the jurisdiction of special Department of Interior forums and, absent a federal statute to the contrary, are not heard in state or Tribal probate courts. These lands are heavily regulated through federal regulations and federal agency approval processes. Tribal members have been left in the dark for over a century on the status of leases of their Tribal lands, the amounts due under the leases entered into by the U.S. Department of Interior as trustee, and how to assert their ownership rights in decision-making for use of their Tribal lands, particularly when those lands are fractionated into a multitude of co-owners.

The United States also holds lands in trust for Tribal Nations. These lands are either lands that remained in Tribal Nation ownership following the allotment process or lands that have been put into trust for Tribal Nations after the 1930s. The Secretary of the Interior has the authority to take lands into trust and routinely does so under 25 U.S.C §§ 5103, 5104, and 5110 as a way of both revamping Tribal land bases and as a way of reaffirming clear U.S.-Tribal Nation jurisdiction over a tract of land. Tribal Nations are actively engaged in repurchasing lands lost through the U.S. government's allotment and surplus policies.

For instance, if a Tribal Nation purchases a tract of fee land that was lost due to the allotment process or other dispossession, the land does not become "Tribal land" by the unilateral action of the Tribal becoming the fee title owner, under U.S. law. In order to guarantee that the Tribal Nation will have presumed jurisdiction over the land and protect the land from state taxation and regulation and operations of state law such as eminent domain or adverse possession that could deprive the Tribal Nation of future ownership in the land, it is necessary to have the land accepted into trust status by the United States. Although there are positive consequences for the Tribal Nations in the Secretary of the Interior's land-into-trust power, there are also downsides for the Tribal Nations to consider.

Trust status creates a restriction on alienation that protects the land from quick sale, but it also takes decision-making authority away from the Tribal Nation and places control in the federal government as the trustee empowered to make decisions regarding leasing, business development, rights-of-way and other considerations. It also means that once tribally controlled land is now "federal" land and subject to federal laws such as environmental controls and other land use regulations that the lands may not be subject to under fee ownership. For example, the fee-to-trust process for a parcel of land purchased by a Tribal Nation must proceed through sixteen steps within the BIA, including step seven, which is a determination under the National Environmental Protection Act (NEPA) on an environmental assessment or the need for an environmental impact statement that can be costly and time-consuming. For more information on this process, see the 2016 *Acquisition of Title to Land Held in Fee or Restricted Fee Status (Fee-To-Trust Handbook)*, available on the U.S. Department of the Interior website. Particularly in the business context, the decision of whether to place land into trust can be a difficult balance of competing concerns, as well as an expensive time-consuming endeavor.

Another example of special federal law provisions for Tribal trust lands occurs when a Tribal Nation plans to operate a Tribal gaming business on land purchased within or contiguous to the reservation boundaries and placed into trust status. Under the provisions of the 1988 Indian Gaming Regulatory Act, 25 U.S.C. 2701 et seq., any newly acquired lands after 1988 must proceed through a two-part test by the Secretary of Interior to allow development of a gaming business on the Tribal lands. Those steps are: (1) that the Secretary of Interior "determine that a gaming establishment on newly acquired lands would be in the best interest of the Indian tribe and its members, and would not be detrimental to the surrounding community," and (2) that the governor of the relevant state concurs in the Secretary's determination. 25 U.S.C. § 2719(b)(1)(A) and 25 C.F.R. § 292 Gaming on Trust Lands Acquired After Oct. 17, 1988. Tribal gaming operations are only available under federal law on Tribal trust lands. 25 U.S.C. § 2710. This is one example of the U.S. federal laws and regulations that may require additional processes for Tribal Nations in the purchase, placement in trust status, and use of their Tribal lands in furthering economic development goals.

b. Restricted Lands

Federal restraints on the alienation of Native American land can also be accomplished by statute or regulation. Under this approach, legal title remains with the Tribal Nation or individual Tribal member, rather than the United States, but legal restrictions keep the land from being sold or otherwise encumbered with liens or subject to state taxation. The land could later revert to fee status, either by operation of an event prescribed by statute such as the expiration of a designated time period, or by a legislative amendment lifting the restriction.

c. Fee Lands

Given the aftermath of the allotment process, where trust and restricted lands lost their protected status or large amounts of "surplus" lands were converted from Tribal Nation ownership, it is now common for both individual non-Natives and Tribal Nations to own parcels of fee lands inside Indian Country. In fact, some Tribal Nations are the minority landowners inside their territory with the majority of lands being owned by non-Tribal individuals or entities, including state and locally owned lands. Fee lands can be freely sold and are subject to state taxation. Fee lands can also be mortgaged without concern for federal or Tribal consent. Probate and other administration of fee lands does not involve the federal government, even for Tribal-owned lands inside Indian Country. Tribal Nations seeking to consolidate land parcels within reservation boundaries may purchase lands initially in fee status and then proceed through the lengthy fee-to-trust process described above. The U.S. Supreme Court has held in *City of Sherrill v. Oneida Indian Nation of N.Y.*, 544 U.S. 197 (2005), that in repurchasing Tribal lands within its Tribal territory, which had been historically sold in violation of the Trade and Intercourse Act provisions, the Oneida Nation held the lands in fee title and was required to follow the BIA fee-to-trust process for state tax exemption and other features of Tribal land status.

Fee land ownership outside of Indian Country is simply subject to the property law rules of jurisdiction where the property is located. If a Tribal Nation or individual Tribal member purchases or acquires an interest in fee lands outside of Indian Country, no special legal status attaches to that land, unless the Secretary of Interior exercises the power to take that property into trust. It is more difficult and more unlikely to see lands taken into trust unless the area where the land is located is on or near a Tribal territory or original homeland.

2. Alaska Native Villages and Tribal Lands

In 1867, Russia purportedly sold all of its rights to the United States in the territory that would become the state of Alaska, which was admitted on January 3, 1959. Alaska Native Villages or Tribal Nations were intermittently contacted by U.S. officials and the Tribal Nations regularly expressed concerns over the encroachment on their Tribal lands and resources. Squatters, non-Native businesses, state officials, and, at times, federal officials utilized Tribal Nation resources and lands without the express consent of the Alaska Native Villages. The U.S. Supreme Court decision in *Tee-Hit-Ton v. the United States*, 348 U.S. 272 (1955), further complicated matters by holding that without federal law recognizing Tribal title no compensation was required if the United States extinguished "Indian occupancy" title and allowed clearcutting of Alaska Native forests. In 1966, Alaska Native leaders formed the Alaska Federation of Nations (AFN) and pressed the U.S. Congress for legislation to recognize Tribal title. After years of negotiation, a compromise federal law was reached with a completely different structure for the settlement of Tribal land title and economic engagement for Tribal Nations.

The Alaska Native Claims Settlement Act (ANCSA) of 1971 divided up the Tribal lands under the authority of Alaska Native Corporations, structured under state law with special features for the Alaska Native Villages. From its enactment, the ANCSA redefined the relationship of small local Alaska Native Villages as Tribal governments to shareholders in Alaska Native Corporations holding Tribal lands as fee lands pursuant to the federal settlement of title. The scheme was complicated in establishing regional for-profit corporations, originally 13, now 12, to share in the valuable mineral, energy, and other resources in the settlement lands held in fee. In addition to regional corporations, over two hundred local Alaska Native Village corporations were authorized, with some consolidating between Tribal Nations. The Alaska Native Village corporations usually retained only surface rights to Tribal lands in fee status under the ANCSA provisions. In the ANSCA, the federal law anticipated the expiration of restrictions on shares and that the diverse and often remote Alaska Native Villages would adapt to corporate practices by 1991.

When this did not occur, the U.S. Congress enacted amendments to ANCSA in 1988 that are often referred to as the "1991 Amendments." The complicated legal status of shareholders led to amendments for "afterborns" of 1971 to be allowed to gain shareholder status by amending the articles of incorporation for Alaska Native Corporations and the extension of restrictions on selling shares into perpetuity to prevent those who are not Alaska Native Tribal members from gaining the shares. Alaska Native Tribal members may gift, will, or bequeath their shares. Under this federally created corporate structure, Alaska Native Corporation shares are not subject to federal securities laws and have state and federal law requirements in their operations.

From the U.S. Bureau of Indian Affairs website on the Alaska Region, "[t]he entire state of Alaska falls under the jurisdiction of the Alaska Region, with the small exception of the Annette Island Reserve, which falls under the Northwest Region. More than 180,000 Tribal members make up the 228 Federally Recognized Tribes under the jurisdiction of the Alaska Regional Office—from Ketchikan in the Southeast Panhandle to Barrow on the Arctic Ocean and from Eagle on the Yukon Territory border to Atka in the Aleutian Chain." Alaska Native Tribal Nations compose almost half of the federally recognized Tribes in the United States and are spread out in urban and remote locations across a vast land area. Travel to some of the Alaska Native Villages requires several modes of transportation from commercial airlines to six-seater airplanes to boats for river crossings to four-wheeler ATVs to navigate mostly mud and gravel roads.

Alaska Native Villages have been subject to conflicting U.S. Presidential Administrations issuing opinions on the ability to take lands into trust. The current federal regulations on taking land into trust status for Tribal Nations allows for the Tribal Nations of Alaska, otherwise known as Alaska Native Villages, to engage in the fee-to-trust process, 25 C.F.R. § 151.1, as of 2014. Prior to this revision in 2014, Alaska Native Tribal Nations had been blocked from placing Tribal lands into trust status. With this fee-to-trust process for Alaska Native Villages reaffirmed in April 2021 in the M-37069 Solicitor's Opinion, these Tribal Nations may begin the process of adding to the Tribal land base for housing, business development, schools, and all other governmental and societal purposes.

3. The Future

At the time lands were allotted, it was presumed by the policy advocates that Tribal Nations would dissolve and, within a generation or two, there would be no Tribal land base or territory. As a result, there was no long range planning or thought given to how individual Tribal members or the Tribal Nations would maintain or administer land tenure systems today. The system that followed, with federal administration of trust land, is plagued with an overall lack of local control and inefficiencies that leave much of the land base encumbered by a broken system. In recent years, it has become clear that reform of the present system is needed from a trust management standpoint. To date, small measures have been taken to place control back at the local Tribal level.

Within many Tribal Nations there exists a Tribal realty or property office that contracts with the Bureau of Indian Affairs to perform federal property functions at the Tribal level, such as approving leases, transfers of property interest, land use management, the acquisition of appraisals, etc. Therefore, instead of dealing directly with the Department of Interior, individual Tribal members and those that seek information on the status of lands can consult local offices rather than relying on federal officials. Yet where these arrangements for Tribal self-government exist, the Tribal officials are carrying out a federal function pursuant to federal laws and regulations rather than implementing a land tenure system prescribed by the Tribal Nations.

Following *Cobell v. Salazar*, 572 F.3d 808 (D.D.C. 2009), a class action lawsuit brought by Tribal citizen allottees against the United States involving claims of federal mismanagement of property and assets, the Department of Interior was charged to reconsider reform to the current system. Past attempts at reform have not been successful in effectuating meaningful change but have led to minor improvements geared toward the reestablishment of Tribal land bases, consolidation of ownership to address fractionated allotments, and estate planning to address a backlog in federal probate of Tribal lands. Following *Cobell*, the Secretary of the Interior appointed a National Commission on American Indian Trust Administration and Reform. The Commission completed its work and filed a report in December 2013. The Commission recommended regulatory and legislative changes as well as significant restructuring of federal offices that administrator Tribal property and resources to avoid future conflicts of interests.

A contemporary "Land Back" movement is underway across Indian Country, driven in part by popular Tribal culture, arts, politics, and stewardship. This movement continues the tradition of past Tribal leaders to assert that unfair practices in the taking of Tribal lands must be remedied through the return of Tribal lands, not merely monetary compensation. As was demonstrated in the 1980 *Sioux Nation* case and the subsequent collective Tribal Nation decision to refuse the payment awarded by the federal courts, Tribal lands are not viewed as fungible resources that can be easily converted into monetary judgments. With Tribal activism continuing in the form of protecting connections to lands separated from the Tribal land base, the "Land Back" movement is raising awareness and allowing for renewed scrutiny on the U.S. claim to gain certain Tribal lands, the need to reform U.S. federal regulations over Tribal trust lands, and the limitations on Tribal Nations through purchase, litigation, or negotiations for the return and recognition of homelands.

CHECKPOINTS

- Tribal Nation property ownership concepts continue to inform contemporary Tribal property laws. Tribal realty offices implement Tribal laws and regulations.
- Native American property law is important to understanding the extent of Tribal regulatory authority. Tribal reservation boundaries provide the basic area of the Tribal land base. The allotment process has changed the status of land within reservation boundaries.
- The Bureau of Indian Affairs, on behalf of the U.S. government, has management authority over the more than 55 million acres of Tribal land in trust status. Tribal lands in trust status are recognized under Tribal regulatory authority and are exempt from state property taxation.
- The Office of Special Trustee within the Department of the Interior has the responsibility of ensuring the accountability of the U.S. government in managing trust fund accounts for Tribal member owners of lands in trust status.
- The three main types of Tribal property are: reservation and trust lands, restricted lands, and fee lands.
- Alaska Native Villages have been subject to unique federal law on the management of Tribal lands in fee status through regional and village corporations and may utilize the federal fee-to-trust process to increase Tribal land holdings.
- Reclaiming Tribal lands and stewardship of those lands is part of a social, cultural, and political movement known as "Land Back" across Indian Country.

CHAPTER 3

Criminal Jurisdiction in Indian Country

ROADMAP

- Learn about Tribal Nation responses to community safety, engaging with criminal law, and using traditional methods of restoring balance to the social order.
- Learn that contemporary Tribal Nations have recognized authority to operate judicial systems with criminal jurisdiction over all Tribal members within the Tribal territory, including Tribal citizens/members of other Tribes. Learn under what circumstances Tribal courts may prosecute any person charged with certain criminal activity in the Tribal territory.
- Learn that criminal jurisdiction on Tribal lands continues to be an area of law that is subject to change due to a history of inconsistent federal prosecutions, limitations on Tribal criminal sentencing authority, and the crisis of Missing and Murdered Indigenous persons in the U.S. Legal scholars have referred to the maze of criminal jurisdiction in Indian Country, due to federal legislation and federal judicial decisions imposing various limitations on prosecutorial authority.
- Learn that the U.S. has enacted federal laws severely limiting the criminal sentencing ability of Tribal courts. In addition, federal laws allow for felony federal criminal jurisdiction over crimes perpetrated by Tribal members or against Tribal members within Indian Country.
- Understand that the U.S. government has enacted legislation to delegate federal criminal authority in Indian Country to state governments on a limited basis under Public Law 280 or in specific federal

laws. Understand that the U.S. Supreme Court has supported state prosecutorial authority in Indian Country over non-Indians committing crimes against Tribal members concurrently with federal prosecutorial authority.

- Know that the criminal jurisdiction analysis requires: identification of the land base upon which the crime allegedly occurred, identification of the perpetrator as a Tribal citizen or not, identification of the victim as a Tribal citizen or not, and cooperation between prosecuting authorities on the Tribal, U.S. and/or state level. Know that the U.S. courts have engaged in tests evaluating the Tribal status of a person for federal prosecution.
- Know that Tribes retain concurrent criminal jurisdiction over any crime perpetrated by a Tribal member of any Tribe within Indian Country and may have concurrent authority for certain crimes by non-Indians within Indian Country.
- Know that "Indian Country" is a legal term of art that serves as a jurisdictional marker as defined by the federal criminal statute, often referred to as the Indian Country statute, 18 U.S.C. § 1151.

Tribal Nations have traditional structures for maintaining societal order that have been translated into the duties of Tribal law enforcement, Tribal prosecutors, Tribal public defenders, and Tribal judges over time. During the sovereign-to-sovereign era of U.S. Indian policy, treaties may have asserted that when a Tribal member was alleged to commit harm that the U.S. would impose a monetary penalty as a fine from Tribal treaty payments with the understanding that the Tribal leadership had authority over any societal action to punish the rule breaker. Other treaties had language that weighed in favor of delivering up any Tribal rule breaker to U.S. authorities. With silence in many treaties, Tribal Nations continued to maintain societal norms and laws through holding any person within the Tribal territory accountable for violation of Tribal law. The shifting authority over law violators in Indian Country continues to be a source of frustration and negotiation between Tribal Nations committed to safe neighborhoods and communities and the U.S. government through, at times conflicting, legislation and judicial decisions.

To determine the extent and scope of criminal jurisdiction in Indian Country, one must consider whether inherent Tribal Nation powers have been recognized as retained and whether federal statutes provide for federal and/or state prosecutions over the matter. It is well-established that Tribal Nations retain criminal jurisdiction to prosecute any Tribal citizen of any Tribal Nation for crimes that take place within Indian Country. Under certain circumstances for specific crimes, Tribal Nations may prosecute non-Indians committing crimes in Indian Country. Depending on the nature of the crime and the parties involved, U.S. laws also provide for federal prosecution of Tribal citizens and non-Indians. Through federal delegations of criminal prosecutorial authority, states may be a second or third prosecutorial authority in Indian Country depending on the parties involved in the crime. A defendant can be prosecuted by more than one sovereign, meaning Tribal, U.S. or state governments, because the power to prosecute stems from different sources of law. This chapter will provide the basic framework of the criminal prosecutorial authority in Indian Country.

A Tribal Nation's power to prosecute is derived from inherent Tribal Nation sovereignty. U.S. power is derived from U.S. congressional authority in Indian affairs and is buttressed by the notion that the federal government is serving as a guardian of Tribal Nations as wards, as discussed in Chapter One. When states have the power to prosecute crimes within Indian Country, that power is derived by delegation of federal power in Indian affairs or a power reserved to the states by the U.S. Constitution. There is limited inherent state power to prosecute inside Indian Country.

In this chapter, inherent Tribal Nation powers will be discussed, followed by an examination of subsequent limitations on inherent Tribal Nation powers imposed by U.S. statutes and judicial decisions. The two key factors of greatest significance in the analysis of criminal jurisdiction in Indian Country are: (1) the race or Tribal citizen status of the alleged perpetrator and victim; and (2) status of the land where the alleged criminal activity occurred. Due to the necessary analysis of these factors and other considerations in this area, criminal jurisdiction in Indian Country is notably a very complex area of law. This chapter will highlight the contours of Tribal Nation criminal jurisdiction, U.S. criminal jurisdiction, and state criminal jurisdiction in Indian Country.

A. Tribal Nation Criminal Jurisdiction

Tribal Nation societies placed a high value on law and order in historical Tribal communities. Often a particular clan or social group had primary responsibility for law enforcement duties in the Tribal structure. As noted in previous chapters, there are many Tribal Nations and philosophies of law and order were diverse. Those who violated Tribal laws would be dealt consequences in line with the Tribal philosophy. For many Tribal Nations, that meant bringing the community back into balance. These concepts of community balance between the perpetrator or rule breaker and society have been adapted by the restorative justice movement in the United States. Historically, Tribal Nation punishments for wrong-doers or rule breakers could range from public shaming, whereby the misdeeds of the community member were announced at a community gathering, to expulsion from the Tribal Nation community. Some Tribes used a permanent facial scar to mark the expelled perpetrator as unworthy of being part of a human society. In contrast and in keeping with the diversity of laws and cultural norms between various Tribal Nations, other Tribes were known to have retributive laws that resulted in public execution or severe flogging for certain offenses. Law and order were maintained as necessary for Tribal societies to flourish with healthy and thriving Tribal members of every generation.

Within communities where communal balance was central, lawbreakers often faced the law enforcement clan and were informed of the actions they would be required to complete to restore the Tribal Nation or society communal balance. Remedial actions could include providing goods and services to a family injured by the lawbreaker's misdeeds and/or periods of solitary reflection and spiritual instruction for the lawbreaker. Behaviors detrimental to others in the community were swiftly and effectively dealt with in historical Tribal communities to maintain social values and prevent further infractions stemming from the original misdeed. For repeat offenders, the consequences were steep. Banishment from the Tribal Nation, community, family and friends was viewed as one of the most severe punishments handed down to an offender. This approach ensured a sense of belonging, protection, and social goodwill, without which the human existence would be desolate and solitary. Another extreme punishment employed by some Tribal communities for a recurring offender would be death.

1. Contemporary Tribal Nation Justice Systems, Tribal Constitutional Rights, and Criminal Sentencing

There are over 300 federally recognized Tribal Nation justice systems currently in operation in the United States. Tribal justice systems may have all or some of the following components: court system, public defender services, prosecutor, probation office, law enforcement department, and Tribal detention center, wellness or specialized courts, and addiction treatment programs. Tribal governments are in the first instance responsible for funding Tribal justice systems along with other governmental functions. The Bureau of Indian Affairs has oversight for federal funding of Tribal Nation justice systems including the Office of Justice Systems. The U.S. Department of Justice also provides grant funding opportunities that are available to Tribal Nations through the Office on Violence Against Women and Office of Justice Programs with a high priority on local governmental safety.

The Indian Self-Determination and Education Assistance Act of 1975, Public Law 93-638, provided a process whereby Tribal Nations may enter into a contract with the BIA for services provided in Tribal communities, often treaty-guaranteed services. Most of the law enforcement departments operated by Tribal Nations are administered under this type of contract from the BIA for federal funding. Components not administered by a Tribal Nation are the responsibility of the BIA for law and order in Indian Country. The BIA provides training for both BIA and Tribal Nation police officers at the Indian Police Academy in Artesia, New Mexico. One of the common constraints of Tribal law enforcement is the underfunding of these departments to the detriment of Tribal Nation communities. The National Congress of American Indians (NCAI) has estimated that the number of active duty BIA and Tribal law enforcement officers is currently at half the amount needed to adequately meet public safety needs in Indian Country. In the regular course of work for Tribal law enforcement, alleged perpetrators in Indian Country are arrested and subject to prosecution as defendants in Tribal courts. For the 200 plus Alaska Native Villages, there is a program known as the Village Public Safety Officer (VPSO) program under the authority of the Alaska State Troopers Division, which is often the only local response to criminal activity in remote locations.

In recent years, drug trafficking has been a major issue in Indian Country with the growing opioid epidemic, a major meth crisis, and the use of heroin, although drug threats differ among Tribal Nation communities and regional-ly. Native Americans experience a higher rate of death by drug overdose than any other demographic. In 2018, the Office of Justice Services received reports from Tribal Nation law enforcement and BIA programs that there was a 47 percent increase in drug cases and an increase of 26 percent in drug-related arrests on reservations across the country. These statistics include the seizure of marijuana in forms that have been legalized in some states but not in others.

Defendants within the criminal jurisdiction of a Tribal Nation may rely on laws and Tribal constitutional provisions to uphold their rights to due process under such laws. The Indian Civil Rights Act (ICRA) passed in 1968 provided guidelines to Tribal Nation justice systems on adopting a thinner modified version of the U.S. Bill of Rights, 25 U.S.C. § 1302(a). The ICRA provisions on the modified individual rights in Tribal Nation criminal proceedings may be adopted into Tribal law as a condition of securing federal funding for the functioning of the Tribal judicial system. The ICRA includes severe criminal sentencing limitations on Tribal courts that have been incrementally modified by federal legislation over several decades of lobbying by Tribal leadership on the necessity of local law enforcement and increased prosecutorial authority to curb lawlessness in Indian Country.

An early U.S. Supreme Court decision involving a Cherokee person-on-Cherokee person murder inside the Cherokee Nation, *Talton v. Mayes,* 163 U.S. 376 (1896), held that the U.S. Bill of Rights was not applicable to Tribal governments as separate sovereigns. In that case, a Cherokee Nation criminal conviction that included a Cherokee grand jury indictment, followed by a criminal jury trial on the merits, appellate review, and a request for Cherokee executive pardon, was challenged under the U.S. Constitution on the grounds that the grand jury had an insufficient number of participants than was required by U.S. law. This decision stands as good law that Tribal Nations are not bound to the provisions of the U.S. Constitution or the U.S. Bill of Rights provisions. Rather, Tribal Nations may adopt individual rights provisions within governing Tribal law or in the Tribal Nation Constitution. Tribal Nations are extraconstitutional or pre-constitutional in relation to the U.S. Constitution, as Tribal Nations did not engage in the adoption or establishment of the U.S. government.

In *Santa Clara Pueblo v. Martinez,* 436 U.S. 49 (1978), the U.S. Supreme Court interpreted the Indian Civil Rights Act as providing only habeas corpus relief for those challenging detention by a Tribal Nation through court processes and not providing any further causes of action in U.S. courts against a Tribal government. 436 U.S. at 69. Therefore, those alleging wrongful detention by a Tribal justice system may seek relief under the ICRA, 25 U.S.C.

§ 1303, and file a habeas corpus petition in federal court seeking release. Other due process rights asserted in a Tribal court proceeding must be based upon the Tribal Nation's laws or provisions in the Tribal constitution and remedied within the Tribal court system, not the federal courts. The necessity of adopting some key constitutional rights outlined in the ICRA is reflected in the increased sentencing ability of Tribal courts when providing procedural safeguards outlined in the Tribal Law and Order Act of 2010 (TLOA).

Tribal courts exercising criminal jurisdiction employ Tribal prosecutors, either through full-time employment or through a contract for services. Increasingly, Tribal court systems also include a tribally-funded public defender position to represent those criminally charged in the court system and unable to afford to pay for an attorney and the right of counsel has been present in many Tribal Nations since the creation of the Tribal justice system. To deal with the cost, some Tribal Nations have required attorneys that are licensed to practice before the courts to agree to accept court-appointed cases in criminal and family law cases, as needed. In *Talton v. Mayes*, mentioned above, the Cherokee defendant in Cherokee courts was represented by an attorney at all stages of the proceeding in the early 1890s.

Under the Indian Civil Rights Act (ICRA), 25 U.S.C. § 1301 et seq., Tribal courts may sentence a Tribal member offender up to one year of incarceration and/or a fine of $5,000 for any one offense. 25 U.S.C. § 1302(a)(7)(B). Recent developments in federal Indian law under the TLOA provide an incentive for offering public defender services by permitting those court systems greater sentencing capabilities than those that do not offer such services. Tribal courts meeting the additional due process safeguard requirements enacted through the TLOA may sentence a Tribal member offender up to three years of incarceration and/or a fine of up to $15,000 for an offense under Tribal law. 25 U.S.C. § 1302(a)(7)(C). These same sentencing standards apply when the Tribal Nation exercises special criminal jurisdiction over non-Native offenders discussed later in this chapter.

For the greater sentencing authority, the Tribal judge may impose the increased sentence where the defendant has a prior conviction in any U.S. jurisdiction for the same or a similar offense or where the defendant is charged with an offense that would be subject to more than one year incarceration in a federal or state criminal proceeding. 25 U.S.C. § 1302(b)(1) and (2). It should be noted that specific federal criminal statutes may provide for increased federal sentencing penalties based on previous Tribal court and/or federal and state convictions, such as in the federal serial domestic violence statute, 18

U.S.C. § 117(a). When sentencing beyond the basic one year incarceration and/or $5,000 fine limitations from the ICRA, there are five basic rights that must be provided to the defendant. 25 U.S.C. § 1302(c) provides the following requirements for Tribal judges to exercise the three year and/or $15,000 fine per offense greater sentencing authority under the TLOA standards.

> (c) Rights of defendants
>
> In a criminal proceeding in which an Indian tribe, in exercising powers of self-government, imposes a total term of imprisonment of more than 1 year on a defendant, the Indian tribe shall—
>
> (1) provide to the defendant the right to effective assistance of counsel at least equal to that guaranteed by the United States Constitution; and
>
> (2) at the expense of the tribal government, provide an indigent defendant the assistance of a defense attorney licensed to practice law by any jurisdiction in the United States that applies appropriate professional licensing standards and effectively ensures the competence and professional responsibility of its licensed attorneys;
>
> (3) require that the judge presiding over the criminal proceeding—
>
> (A) has sufficient legal training to preside over criminal proceedings; and
>
> (B) is licensed to practice law by any jurisdiction in the United States;
>
> (4) prior to charging the defendant, make publicly available the criminal laws (including regulations and interpretative documents), rules of evidence, and rules of criminal procedure (including rules governing the recusal of judges in appropriate circumstances) of the tribal government; and
>
> (5) maintain a record of the criminal proceeding, including an audio or other recording of the trial proceeding.

When a Tribal Nation court meets all of these requirements, then the imposition of greater sentences will allow the court to better match punishment with the severity of an offense committed by a defendant subject to Tribal prosecution. There are added financial costs for a Tribal judicial system to meet the increased procedural safeguards.

Federal criminal courts in Indian Country also exist for those Tribal Nations without an established court system. Originally established as instruments of eliminating cultural and spiritual practices of Tribal Nations and enforcing labor and assimilation policies, the Courts of Indian Offenses were established in 1886 as control mechanisms with nearby military forts for added threat. These Courts of Indian Offenses have been updated to the contemporary "CFR courts" because the operative criminal law is contained in the Code of Federal Regulations for Indian Country crimes. 25 CFR 11.100 provides a listing of the Tribal Nations utilizing such courts at present. CFR courts are trial courts with appeals taken to the Court of Indian Appeals. A majority of the CFR courts that remain are within the state of Oklahoma and are serving Tribal Nations in that region, although the number of CFR courts is in decline due to Tribal Nations taking over this function with their own Tribal Nation justice systems. In the U.S. Supreme Court decision *Denezpi v. United States*, 596 U.S. 591 (2022), the Court held that a CFR court conviction of a Navajo Nation person for a crime on the Ute Mountain Ute Reservation under an offense in the Tribal Nation criminal ordinance did not present a double jeopardy bar to a federal prosecution when the U.S. criminally charged Denezpi in federal court on a different offense.

2. Tribal Nation Criminal Jurisdiction Imposing and Removing Limitations by the U.S.

Tribal Nations exercise criminal jurisdiction from inherent powers of governing. The U.S. government through legislation has imposed restraints on Tribal Nations' ability to govern in the area of criminal jurisdiction. The U.S. Supreme Court has contributed to restraints on Tribal Nation governing authority over criminal activity occurring within Tribal Nation reservations and communities. The U.S. Indian Civil Rights Act of 1968, 25 U.S.C. §§ 1301 and 1302, provides the severe limitations imposed by the federal government on the exercise of Tribal Nation criminal jurisdiction. While Tribal Nation criminal codes provide the punishable offenses in Tribal courts accompanied by Tribal sentencing guidelines, the ICRA limited the extent of Tribal court sentencing power and, thereby, interfered with a Tribal Nation's ability to fully address public safety concerns.

In addition, the U.S. Supreme Court in *Oliphant v. Suquamish,* 435 U.S. 191 (1978), has imposed limitations on Tribal Nation criminal jurisdiction over non-Indians through the concept known as "implicit divestiture." This divestiture is purportedly a result of the categorization of Tribal Nations as "domestic dependent nations." The U.S. Supreme Court ruled in *Oliphant* that through the incorporation of Tribal Nations within the geographic boundaries of the

United States and due to the guardian-ward relationship, certain aspects of Tribal Nation sovereignty have been lost, including criminal jurisdiction over non-Indians. In reaching the decision, the Supreme Court determined that criminal jurisdiction over "non-Indians" was not a power that Tribal Nations historically exercised and therefore it was not an inherent Tribal Nation power. The historical record on this point is in conflict with noted examples of Tribal Nations exercising such jurisdiction. In the *Oliphant* decision, the U.S. Supreme Court noted that the respondent Suquamish Indian Tribe had adopted a law and order code in 1973 that applied to crimes committed by "Indians and non-Indians." When the case was decided in 1978, over 45 Tribal Nations had Tribal statutes for criminal jurisdiction that could include application to Tribal members and non-Indians who commit crimes within Indian Country. Nonetheless, *Oliphant* stands as a bright line federal rule barring the Tribal Nation criminal jurisdiction over non-Indians and appears to apply to all Tribal Nations, absent a treaty provision or federal law to the contrary. This barrier to prosecution of non-Indians has given way in certain instances through federal legislation removing limitations and supporting "Special Tribal Criminal Jurisdiction" described later in this chapter.

In some instances, the U.S. Congress has responded to provide recognition for the inherent sovereign authority of Tribal Nations and judicial systems where the U.S. Supreme Court has previously initiated a limitation. Following *Oliphant* the U.S. Supreme Court extended the same logic in *Duro v. Reina,* 495 U.S. 676 (1990), holding that Tribes lack inherent authority to prosecute persons who are members of other Tribal Nations. *Duro* limited Tribal Nation authority to the Tribal citizens/members of the prosecuting Tribal Nation only and, in doing so, created a gap in jurisdiction where no sovereign had the authority to prosecute misdemeanor crimes committed by persons who were members of other Tribal Nations. Tribes could no longer prosecute based on the U.S. Supreme Court's decision in *Duro*. There was no federal statute creating federal jurisdiction over misdemeanors in Indian Country. States generally lack the authority to prosecute Tribal members for crimes that are committed inside Indian Country.

Both of the U.S. Supreme Court holdings limiting Tribal Nation criminal jurisdiction have been modified, to some extent, by later federal law. Closely following the *Duro* decision, Tribal leadership joined together nationally to seek federal legislation remedying the jurisdictional gap that was created through the Court's decision—namely, the complexity that would follow requiring law enforcement to first identify specific Tribal enrollment for al-

Prairie Band Potawatomi Signs. Photo credit: Mona Nozhackum.

leged Native American perpetrators before handling criminal situations. The U.S. Congress swiftly passed an amendment to the ICRA on November 5, 1990, acknowledging Tribal Nation criminal jurisdiction over all "Indians" in the Tribal territory. The definitional section of the ICRA was amended at 25 U.S.C. § 1301(2) to read: "'powers of self-government' means and includes all governmental powers possessed by an Indian tribe, executive, legislative, and judicial, and all offices, bodies, and tribunals by and through which they are executed, including courts of Indian offenses; and means the inherent power of Indian tribes, hereby recognized and affirmed, to exercise criminal jurisdiction over *all Indians*" (emphasis added). This amendment is commonly referred to as the "*Duro* fix," which effectively negated the U.S. Supreme Court's limitation on Tribal Nation criminal jurisdiction in the *Duro v. Reina* decision. The statute stands as federal recognition of the inherent power of Tribal Nations to govern in Tribal territories. Today, Tribal Nation court systems handle prosecutions of Tribal members from any Tribal Nation committing crimes within Indian Country.

In the mid 2000s, reports of widespread violence against Native American women in Tribal territories due to non-Native perpetrators were widely publicized. With the jurisdictional gap created by the *Oliphant* decision leaving prosecution of non-Indians committing crimes in Indian Country to either federal or state law enforcement, the victimization of Native American women reached epidemic proportions when those external law enforcement entities were not diligent in bringing prosecutions. This jurisdictional gap was particularly apparent when sexual violence was perpetrated by a non-Native male against a Tribal citizen female on Tribal lands. The seriousness of such widespread sexual violence was reported on by Amnesty International USA in 2007 through a report titled, *Maze of Injustice: The Failure to Protect Indigenous Women from Sexual Violence in the USA*. In the introductory chapter of the report, an overview of the violence experienced by Native American women revealed staggering statistics.

> Over the past decade, federal government studies have consistently shown that American Indian and Alaska Native women experience much higher levels of sexual violence than other women in the USA. Data gathered by the US Department of Justice indicates that Native American and Alaska Native women are more than 2.5 times more likely to be raped or sexually assaulted than women in the USA in general. A US Department of Justice study on violence against women concluded that 34.1 percent of American Indian and Alaska Native women—or more than one in three—will be raped during their lifetime; the comparable figure for the USA as a whole is less than one in five. Shocking though these statistics are, it is widely believed that they do not accurately portray the extent of sexual violence against Native American and Alaska Native women.

Maze of Injustice, p. 2. Also noted in the report is the maze that a Native American woman must navigate in bringing a non-Native perpetrator to justice for rape and/or acts of sexual violence. Response times are impacted when Tribal, state, and federal law enforcement need to determine the proper jurisdiction. When an alleged perpetrator is a Tribal member on Tribal lands, felony criminal acts of sexual violence would be within both Tribal Nation and federal criminal jurisdiction. Further, due to the known barriers to bring charges against alleged perpetrators, a substantial number of these types of crimes go unreported.

One of the attempted solutions Tribal Nations have employed for this law enforcement problem is to enter into cross-deputization agreements with local county and state law enforcement agencies to allow joint Tribal and state officers response authority when criminal activity occurs in Indian Country regardless of the racial or political status of the perpetrator. In these arrangements, all law enforcement are first responders to 911 and other emergency calls and the arresting officer is acting pursuant to the jurisdiction that has authority to arrest the suspect and try the case. When the immediate safety concerns are addressed and an arrest is made, the suspect is then delivered to the proper authority. The challenge is to have sufficient agreements in place. A Tribal Nation with a large land base that encompasses several state towns and counties could have as many as 50 different cross-deputization agreements in place with the various municipalities, sheriff's offices, state patrols, natural resources officers, and other Tribal law enforcement departments. Support for streamlining this type of law enforcement collaboration in Indian Country was affirmed by the U.S. Supreme in the *U.S. v. Cooley*, 593 U.S. 345 (2021), unanimous decision that upheld the ability of Tribal Nation police officers to temporarily detain and search non-Indians within Tribal territorial boundaries on suspicion of federal and/or state criminal activity. The Court noted that "no treaty or statute has explicitly divested Indian tribes of the policing authority at issue." 593 U.S. at 350. After a temporary detention and search, Tribal Nation police officers are expected to notify proper federal or state authorities of any probable cause for the violation of federal and/or state criminal law.

Tribal law enforcement also works closely with the U.S. Department of Justice and U.S. attorneys for interagency coordination to respond to non-Native crime on Tribal lands and to respond to violent crimes and drug trafficking where federal prosecutions could result. Without full criminal jurisdiction over all those who enter the Tribal Nation territory, Tribal Nations and communities must rely on external agencies to curb lawlessness and violence stemming from non-Native activity within the Tribal jurisdiction.

After the enactment of the TLOA, collaboration and reporting standards were set in place, as the law directed the U.S. attorneys serving Indian Country to provide information on when federal prosecutions are declined; the appointment of a Tribal Liaison in each district office serving Indian Country; and coordination with Tribal Nation law enforcement on criminal investigations and prosecutions in Tribal courts. The TLOA required an assessment by U.S. and Tribal Nation officials on the needs for Tribal detention facilities in Indian Country, including juvenile detention facilities and construction of federal detention centers. Under 25 U.S.C. § 1302(a), the federal Bureau of Prisons was authorized to contain Tribal court convicted persons sentenced to a minimum of one year incarceration at the expense of the United States as long as the number of Tribal Nation convicted persons did not exceed 100 persons. The U.S. Department of Justice maintains a website on "Tribal Justice and Safety," https://www.justice.gov/tribal, that provides information on collaboration with Tribal Nations, reports on federal law enforcement efforts in Indian Country, current grant opportunities for Tribal Nations to participate in law enforcement training, and reports from Tribal Nation consultations and advisory groups. In recent years, the process for Tribal Nations to apply for Office of Tribal Justice funding has been streamlined to permit one application for multiple grant programs. The work continues to provide better means to collaborate and provide support on all levels for safe and healthy Tribal Nation communities.

3. Partial Federal Response to Non-Native Perpetrators in Indian Country: The Exercise of Special Tribal Criminal Jurisdiction under Federal Law

In response for the repeated calls for removing restraints on Tribal Nation criminal jurisdiction to address local criminal activity by non-Indians, the U.S. Congress has responded through provisions in the 2013 and 2022 reauthorizations of the Violence Against Women Act. In March of 2013, the Violence Against Women Act (VAWA) was reauthorized and included amendments to the Indian Civil Rights Act recognizing the inherent authority of Tribal governments and judicial systems "to exercise special domestic violence jurisdiction *over all persons* (emphasis added)." The 2013 VAWA "Special Tribal Domestic Violence Jurisdiction" (STDVJ) focused on the crimes of domestic violence, dating violence, and criminal violations of protection orders. In 2017, the Pascua Yaqui Tribe was the first Tribal Nation to successfully prosecute a non-Native under the new VAWA provisions with a conviction for domestic violence and malicious mischief under Tribal Nation law. The defendant in that case was a repeat offender out on probation from prior domestic violence crimes at the time of violence that gave rise to the new charges. With this lessening of limitations on Tribal Nation criminal sentencing for domestic violence offenses, many Tribal Nations revised Tribal criminal codes to adapt to the federal law provisions.

With the 2022 reauthorization of VAWA, Tribal Nations may choose to participate in the "Special Tribal Criminal Jurisdiction" (STCJ) removal of restraints to permit Tribal Nation courts to prosecute all persons, including non-Indians, within Indian Country for the specific listed crimes in 25 U.S.C. § 1304(5).

> (5) Covered crime
>
> The term "covered crime" means—
>
> (A) assault of Tribal justice personnel;
> (B) child violence;
> (C) dating violence;
> (D) domestic violence;
> (E) obstruction of justice;
> (F) sexual violence;
> (G) sex trafficking;
> (H) stalking; and
> (I) a violation of a protection order.

As with the greater sentencing available under the TOLA, the Special Tribal Criminal Jurisdiction has additional requirements for Tribal Nation courts to implement the federal law. First, the STCJ applies to all persons within Tribal lands. Within the 2022 enactment, the U.S. Congress affirmed the inherent authority of Tribal Nations to exercise this criminal jurisdiction. "Notwithstanding any other provision of law, in addition to all powers of self-government recognized and affirmed by sections 1301 and 1303 of this title, the powers of self-government of a participating tribe, including any participating tribes in the State of Maine, include the inherent power of that tribe, which is hereby recognized and affirmed, to exercise special Tribal criminal jurisdiction over all persons." 25 U.S.C. § 1304(b)(1). In the next section, the federal law provides that concurrent jurisdiction continues to exist with any exercise of Tribal Nation jurisdiction. "The exercise of special Tribal criminal jurisdiction by a participating tribe shall be concurrent with the jurisdiction of the United States, of a State, or of both." 25 U.S.C. § 1304(b)(2). The Alaska Native Villages as Tribal Nations have the ability to participate in exercising this updated authority as well. Thus, the holding in the 1978 *Oliphant* decision has been partially modified by federal law recognizing that when the offense alleged is a listed crime within the Special Tribal Criminal Jurisdiction law, then federally approved Tribal Nation courts may prosecute any person committing such an offense against a Native American person within the Tribal territory.

Next, the Tribal Nation court must ensure threshold procedural safeguards to exercise the STCJ over all persons. Two particular safeguards include the right to an impartial jury and the right to file a federal habeas corpus petition to federal court challenging the Tribal Nation court's jurisdiction and an additional petition to stay detention by the Tribe. The impartial jury requirements include drawing from a cross-section of the community and not systematically excluding non-Indians or other distinctive community groups from serving on the Tribal court jury. 25 U.S.C. § 1304(d).

With this removal of limitations on Tribal Nation criminal jurisdiction, Tribal Nation courts will be in a better position to address the violence suffered by Native American women, children, and all other Native persons caused by any person engaging in the listed criminal activity on Tribal lands. As Tribal Nations are restored to exercise their inherent governmental powers in the criminal law sphere, Tribal peoples and all residents are able to live in safety knowing reservations and Tribal communities are properly patrolled and perpetrators of violence are dealt with. This section has noted significant removal of limitations for specific criminal activity, but there remain large swaths of criminal offenses that require greater criminal sentencing than that currently permitted under the Indian Civil Rights Act for Tribal Nation courts. The extent of federal and state criminal jurisdiction will be more fully discussed in the next sections.

B. Federal Criminal Jurisdiction: Federal Court Decisions and Federal Legislation Impacting Tribal Nation Criminal Jurisdiction

A major impetus for the development of federal Indian law has arisen from the area of criminal law. Prior to the removal and reservation eras, the United States entered into treaties with Tribal Nations often with terms requiring each side to punish offenders harming the other side. Some treaties required a Tribal Nation to turn over detained U.S. citizens and others recognized Tribal Nation authority to punish trespassing U.S. citizens in Tribal Nation territories. As the removal and reservation eras were underway, the federal officials in the BIA sought greater control over criminal matters in Indian Country.

The next section will provide the relevant federal statutory and federal judicial opinion underpinnings for four types of criminal jurisdiction in Indian Country: (1) federal criminal jurisdiction over Tribal citizen perpetrators; (2) federal prosecution of crimes between Tribal citizen and non-Indians; (3) criminal jurisdiction over non-Native perpetrators; and (4) state criminal jurisdiction within Indian Country. The following laws apply only when the alleged crime occurred in Indian Country as defined in 18 U.S.C. § 1151.

1. Extension of Federal Criminal Jurisdiction into Indian Country over Indian/Tribal Citizen Perpetrators

The primary historical case demonstrating the tension between federal officials seeking criminal prosecution of Tribal citizens and Tribal Nation sovereignty was *Ex Parte Crow Dog,* 109 U.S. 556 (1883). The lawsuit reached the U.S. Supreme Court as a habeas corpus petition for wrongful imprisonment by the U.S. of Lakota Tribal citizen Crow Dog in the Dakota Territory for the crime of murder of another Tribal leader, Chief Spotted Tail. Crow Dog had been tried and sentenced to execution in federal court. The U.S. Supreme Court held that the U.S. lacked jurisdiction over Crow Dog for his actions in his Tribal Nation territory against another Tribal person, rejecting arguments that treaties or federal statutes extended federal authority into Tribal Nation jurisdictions for Tribal citizen prosecution. The BIA seized upon the case to build political pressure to extend federal criminal jurisdiction into Indian Country. The efforts led to the passage of the Major Crimes Act (MCA) of 1885, 18 U.S.C. § 1153, listing the felony level crimes permitting an alleged Native American perpetrator to be charged and tried in federal court. The listed crimes have been updated and modified since 1885. A recent modification included expanding the specific felony assault crimes listed to match the general broader catalog of federal assault crimes contained in 18 U.S.C. § 113 as under the MCA federal jurisdiction if committed in Indian Country.

The Major Crimes Act represented a significant departure from the limited authority of the U.S. Congress in the U.S. Constitution to regulate commerce with Tribal Nations. The constitutional authority for the MCA was swiftly challenged in *U.S. v. Kagama,* 118 U.S. 375 (1886). The U.S. Supreme Court addressed the central issue as a question of federal or state criminal jurisdiction over the alleged Tribal citizen perpetrator on the Hoopa Valley Reservation. The Court reasoned that the federal government should act as a shield for the defendant from state prosecution.

> These Indian tribes *are* wards of the nation. They are communities dependent on the United States.... Because of the local ill feeling, the people of the States where they are found are often their deadliest enemies. From their very weakness and helplessness, so largely due to the course of dealing of the Federal Government with them and the treaties in which it has been promised, there arises a duty of protection, and with it the power. This has always been recognized by the Executive and by Congress, and by this court, whenever the question has arisen. 118 U.S. at 383–384.

Thus, the constitutionality of the MCA was upheld as within a protective power of the U.S. Congress over Indian affairs in this decision. The Court relied on a policy rationale rather than finding support in the text of the U.S. Constitution to uphold this extension of federal jurisdiction into Tribal Nation community affairs.

To apply the Major Crimes Act for federal prosecution, it must be included in the indictment and proven beyond a reasonable doubt that the defendant is an "Indian" and the crime occurred in Indian Country, as one of the listed major crimes. Different tests have arisen in the Eighth Circuit courts and the Ninth Circuit courts to determine whether a person qualifies as "Indian" for federal prosecution under the MCA. The reach to uphold federal prosecution has led to some federal courts espousing a standard of whether a person is viewed as a Tribal person for federal or Tribal Nation services or socially participating in Tribal activities on Tribal lands, which are easier thresholds to reach than actual verified Tribal membership in a federally recognized Tribal Nation.

The Eighth Circuit Court of Appeals in *U.S. v. Stymiest,* 581 F.3d 759 (8th Cir. 2009) announced five factors to be considered equally for a jury determination on whether the defendant qualified as an "Indian" person as a factual matter beyond a reasonable doubt: (1) enrollment in a Tribal Nation, (2) government recognition formally or informally through providing the defendant assistance reserved only to Tribal members, (3) Tribal Nation recognition formally or informally through subjecting the defendant to Tribal court jurisdiction, (4) enjoying benefits of Tribal affiliation, and (5) social recognition as a Tribal person through living on a reservation and participating in the local social life, including whether the defendant holds himself out as a Native

American. 581 F.3d at 763. The Ninth Circuit Court of Appeals test is composed of two parts: (1) defendant must have some "Indian" blood "whether or not traceable to a federally recognized" Tribal Nation; and (2) defendant must be "a member of, or is affiliated with a federally recognized" Tribal Nation. See *U.S. v. Zepeda,* 792 F.3d 1103 (9th Cir. 2015). In this decision, the Ninth Circuit further stated that a federal judge as a matter of law may determine whether a Tribal Nation is federally recognized. 792 F.3d. at 1107.

In sum, the Eighth Circuit test is much broader, allowing the inclusion of a person for federal criminal prosecution as an "Indian" when the same person may not be eligible for Tribal Nation citizenship or federal services. The Ninth Circuit's inclusion of language on "affiliation" may be read as expanding the category of persons beyond the purview of the Tribal Nation's membership process. For persons who do not qualify for Tribal membership or do not satisfy the federal court tests for federal prosecution as an "Indian" under the Major Crimes Act, other federal laws and federal court decisions are pertinent. Since the passage of the MCA, Congress has passed several other notable statutes regarding criminal jurisdiction in Indian Country.

2. Federal Prosecution for Crime between Indians/Tribal Citizen and Non-Indians in Indian Country

For crimes not specifically listed in the MCA, federal criminal jurisdiction extends over Tribal citizens that commit crimes in Indian Country against non-Indians under the Indian Country Crimes Act (ICCA), 18 U.S.C. § 1152, commonly referred to as the "General Crimes Act." The ICCA also applies when a non-Native perpetrator commits a crime against a Tribal member in Indian Country. This federal law does not apply if any of the following exceptions are met: (1) as mentioned, the crime(s) was by Tribal member against a Tribal member or the property of a Tribal member; (2) crimes by a Tribal member where the Tribal Nation jurisdiction has provided punishment under local Tribal law; or (3) to offenses under the exclusive jurisdiction of the Tribal Nation by treaty.

The U.S. Supreme Court held in *Williams v. U.S,* 327 U.S. 711 (1946), that the Assimilative Crimes Act, 18 U.S.C. § 13, is operative in Indian Country to allow federal prosecutions based on state criminal law where federal criminal law over an offense is lacking. This federal statute provides further federal criminal jurisdiction over Indians/Tribal member perpetrators committing acts against non-Indians in Indian Country. By applying the Assimilative Crimes Act, federal prosecutions of Tribal citizen perpetrators extend to crimes listed under a state criminal code. When the federal criminal code does not have a particular crime listed and the state criminal code does include the offense, Tribal member perpetrators can be federally prosecuted using the Assimilative Crimes Act to bring the offense to federal court.

3. Criminal Jurisdiction over Non-Indian Perpetrators in Indian Country

As discussed previously, Tribal Nation criminal jurisdiction over non-Indians has been sharply curtailed by the U.S. Supreme Court's decision in *Oliphant v. Suquamish Tribe*, 435 U.S. 191 (1978). In the *Oliphant* decision, the Court opined that Tribal Nation governments lacked inherent criminal jurisdiction over non-Indians, or those lacking Tribal membership, as a general matter since the formation of the United States and the extension of U.S. boundaries surrounding the Tribal Nations. Further, the Court found significant that the U.S. Congress had not enacted a federal law recognizing Tribal Nation criminal jurisdiction over non-Indians and thus, held that Tribal Nations could not exercise such jurisdiction absent an act of the U.S. Congress. Due to this U.S. Supreme Court opinion, Tribal Nation courts do not generally exercise criminal jurisdiction over non-Indian, or those lacking Tribal membership, perpetrators committing crimes within the Tribal Nation territory. Native American law scholars have criticized this judicial result and the subsequent lack of law enforcement supervision over non-Indians occurring in many parts of Indian Country.

With the 2013 and 2022 passage of the VAWA amendments to the Indian Civil Rights Act, Tribal Nation courts may exercise Special Tribal Criminal Jurisdiction (STCJ) over all persons when meeting certain federal requirements. This STCJ partially modified the *Oliphant* decision and recognized the inherent authority of Tribal Nations to exercise criminal jurisdiction over all persons committing certain criminal acts against Tribal members in the Tribal Nation territory. This Special Tribal Criminal Jurisdiction exists concurrently with federal criminal jurisdiction and/or state jurisdiction where appropriate.

If a non-Native person, or a person who lacks Tribal membership, commits a crime against a Tribal member in Indian Country, then under the ICCA federal criminal jurisdiction applies. If the crime is not a federal crime, but would be considered a state crime, then the Assimilative Crimes Act allows federal prosecution of the criminal act(s) with state criminal law underlying the prosecution. In *Oklahoma v. Castro-Huerta*, 597 U.S. 629 (2022), the U.S. Supreme Court broke from years of precedent to find state prosecutorial authority existed in Indian Country over non-Indians committing crimes against Tribal members without a federal delegation of criminal jurisdiction. As a result of this decision, non-Indian persons, or persons lacking Tribal membership, may be prosecuted by both federal and state courts for criminal acts occurring in Indian Country where Tribal members are the victims of those crimes.

Where a non-Native person, or person lacking Tribal membership, commits a crime against a Tribal member in Indian Country that falls within the listed crimes for Special Tribal Criminal Jurisdiction under 25 U.S.C. § 1304(b)(5), there may exist three prosecuting sovereigns—the participating Tribal Nation under the federal law, federal government prosecution, and state government prosecution. Whether this multi-jurisdictional approach curbs lawlessness by non-Indians and reduces the victimization of Tribal members will be a subject of study in years to come.

The next category of criminal prosecution is when a non-Native person, or person lacking Tribal membership, commits a crime in Indian Country where the victim is another non-Native person, or person lacking Tribal membership. The U.S. Supreme Court has held that federal criminal jurisdiction does not apply. In *U.S. v. McBratney,* 104 U.S. 621 (1881), the Court held that exclusive state criminal jurisdiction existed where only non-Indians are the perpetrator and the victim in criminal acts occurring within Indian Country. Therefore, state law enforcement are empowered to prosecute these types of crimes within Indian Country with the non-Native, or person lacking Tribal membership, perpetrators to be tried under state law in state courts.

4. Limited State Criminal Jurisdiction over Indian/Tribal Citizen Perpetrators in Indian Country

To discuss state criminal jurisdiction over Tribal Nation citizens in Tribal territories, the primary authority of the U.S. Congress is foundational to understanding federal law enactments delegating responsibility to state governments. During the termination era of U.S. Indian policy, the U.S. Congress passed legislation in 1953 delegating federal criminal jurisdiction over all persons, both Tribal members and non-Native persons, in Indian Country to certain state governments through passage of Public Law 280, commonly referred to as "PL-280." 18 U.S.C. § 1162(a). Six states assumed mandatory criminal jurisdiction under PL-280: Alaska, California, Minnesota, Nebraska, Oregon, and Wisconsin. Exceptions to the reach of PL-280 exist for the mandatory states. For example, the Metlakatla Indian Community has concurrent criminal jurisdiction with the state in Alaska. In Minnesota, the Red Lake Band of Chippewa is excepted from state criminal jurisdiction. The Warm Springs Reservation is not within Oregon's PL-280 jurisdiction. Wisconsin does not have state criminal jurisdiction over the Menominee Tribe.

In the mandatory PL-280 states, the Major Crimes Act and the Indian Country Crimes Act were no longer operative, 18 U.S.C. § 1162(c). Thus, there is state criminal law and state criminal prosecution for all crimes committed in Indian Country by all persons in the mandatory states. PL-280 has worked as a delegation of federal authority to state governments for criminal jurisdiction in Indian Country. PL-280 also contained a civil component providing access to state courts in civil action matters involving Tribal members where those matters arose in Indian Country, 28 U.S.C. § 1360.

Up through 1968, other state governments could optionally accept the delegation of federal criminal jurisdiction and tailor the delegation to certain types of criminal activity. For example, Idaho optionally accepted PL-280 authority under state legislation for seven specific areas: (1) compulsory school attendance; (2) juvenile delinquency and youth rehabilitation; (3) dependent, neglected and abused children; (4) insanities and mental illness; (5) public assistance; (6) domestic relations; and (7) operation and management of motor vehicles upon highways and roads maintained by the county or state, or political subdivisions. I. C. § 67-5101. All other areas of criminal jurisdiction enforced federally remain available for federal prosecution either under the Major Crimes Act or the Indian Country Crimes Act.

The option for states to immediately receive federal criminal jurisdiction in Indian Country existed up until the passage of the Indian Civil Rights Act of 1968 that included a provision that Tribal Nation consent was necessary prior to assumption of federal criminal jurisdiction by states, 25 U.S.C. § 1321(a). PL-280 has been critically regarded based upon lack of federal funding to those states assuming jurisdiction and lack of state law enforcement with jurisdiction adequately policing Indian Country. State retrocession of criminal jurisdiction is available under 25 U.S.C. § 1323 by sending a state resolution to the Secretary of the Interior for consideration of a request to relinquish the delegation of federal criminal jurisdiction in Indian Country. With passage of the Tribal Law and Order Act (TLOA) in 2010, Tribal Nations also have the authority to request a return of federal criminal jurisdiction where PL-280 jurisdiction has been exercised by the state. 18 U.S.C. § 1162(d). States may also pass legislation for a process for retrocession of PL-280 jurisdiction initiated by a Tribal government request, which the state of Washington did in March 2012.

Over time, state criminal jurisdiction under PL-280 has been influenced by Tribal Nation processes and interactions. In the state of Minnesota, the Bois Forte Band of Chippewa successfully received retrocession of the state's PL-280 jurisdiction in 1973. Since that time, the Tribal Nations of the White Earth Reservation in 2013 and the Mille Lacs Reservation in 2017 both requested the return of partial federal concurrent criminal jurisdiction. The state of Alaska is a mandatory PL-280 state and provides that under the Alaska State Troopers Division training and funding of the Village Public Safety Officer (VPSO) program. The VPSOs are usually Alaska Native persons who are known in the local community. Alaska Native Villages operate Tribal courts and have the ability to enter into diversion and other agreements for culturally appropriate sentencing plans for Tribal citizens subject to state prosecution. These types of cooperative sentencing are also entered into on a county-by-county basis in the lower 48 states, in both PL-280 states and non-PL-280 states. With the focus on safe Tribal Nation territories and curbing criminal activity, collaboration and seeking criminal justice partnerships and flexibility have been avenues pursued by Tribal Nations in response to federal and/or state assertions of criminal jurisdiction.

State criminal jurisdiction in Indian Country may also exist based upon state-specific legislation passed by Congress. Under 25 U.S.C. § 232, New York in 1948 assumed all criminal jurisdiction in Indian Country within state borders. Similarly, Kansas in 1948 obtained specific legislation for state criminal jurisdiction in Indian Country. 18 U.S.C. § 3243. North Dakota also has a federal grant of criminal jurisdiction over Indian Country under 60 stat. 229 passed in 1946. Congress may also pass specific criminal jurisdiction laws on a Tribal Nation-specific basis or in Tribal Nation land claim settlement acts.

State governments sometimes move forward with criminal jurisdiction over persons in Indian Country on the theory or presumption that reservation boundaries have been modified or dissolved and therefore the Tribal Nation territorial jurisdiction component of 18 U.S.C. § 1151(a) is lacking. In a 1984 case involving the Cheyenne River Sioux Tribe in South Dakota, the U.S. Supreme Court ruled that opening up lands during the allotment process did not constitute a diminishment of Tribal reservation boundaries. *Solem v. Bartlett*, 465 U.S. 463 (1984). Even if the land holdings inside the reservation include fee or patented lands owned by non-Indians, the reservation boundary remains as a jurisdictional marker unless the U.S. Congress expressly terminates the reservation boundaries. Where boundaries remain intact, the area meets the 18 U.S.C. § 1151 definition for Indian Country with prosecutions of Tribal members falling to the Tribal Nation and federal courts to the exclusion of the state courts.

Most notably, the state of Oklahoma has overreached into the Muscogee (Creek) Nation territorial boundaries to prosecute a Tribal citizen under the theory that Oklahoma statehood and a prior 1901 allotment act changed the status of the Muscogee (Creek) Reservation. In *McGirt v. Oklahoma*, 140 S.Ct. 2452 (2020), the U.S. Supreme Court upheld the rule of law standard that only the U.S. Congress by express language can modify a reservation's boundaries or status, which was not evidenced for the treaty-guaranteed reservation of the Muscogee (Creek) Nation. Thus, federal criminal jurisdiction under the Major Crimes Act was proper, rather than state court prosecution for the defendant Tribal member on Tribal lands as defined in 18 U.S.C. § 1151. Oklahoma has continued the argument for other Tribal Nations that reservation boundaries did not survive allotment and Oklahoma statehood. To date, nine Tribal Nations in Oklahoma have had their reservations judicially reaffirmed in the *McGirt* aftermath. This highlights how the allotment process discussed in Chapter Two may directly impact criminal jurisdiction depending on the determination of whether Indian Country exists.

C. Concurrent Prosecutions of Indian/Tribal Citizen Perpetrators in Federal, State, and Tribal Courts

Tribal courts have inherent criminal jurisdiction over Tribal citizen perpetrators committing crimes in the Tribal Nation territory. With the extension of federal criminal jurisdiction, and at times state criminal jurisdiction, in Indian Country, the question has arisen whether Tribal court prosecution of the Tribal member perpetrator for a crime bars a second prosecution in federal or state court. The Fifth Amendment of the U.S. Constitution prohibits double prosecution, known as "double jeopardy," of the same individual by the same sovereign jurisdiction. In *U.S. v. Wheeler,* 435 U.S. 313 (1978), the U.S. Supreme Court held that a Tribal Nation criminal prosecution of a Tribal citizen was the action of a separate sovereign and therefore, the federal prosecution of the same individual for the same criminal activity was not in violation of the double jeopardy clause. After the Indian Civil Rights Act was amended to recognize Tribal Nation inherent jurisdiction over all Tribal members within a Tribe's territory, a case was brought into the U.S. Supreme Court challenging that provision and the prosecution of a Tribal member of another Tribal Nation by both the local Tribal court and a federal court.

In *U.S. v. Lara,* 541 U.S. 193 (2004), the U.S. Supreme Court upheld the authority of the U.S Congress to recognize inherent Tribal Nation criminal jurisdiction over Tribal members of other Tribes, in essence upholding the "*Duro* fix." Further, the Court determined that no double jeopardy violation occurred when the Tribal member from another Tribe was prosecuted in a local Tribal court with jurisdiction and subsequently in federal court for the same criminal actions. It reasoned that each court was maintained by a separate sovereign and therefore, no double jeopardy had occurred for the defendant in the two separate criminal prosecutions. This reasoning holds true for defendants prosecuted in a Tribal court system and subsequently in a state court system with proper criminal jurisdiction. It should be noted that few defendants in Tribal Nation justice systems seek to challenge the authority of Tribal Nation prosecutions.

In conclusion, Tribal Nation courts continue to have concurrent criminal jurisdiction under Tribal laws to prosecute Tribal members where there is federal criminal jurisdiction or where state criminal jurisdiction exists by virtue of PL-280 or a specific federal law. Because of inherent Tribal Nation criminal jurisdiction over any Tribal member, a Tribe does not relinquish its authority over criminal matters in the Tribal Nation territory by not exercising that authority. It is within the Tribal prosecutorial authority to charge all offenses committed in the Tribal territory to the limits of Tribal sentencing maximums. One of the major federal limitations on the Tribal Nation prosecutorial authority is derived from the *Oliphant* decision barring prosecutions of non-Indians by Tribal Nation courts. With the now authorized Special Tribal Criminal Jurisdiction, participating Tribal Nations may prosecute all persons, including those who are not Tribal members, for committing any of the specifically listed crimes under 25 U.S.C. § 1304(b)(5), which is a significant relaxation of the limitations under the *Oliphant* decision. Secondly, federal law has placed maximum sentencing limitations on Tribal Nation courts per offense for Tribal member defendants under the ICRA of one year incarceration and/or up to a $5,000 fine with those maximums increasing up to three years of incarceration and/or up to a $15,000 fine when procedural safeguards are met under the federal law.

Overall, Tribal Nation courts are effectively dealing with the daily prosecutions of offenders in Indian Country. Tribal law enforcement has the task of handing over Tribal member perpetrators to the Tribal Nation justice system. Tribal law enforcement may stop, temporarily detain, and search all persons within the Tribal Nation jurisdiction. For those in violation of the Special Tribal Criminal Jurisdiction provisions who lack Tribal membership, federally approved Tribal Nation courts may exercise criminal jurisdiction. When other criminal activity under federal and/or state law is apparent, Tribal law enforcement may refer the non-Native perpetrators to state and federal authorities. The jurisdictional gap is found when there is not a proper response from state and federal authorities with jurisdiction over offenders committing crimes in Indian Country. Through removing limitations on Tribal Nation's exercising criminal jurisdiction, Tribal communities become safer for all residents and travelers.

CHECKPOINTS

- Criminal jurisdiction in Indian Country requires an analysis of the land status where the crime allegedly occurred. Next, the determination of whether the perpetrator and/or victim was or was not a Tribal citizen will establish what authorities have criminal jurisdiction.
- The U.S. Supreme Court has held that a non-Native perpetrator committing a crime against a non-Native victim in Indian Country is subject to state criminal jurisdiction.
- Tribal Nations have concurrent jurisdiction with any other prosecuting authority for crimes involving Tribal member perpetrators on Tribal lands. Criminal sentencing in Tribal courts is limited by the Indian Civil Rights Act.
- The U.S. Supreme Court has held that Tribes lack full criminal jurisdiction over non-Native perpetrators committing crimes against Tribal members in Indian Country. Federal legislation has allowed for Tribal Nations to participate in exercising Special Tribal Crimi-

nal Jurisdiction over all persons committing specified crimes in Indian Country, which is a removal of limitations on Tribal Nation criminal jurisdiction.

- Under Public Law 280, certain states have been delegated federal criminal jurisdiction over Tribal members in Indian Country. Each reservation requires an analysis of this delegated jurisdiction in those states. Tribal criminal jurisdiction is concurrent with those state governments. States may also exercise concurrent prosecutorial authority with the federal government over non-Indians committing crimes against Tribal members in Indian Country.
- Prosecution of a Tribal citizen by a Tribal Nation and a federal or state authority for offenses arising out of the same criminal activity does not constitute double jeopardy under the U.S. Constitution.

CHAPTER 4

Tribal Government, Civil Jurisdiction, and Regulation

ROADMAP

- Learn that Tribal Nations are fully operational within Tribal jurisdictions, providing basic governmental services to residents of their communities including both Native Americans and non-Native persons.
- Learn that Tribal Nation governance has been greatly impacted by shifting U.S. Indian policies and the current U.S. Indian policy is known as the Indian self-determination era.
- Understand that many Tribal Nations currently operate under Tribal Constitutions modeled after the U.S. system as a result of the Indian Reorganization Act of 1934.
- Understand that U.S. Supreme Court decisions have limited Tribal Nation regulatory authority in some instances over non-Native persons activity on fee lands within Tribal Nation territorial boundaries.
- Know that Tribal Nations are governments with various levels of administrative agencies and engage in legislative and rule-making processes similar to other governments.

For thousands of years, Tribal peoples have governed their own societies with laws and dispute resolution processes in the western hemisphere. This chapter will provide a broad view of contemporary Tribal Nations and the operation of civil adjudicative and regulatory jurisdiction in Indian Country. Civil jurisdiction covers the day-to-day operation of government and law and includes everything outside of the criminal jurisdiction context and encompasses all aspects of local governance, including court systems. Criminal jurisdiction, as discussed in Chapter Three, involves ensuring public safety by bringing legal actions against a defendant for the elimination and deterrence of bad behavior. This is carried out by a Tribal prosecutor and Tribal Nation court system. The broad sphere of civil jurisdiction includes resolution of family law cases; providing food safety measures; enforcing private and public contracts and agreements; regulating and stewarding the environment; collecting taxes; providing for health, safety, and welfare; ensuring safe roads; and an endless list of powers required to be responsive to the community's infrastructure and governmental services.

Civil jurisdiction, the focus of this chapter, involves the private and governmental sectors operating across a variety of areas of law. Civil jurisdiction includes a wide variety of governmental action, commercial activity, the enforcement of rights and benefits, and all other legal interactions that are non-criminal. In civil cases, the end result can be one of the following: money damages, a government order to stop an action or to require action, a declaratory order setting forth the legal rights of the parties, child custody decisions, dissolution of marriages, enforcing an action to fulfill promises previously made between parties, and other types of administrative and regulatory outcomes. Administrative processes, such as licensing and permitting, fall within the civil jurisdiction of Tribal Nation governments. The civil jurisdiction stemming from Tribal Nation sovereignty will be discussed in this chapter.

A. Tribal Governments and Shifting U.S. Policies

To understand the current structure and function of Tribal Nations, two important elements provide context. First, Tribal Nations have had a system of governance from time immemorial. Second, the U.S., since the late 1800s, has heavily impacted the contemporary organization of Tribal Nation governance. As governments, Tribes are sovereign by consent of the Tribal citizenry. In the discussion to follow, the sovereignty of Tribal Nations has been redefined, generally in increasingly limiting ways, by U.S. federal Indian law through various policy eras and political movements. Tribal governance has been adaptive through contact with Euro-American politics and ideology. The

Jicarilla Apache Nation Veterans in Summer Parade. Photo credit: Angelique EagleWoman.

negotiated relationship between Tribal Nations and the U.S. is ever-changing and evolving on issues of jurisdiction and sovereign authority. As the original governments exercising inherent powers, Tribal Nations seek a balance with the U.S. as treaty partner that rests on mutual respect and shared goals of flourishing communities.

1. Overview of Historical Tribal Governments

Historically, Tribal Nations were among the earliest democracies in the world. The authority of a government, known as sovereignty, was fully enjoyed by Tribal governments prior to engaging in trade with Europeans. Tribal Nations were generally organized with distinct internal societies responsible for governance over specific aspects of Tribal life. Family groupings occurred within clan systems that organized domestic events and coordinated social roles. Societies, on the other hand, operated as closed associations that required an invitation to join based upon a citizen's qualifications for the particular society. For example, men's societies included warrior societies, spiritual leader societies, and other focused activities. Women's societies included community leader societies, spiritual leader societies, and other focused activities. Authority passed from society to society based on the needs and events of the community in peace times. In war times, authority was grounded in the societies dealing with crisis activities, such as moving the community or harvesting crops for transport. As noted throughout the book, however, there are hundreds of Tribal Nations and their cultures and lifeways, including views on governance vary considerably.

Consistent with the theme of political complexities, Tribal Nations entered into larger alliances and confederacies based upon kinship and regional cooperation. Along the eastern seaboard, the Haudenosaunee or Iroquois Confederacy is an example of six separate Tribal Nations joining together for regional strength, commercial benefits and diplomatic relations. In many regions of North America, Tribal Nations joined with each other to form stronger, larger communities and commercial networks and military alliances. This practice has continued in contemporary times with the formation of organizations, such as the National Congress of American Indians (NCAI) providing the means for unifying Tribal Nation leadership on national issues of common concern and increasing the power of Tribal voices.

2. The Impact of U.S. Indian Policy Eras on Tribal Nations

With the formation of the United States, Tribal Nations dealt with two opposing policies of the new government. One was respect for, or at least necessary alliance with, Tribal Nations due to their size and political strength and the other was an intention to overtake the lands and resources of Tribal Nations for the benefit of the United States. During the sovereign-to-sovereign era of U.S. Indian policy, many treaties were negotiated between U.S. officials and Tribal Nation leaders across the country. However, in some instances, U.S. representatives purposefully bypassed legitimate Tribal leadership to negotiate uneven bargains with unauthorized Tribal citizens for large land cessions. As the pendulum swing began in U.S. Indian policy between the two divergent goals of recognizing Tribal Nation sovereignty and denying Tribal Nation sovereignty, the next three eras demonstrated the shifting relations between Tribal Nations and the United States.

The removal and reservation eras of U.S. Indian policy overlap and reflect the divergence in policy-making by U.S. officials. In contravention of treaty boundaries, the U.S. through the passage of the 1830 Indian Removal Act shifted into a federal push to remove all Tribal Nation citizens on the eastern seaboard to a territory west of the Mississippi River. Contemporaneously and subsequently, U.S. officials were entering into new treaties recognizing Tribal Nation territorial boundaries and land cessions in the interior and western regions of mid-North America. Therefore, the recognition of Tribal Nation reserved lands as reserved permanent homelands overlapped with the history of removal for other Tribal Nations from ancestral lands.

For most Tribal Nations, a complete disruption in Tribal governmental authority occurred during the allotment/assimilation era of the late 1800s and early 1900s. This era was marked by detrimental U.S. laws and actions intended to exert complete social control over Tribal citizens including federal laws declaring Tribal Nation actions void. In some instances, federal statutes expressly abolished entire Tribal Nation judicial systems and set expiration dates for the end of Tribal governmental rule.

Tribal leadership was undermined by U.S.-appointed "Indian agents" with totalitarian control on most reservations and usually with a nearby military fort to implement agent action. During this time period, the majority of treaty-recognized reserved homelands became subject to the General Allotment Act of 1887, which is more fully discussed in Chapter Two. Through this U.S. law, tribally-owned lands were divided into small allotments distributed to individual Tribal Nation citizens/members over the objection, or coerced consent, of the Tribal Nations. This policy stripped most powers of local government away from Tribal governments. External pressure from U.S. officials, agents, and policymakers devastated Tribal Nation economies, governance, territorial stewardship, and, through the mandatory boarding school policy for Tribal Nation children, the fabric of the Tribal family. Underground Tribal leader meetings allowed for a sense of continuity for those able to escape the attention of the U.S. Indian agents. During this era, the Courts of Indian Offenses came into existence and imposed criminal punishments for engaging in Tribal ceremonial or social activities outlawed by the agents of the BIA. By 1928, a government-commissioned task force headed by Lewis Meriam released a report, commonly known as the Meriam Report, detailing the deplorable living conditions for most Tribal Nation citizens under the authority of the BIA.

To address the deteriorating situation on reservations, federal legislation was passed in 1934 partially reaffirming recognition for Tribal Nation authority, the Indian Reorganization Act (IRA), 25 U.S.C. § 5101 et seq. Critically analyzing the IRA, one of the strongest components of the federal law was to authorize the BIA to provide template constitutions for adoption by Tribal citizens, restructuring Tribal Nation governance into a centralized Tribal Council. A primary benefit of restructuring under the IRA was the partial relinquishment of U.S. Indian agent control over Tribal Nation resources, laws, and citizenry. As discussed in Chapter Two, the IRA also halted the allotment of Tribal lands and allowed for the reacquisition of land into Tribal ownership.

With Tribal Nations organized under constitutions, Tribal leaders began the long process of rebuilding Tribal societies, implementing written laws, and adapting to the changing political circumstances of the times. Few federally-recognized Tribal Nations resisted the new "IRA-Constitution" government structure and there is great similarity in the adopted Tribal constitutions across Indian Country. Notable non-IRA Tribes are the Navajo Nation, the Sisseton-Wahpeton Oyate of the Lake Traverse Reservation, and the Confederated Tribes of the Colville Reservation. The Oklahoma Indian Welfare Act of 1936, 25 U.S.C. § 5201 et seq., provided the Tribal Nations in Oklahoma a similar opportunity to organize under the Tribal constitution model with minor differences. For Alaska Natives, the Alaska Reorganization Act of 1936, 25 U.S.C. § 5119, also extended the general provisions of the IRA to the Alaska Native Villages.

Tribal constitutions often contain clauses that require approval by the U.S. Secretary of the Interior or even the President of the United States to amend the Tribal Nation constitution. It is important to note that this legislation was merely a re-recognition of inherent Tribal Nation sovereignty and not a delegation of federal authority. Tribal Nations that moved forward in the exercise of sovereignty and self-governance without invoking the IRA's self-governance provisions have been free to do so and these Tribal Nation powers have been recognized by the federal government. In *Kerr-McGee v. Navajo Tribe*, 471 U.S. 195 (1985), the U.S. Supreme Court upheld the inherent governmental authority of the Navajo Nation to exercise taxation powers enacted by Tribal law, rather than receiving approval by the Secretary of the Interior or operating under the IRA constitutional framework.

With the barriers lifted allowing for greater Tribal Nation authority, political backlash led to a change in U.S. policy embodied in the termination era. Through House Resolution No. 108 of the U.S. Congress, the policy goal of withdrawing federal recognition of Tribal Nations and the "Indian" status of Tribal citizens began in 1953. The justification for termination of federal recognition was to allow Tribal members to join the mainstream U.S. society and abolish the separate status of reservation Natives. The impact of the termination era on Tribal Nation sovereignty was severe as the U.S. government's actions allowed state and county assertions of jurisdiction over territories no longer considered Indian Country. Furthermore, loss of federal recognition ended individual eligibility for treaty-guaranteed health, education and other benefits. Several national Tribal leadership associations were formed in resistance to the U.S. termination policy, such as the regional Tribal Chairman's associations and the National Congress of American Indians.

Since the late 1960s, the U.S. Indian policy era has been heralded as the Indian self-determination era. President Richard Nixon in his special address on Indian affairs to the U.S. Congress on July 8, 1970, announced his intention to abandon the termination policy in Indian affairs and move towards a policy of self-determination through Tribal Nation decision-making in relation to federal programs and services. This is the present policy of U.S. Indian affairs and the one in which Tribal Nations continue to operate within to rebuild and strengthen Tribal communities with the assistance of the U.S. government as a treaty partner and in furtherance of the trust relationship.

B. Civil Jurisdiction in Indian Country

As sovereigns, Tribal Nations have an obligation to Tribal citizenry, residents, and visitors to the Tribal territory to provide basic services for health, education, safety, transportation routes, communication networks, support for commerce, employment opportunities, and forums to resolve disputes. All of these governmental roles fall within the civil jurisdiction of the Tribal government.

1. Tribal Councils, Laws and Courts

Under Tribal constitutions and laws, Tribal legislative branches, generally called the Tribal Council or the Tribal Business Committee, serve as the governing body of the Tribal Nation. Tribal Councils can serve executive, legislative, and judicial functions or a Tribal Nation may adopt separate government branches for executive and judicial functions. Early IRA templates for Tribal constitutions did not provide for three separate branches of government; rather, all three functions were consolidated in the elected Tribal Council. Amendments to these constitutions have occurred providing for separate judicial functions, deleting language that would require the U.S. Secretary of the

Interior to approve Tribal Nation laws and future constitutional amendments, and redefining citizenship/members laws often broadening threshold blood quantum qualifications.

Tribal constitutions vary across Indian Country and some Tribal Nations operate as civil law jurisdictions with no constitution. Variances are often found in the number of elected representatives, qualifications for Tribal citizens/members to vote or hold office, and whether the judicial branch is a separate constitutional entity or created by legislation. Qualifications for elected office and the election process are generally governed by a Tribal Nation election commission charged with verifying the eligibility of candidates, providing notice and holding elections, and, finally, certifying election results. Terms of office for Tribal Council members are usually set at two-, three-, or four-year terms with some Tribal Nations providing for staggered terms to provide continuity on government projects that outlive terms of office. There are some Tribal constitutions that provide for meetings of all Tribal citizenry in a General Council annual or bi-annual session with the authority, based upon a quorum present, to veto or modify actions of the Tribal Council. Each Tribal Nation's governing documents should be reviewed prior to any dealings with the Tribal government to understand the particular governance structure of the Tribal Nation.

Commonly, Tribal Councils include the role of a leader known as President or Chairperson with the authority of the executive powers to oversee the Tribal Nation's activities and speak as an authoritative voice on Tribal governance and issues. The Tribal Council may also share in the executive function, and the Tribal Council may provide enforcement and oversight of the Tribal laws through supervision of all governmental departments, services, contracts, and programs. Tribal Council members may be ex-officio members of Tribal committees over a wide range of agencies, such as education, business, law enforcement, judicial services, child protection, culture and language preservation, construction management, and healthcare, among others. With the tensions for the Tribal Council to strengthen the Tribal Nation, oversee financial situations, increase the economic capacity of the Tribal businesses, and engage on all issues with local, state, and federal entities, the pressures to govern and be responsive to carry out the operations of government are numerous.

The Tribal Council also carries forth the legislative function by creating the laws of the Tribe along with adopting revisions and amendments to those laws. The body of Tribal laws is commonly called the Tribal code with many Tribal Nations now making the code of laws available online, some included in Westlaw and Lexis databases or hosted on the Tribal government's website or in shared municipal code online services. Due to the common needs of Tribal governments, Tribal Councils may choose to model new laws on those of other Tribal codes and revise existing laws to better suit the needs of the particular Tribal Nation.

Tribal attorneys often work closely with Tribal Councils in developing new laws, providing drafting services, and researching legal issues involved. Tribal judicial committees and in-house legal counsel offices may share the work of drafting and proposing legislation with the Tribal Council. With only approximately 25 Native attorneys in the late 1960s, the majority of attorneys assisting Tribal governments with Tribal code drafting from 1934 on were non-Indians and versed in U.S. law. With the current number of 2500+ Native attorneys, there is an emphasis on revising, updating, and enacting Tribal laws that more accurately reflect Tribal values, processes, and understandings.

Many Tribal Nations are reviving traditional dispute resolution circles and courts. Tribal Healing to Wellness Courts may operate with a healing plan for participants to address cultural disconnection and focus on the whole person, rather than a criminal act. Wellness concepts are based on a person becoming well, able, and strong so that they can contribute to their Tribal society. One of the most world-renowned dispute resolution systems is the Navajo Nation Peacemaking Program, which implements traditional Navajo Fundamental Law with peacemaking sessions organized to facilitate family and community involvement in seeking dispute resolution. Participants are guided by respected peacemakers who offer teachings to further the understanding of all involved. Judges from all over the world have visited the Peacemaking Program to learn more about alternatives to the Anglo-Saxon based adversarial approach to court proceedings.

To implement traditional Tribal Nation practices, there is often a need to organize, update, and revise Tribal codes to infuse traditional legal principles, customs, and processes into the Tribal laws. Tribal legislation and Tribal courts often balance the incorporation of U.S. legal standards with the incorporation of Tribal legal principles based in culture and tradition. There can be legitimacy issues when Tribal laws seem foreign to Tribal peoples, especially in Tribal court decisions where there is a vested interest in seeking justice on an issue.

As Tribal Nations seek to implement new policies, Tribal laws are developed to govern the efforts. For example, Tribal Nation gaming businesses are subject to specific federal laws that require Tribal legislation governing Tribal

Nation gaming operations to conform to minimum federal regulatory standards. To keep pace with governmental goals and federal requirements, Tribal Councils must devote considerable time to legislative matters. Tribal laws may be comprehensive code sections, such as an environmental standards code, or isolated specific laws, such as declaring a Tribal Nation holiday commemorating a historic treaty council.

There are over 570 federally recognized Tribal Nations in the United States. All exercise self-government and have the option to operate a Tribal court, of which more than 330 are currently in operation. Tribal laws become subject to judicial interpretation when parties seek to resolve disputes in Tribal courts. The authority of Tribal Nation courts to resolve cases is referred to as the court's adjudicative authority. Tribal courts may exercise only civil adjudicative authority or may have both criminal and civil adjudicative authority. Tribal judges and court personnel often experience high volumes of civil cases on court dockets while dealing with issues of being underfunded, lack of adequate facilities and technology, and, at times, external pressure by Tribal politicians, Tribal citizenry, or non-Indians or those who lack Tribal citizenship. In recent years, there has been a growing emphasis on wellbeing and self-care practices for Tribal court personnel due to the many stresses that may be experienced on the job.

The decisions of Tribal Courts form the common law of the particular Tribal Nation. In the civil litigation context, Tribal Nation court decision archives are important to determine how a court has ruled on any previous similar legal issue. Accessing extensive Tribal court archives can require museum archive searches and/or the assistance of Tribal court clerks and staff. More recent case decisions are available with online access to Tribal laws, court decisions, and regulations. This access has increased through legal information service providers. Yet, a full range of online access is still limited due to resource constraints from the underfunded nature of Tribal Nation judicial systems. It is the current trend to archive Tribal court decisions for retrievable purposes to assist parties, attorneys, and judges in all court systems. Tribal court staff members are often highly knowledgeable on the Tribal court system they serve and are key to working competently and effectively in legal research.

Tribal judges may serve as full-time employees of the Tribal court or under part-time arrangements with the Tribal Nation based on the term of appointment, such as two-, three- or four-year terms. It is typical for Tribal judges to be present for court hearings and on designated docket dates during the month if the number of cases before the court does not warrant a full-time judge. For those with a more extensive docket, the Tribal court may be overseen by a full-time Chief Judge who also serves as the manager and supervisor of Tribal court staff. It is common for Tribal Nations with more active dockets to employ a court staff of several employees, including trial and appellate judges, court clerks, research clerks, bailiffs, and probation officers.

Judges may also be elected for a set term by the entire Tribal citizenry and are then subject to re-election every term on a more permanent basis. Formal legal training has become the norm for serving in a Tribal judge position, although, like some state courts, lay persons can sometimes serve as justice of peace over certain matters. In some Tribal courts, lay judges may preside only over certain types of cases or may have the same status as law-trained judges to hear all types of cases before the court. The National American Indian Court Judges Association (NAICJA), founded in 1969, provides online training videos and in-person workshops for all levels of Tribal courts, from Tribal judge sessions and Tribal court clerk trainings to Tribal court administrator processes and best practices.

For appellate review of Tribal court decisions, Tribal Nations may operate a standalone appellate court or may join an association for appellate services on an as-needed basis. Tribal courts of appeals tend to be filled with lawyers and most Tribal citizen law professors at U.S. law schools serve on one or more Tribal Nation appellate courts. Some Tribal Nations maintain a list of qualified appellate judges to call upon for appointments when an appeal is filed. The appeals court may consist of one appellate judge per appeal or a panel of three or more judges to rule on an appeal en banc. The Chief Justice of the appeals court may be responsible for convening the judicial panels and determining the briefing and hearing schedule for the immediate appeal. Inter-Tribal judicial associations for specific regions may be joined by local Tribal Nations to provide an appellate court of neutral decision-makers. Examples of these types of associations include the Northern Plains Intertribal Court of Appeals and the Southwest Intertribal Court of Appeals. Practitioners of Tribal law, law professors in the field, and judges of other court systems may all serve as appellate judges in Tribal court systems.

Court dockets with a wide variety of cases may require several Tribal judges with each assigned to particular types of cases. Like other jurisdictions, a Tribal judge may oversee only cases on the domestic issues docket concerning family matters, such as marriages, divorces, child custody and support, guardianships, and probate matters. In other court systems, the Tribal judge will oversee all matters before the court. As with other court systems, Tribal laws provide the civil procedure for litigants. Practitioners in a Tribal court system are expected to become familiar with the rules of civil procedure and other local court rules prior to filing a case in Tribal court.

Tribal courts should reflect the Native society's concepts of law and harmony. Tribal judges must engage customary and traditional law in their decisions for the future development of Tribal Nation justice systems as best practices. Tribal courts may take judicial notice of customary law that is well-known in a particular Tribal Nation. For Tribal Nation customary law to be embedded into the understanding of Tribal court decisions, lawyers and practitioners in Tribal courts must incorporate this type of law, through expert statements and traditional law sources.

When a lawyer plans to file a case in Tribal court, the Tribal Nation's rules for admission to practice law must be followed. Although some Tribal Nations require applicants to pass a tribally-specific bar examination as a threshold to attorney or lay advocate practice before the court, most Tribes have a system of admitting practitioners who can demonstrate an active license to practice law in good standing in another jurisdiction. Once admitted to practice law, a lawyer must abide by the ethics and professional responsibility laws of the Tribal Nation. Failing to do so may result in disciplinary proceedings and actions in the Tribal forum and also ethics complaints filed in other jurisdictions where the attorney is licensed to practice. Depending on the local court rules, attorneys may be admitted for the limited purpose of filing a single case with a pro hac vice motion to the Tribal Nation court. Local rules may also provide for law students to obtain limited-action approval to represent clients in certain cases that are limited in scope and/or under the supervision of a licensed attorney.

With the proliferation of Tribal courts, state governments may adopt legislation on recognizing Tribal court orders for matters or persons subject to state jurisdiction. In some states, the highest court of the state may adopt a court rule on granting comity, or lateral recognition, of Tribal court orders. This is particularly necessary for protection orders, domestic cases with orders requiring ongoing monitoring, and the enforcement of monetary judgments when assets and/or accounts are located off-reservation or outside of the Tribal Nation territory to satisfy a Tribal court order. Some states have active Tribal-state court forums that allow for cooperation across jurisdictions to ensure the best services of all persons.

Despite the adaptation to the constitutional forms of government, the ability of Tribal Nations in the U.S. to continue self-government, self-determination, and exercise sovereignty serves as models for other Indigenous communities around the world. The policy shift with the enactment of the 1934 Indian Reorganization Act has significantly provided the means for Tribal leadership to re-assert traditions of governance through the new frameworks. Today, many Tribal Nations are revising the adopted constitutions from ninety years ago to more accurately reflect Tribal Nation governance norms and traditions.

Indigenous peoples around the world may seek national legislation to provide a similar pathway to assert self-governance and begin the rebuilding process of traditional governmental, legal, judicial, and economic systems. There remain issues to be addressed in the limitations imposed by the U.S. on the authority and jurisdiction of Tribal Nations, but the exercise of Tribal Nation self-government, self-determination, and sovereignty is firmly embedded in the political fabric of the Tribal Nation-U.S. relationship.

2. Federal Limitations on Tribal Nation Adjudicative Authority

As covered in Chapter Three, in the criminal jurisdiction context, the U.S. Supreme Court ruled in 1978 that Tribal Nations lack criminal jurisdiction over non-Indians, or those who lack Tribal membership, who commit crimes in Indian Country. Since that decision in *Oliphant*, the U.S. Congress has significantly responded and provided federally approved Tribal Nations the ability to exercise some forms of criminal jurisdiction over all persons under 25 U.S.C. § 1304(b)(5). In the civil jurisdiction context, the U.S. Supreme Court has imposed limitations that are less concrete, but ever-evolving, building on the rationale in *Oliphant* through the use of the "implicit divestiture doctrine" to find governance limitations on Tribal Nations as a consequence of the "domestic dependent nation" status from early U.S. Supreme Court decisions.

The vast majority of civil cases heard by Tribal Nation courts do not involve an analysis of U.S. Supreme Court decisions. Only in the limited situations where a non-Native, or person lacking Tribal membership, is sued in Tribal court and challenges the jurisdiction of the court to hear the action does the analysis that is described below follow. This review, of Tribal Nation courts determination of Tribal jurisdiction to hear a civil action, by the U.S. Supreme Court has been a matter of providing disincentives to filing in Tribal court as the time commitment and steps involved in resolving jurisdictional issues may be too burdensome for a party seeking relief. For those who consent to the Tribal court's jurisdiction in civil actions as non-Indians or non-members, the case may proceed in a timely and efficient matter through the Tribal court process.

A series of U.S. Supreme Court decisions must be taken into consideration to determine whether the federal government will recognize Tribal adjudicatory authority over civil cases when a non-member/non-Native person is a defendant challenging Tribal court authority. The starting point for an analysis of a Tribal Nation's civil jurisdiction begins with inherent Tribal Nation jurisdiction within the Tribal Nation territory. Through federal court decisions, the next steps are to determine: (1) whether each party to the litigation in Tribal court is a Tribal Nation citizen or not, (2) whether the land where the activities occurred is within the Tribal Nation jurisdiction, and (3) whether the conduct at issue gives rise to Tribal Nation jurisdiction.

The foundational federal case on Tribal Nation civil jurisdiction limitations is *Montana v. United States,* 450 U.S. 544 (1981), a case that reviewed regulatory authority to regulate hunting and fishing on fee lands inside the reservation of the Crow Tribe. The U.S. Supreme Court set out a general principle that inherent Tribal Nation civil authority does not extend over the activities of non-Native persons on non-Native fee owned land inside the reservation, subject to two exceptions. From this case, the *Montana* test was formed as a two-part test to determine whether inherent Tribal Nation civil jurisdiction has been retained over civil suits with defendant non-Native persons for conduct on fee lands within reservation boundaries. The first prong of the test questions whether the "non-Indian" person or non-member, entered into "consensual relationships with the [T]ribe or its members through commercial dealing, contracts or other arrangements." 450 U.S. at 565. This is referred to as the "consensual relations" test. If this first prong of the test is met, then the Tribal court has civil authority over the case and the non-member for the conduct that gave rise to the litigation.

The second prong of the *Montana* test questions whether the conduct of the non-Native person or non-member "threatens or has some direct effect on the political integrity, the economic security, or the health or welfare of the [T]ribe." 450 U.S. 566. This is referred to as the "direct effects" prong. If this prong of the *Montana* test is met, then the Tribal court may exercise civil authority over the case and the non-member for the conduct that created the cause of action for the litigation.

The *Montana* "consensual relations" and "direct effects" test are applied by federal courts to civil actions from conduct arising on fee lands within the Tribal territory, including regulatory jurisdiction exercised by Tribal Nation administrative agencies, and to Tribal court cases where a non-member defendant is involved. Most recently, the United States Supreme Court was equally divided in a 4–4 ruling on whether a Tribal Nation court retained jurisdiction in a civil action over a retail company that entered into a commercial lease with the tribe. *Dollar General Corp. v. Mississippi Band of Choctaw Indians*, 579 U.S. 545 (2016). Due to the split in the U.S. Supreme Court, the 5th Circuit Court of Appeals decision was affirmed, leaving intact Tribal Nation civil jurisdiction over the lawsuit over an alleged sexual assault of a minor Tribal citizen by a non-Native store manager where the business leased land from the Tribal Nation. The Tribal court and the lower federal courts had found that the retailer entered into a consensual relationship through the lease agreement with the Tribe, and thus was subject to Tribal civil jurisdiction.

In another series of cases, the U.S. Supreme Court held that the Tribal Nation court is the proper forum to first decide whether it has civil jurisdiction before a non-member can seek to challenge Tribal jurisdiction in a federal court. In *National Farmers Union v. Crow Tribe*, 471 U.S. 845 (1985), the Court held that a non-member must exhaust all Tribal court levels for remedies before challenging Tribal court jurisdiction in a federal court. This is referred to as the "tribal exhaustion doctrine," which requires a challenging party to receive final judgment at all levels of the Tribal court system, raising the issue of whether Tribal Nation civil adjudicatory authority is proper before the party can file suit in federal court to bring a challenge to Tribal court authority. The Court reasoned that there was a federal question involved when a party challenged Tribal court authority that gave the federal courts jurisdiction to ultimately determine the matter once Tribal court remedies were exhausted. This framing of a federal question for federal court review has been criticized as novel and outside the scope of the bounds of federal question jurisdiction as commonly understood under the U.S. Constitution.

In *National Farmers Union*, the Court provided three exceptions to the application of the Tribal exhaustion doctrine. First, the Court stated a challenging party need not exhaust all levels of Tribal court review prior to filing in federal court if the assertion of Tribal Nation jurisdiction "is motivated by a desire to harass or conducted in bad faith." Second, the doctrine will not apply "where the action is patently violative of express jurisdictional prohibitions." Third, the challenging party can file in federal court without exhaustion of Tribal court review and remedies "where exhaustion would be futile because of the lack of an adequate opportunity to challenge the court's jurisdiction." 471 U.S. at 856 fn. 21.

Two U.S. Supreme Court cases following the *National Farmers Union* case sharpened the Tribal exhaustion doctrine's application for Tribal Nation court civil cases. In *Iowa Mutual Insurance Company v. LaPlante,* 480 U.S. 9 (1987), the Court stated that the "tribal exhaustion doctrine" was operative when a non-member filed suit in federal court on a diversity of citizenship basis at the same time a Tribal court case was in process over the matter. The Court rejected the challenging party's assertion that the Tribal court was incompetent and therefore, the Tribal exhaustion doctrine should not apply. This case upheld the Tribal exhaustion doctrine and required the non-member to go through all levels of the Tribal judicial system before filing a case in federal court challenging the Tribal court's authority.

In *Strate v. A-1 Contractors,* 520 U.S. 438 (1997), the Court determined that a civil action brought in Tribal Nation court involving a collision between a truck and a car both driven by non-members that occurred on a right of way running through Tribal land was outside of the Tribal civil adjudicatory authority. The Court held that the Tribal exhaustion doctrine did not apply to this case based upon the reasoning that exhaustion would "serve no purpose other than delay," 520 U.S. at 459 fn. 14. In finding that the Tribal court lacked adjudicatory authority in the case, the Court stated that the *Montana* test exceptions were not met in this personal injury case because the conduct by the defendant non-member did not meet either the consensual relations or the direct effects prong. The facts surrounding the vehicle collision include that the truck driver was on the reservation due to a construction contract with the Tribal Nation and the car driver was a reservation resident of her deceased Tribal member husband's allotment and mother to five Tribal member sons.

In sum, inherent Tribal Nation civil authority has been limited by federal court decisions when that authority is applied to non-members on non-Tribal lands within Tribal Nation boundaries. Tribal Nations retain civil jurisdiction on fee lands within reservation boundaries over non-members who enter into consensual relations with the Tribe or its Tribal members and when a non-member's conduct has a direct effect on the Tribe. Tribal courts have the authority to determine the extent of their civil jurisdiction before a challenge can be brought into federal court under the Tribal exhaustion doctrine.

In recognition that federal cases involve incredibly high stakes for the future of all Tribal Nations, and not only the Tribal Nation(s) involved in a fact-specific lawsuit, the Native American Rights Fund oversees a Tribal Supreme Court Project. The project was established in 2001 and includes an advisory board of Tribal leaders and a working group of over 200 attorneys including attorneys from the Native American Rights Fund with the National Congress of American Indians as the co-sponsoring national inter-Tribal organization. The project assists with high profile federal cases by providing strategy and legal writing assistance and coordinates amicus brief submissions.

C. Regulatory Authority in Indian Country

As a general rule, Tribal Nations retain inherent regulatory authority within Indian Country. This inherent authority has been discussed at length in federal court decisions when states have sought to regulate within Indian Country. The major court decisions and tension between Tribal and state regulatory jurisdiction will be discussed in this section. In specific areas, such as meeting federal environmental standards, federal regulatory authority is the default when a Tribal Nation does not provide regulatory oversight. Additionally, the BIA has regulatory authority in certain matters based on trust land status and federal service delivery in Indian Country. When a question arises over regulatory authority in Indian Country, a Tribal Nation should be the first point of inquiry to determine the proper authority for a regulatory issue.

1. Tribal Nation Law and Administrative Bodies

As Tribal Nations have established governmental services and agencies to administer those services, dispute resolution processes have been necessary outgrowths as part of the delivery of services in the Tribal Nation territory. A foundational service provided by Tribal government is employment within its branches. The majority of Tribal Nations have formal personnel policies and employment dispute resolution processes. Best practices for the exercise of Tribal Nation regulatory authority include: allowing comment periods prior to the adoption of new regulations or policies; clear and concise written regulations/policies readily available to those impacted; and non-interference on the political level towards administrative agency actions. Agency administrative action is at its most effective when regulations and policies are well-known, easily understood, accessible, and consistently followed.

Dispute resolution processes in the regulatory context can range from an immediate petition to the Tribal Council for hearing to a multi-tiered review panel process allowing an appeal to the Tribal Nation court. Tribal Nations have the option of establishing subject matter specific dispute resolution forums. For example, the Prairie Band Potawatomi Nation has created a forum, the Employment Disputes Tribunal, with five individuals as magistrates appointed by both the Tribal Council and Tribal government employees for resolving employment issues. Another route is for the Tribal Council to provide dispute resolution mechanisms in the same set of Tribal laws establishing the administrative agency as a delegation to that agency.

Many Tribal Nations have created Tribal Employment Rights Offices (TEROs) that serve a variety of administrative functions. A primary role of the TEROs is to maintain the Tribal preference status in employment and government contracting under Tribal Nation law. The enforcement of the Tribal preference status requires an administrative oversight body to provide lists of eligible tribally-owned businesses when opportunities arise within the Tribal territory. TEROs may also provide lists of skilled Tribal member workers available for temporary hire or for hire on projects as subcontractors. Tribal law may provide that the TEROs exercise the ability to assess sanctions and fines for non-compliance by employers and contractors doing business within the Tribal Nation boundaries. On the national level, the Council for Tribal Employment Rights holds annual meetings to provide updates on Tribal Nation and federal legislation developments; to provide a networking opportunity among TEROs; and to exchange information on opportunities for Tribal employment. Tribal member preference by Tribal Nations is recognized in the U.S. employment statutes at 42 U.S.C. § 2000e-2(i) as an exemption "for any business or enterprise on or near an Indian reservation."

For the related areas of commercial activity and contracting, Tribal Councils have commonly created Tribal revenue and taxation departments to administer business licenses within the Tribal Nation jurisdiction and to collect business-related taxes. With the development of Tribal gaming enterprises, Tribal Nations put in place Tribal gaming laws and regulations on a full-scale level for almost every aspect of the gaming operations. The chief regulatory agency for Tribal gaming is often called the Tribal Gaming Commission, which operates under a delegation of authority from the Tribal Nation to enforce the Tribal gaming laws and establish regulations as needed for the lawful and efficient performance of the Tribal business.

Domestic relations services are part of the purpose of Tribal government. Providing for the health, education, and welfare of the Tribal citizenry is at the forefront of Tribal Nation governmental priorities. Tribal Nations have put time and energy into the creation of child support enforcement offices, child protection and social work services, domestic violence prevention agencies, and elder community centers. Programs, agencies, and offices working in the domestic service delivery sector require dispute resolution processes and proper regulations in determining service eligibility, level of service provisions, and resolving service-related issues.

A major undertaking of most Tribal Nations is to provide residential homes and planned neighborhoods for Tribal citizens. U.S. governmental grant funding has served as the historical method of providing Tribal housing. Through the Native American Housing Assistance and Self-Determination Act (NAHASDA) of 1996, Tribal Nations had the opportunity to receive direct block grant funding and utilize a guaranteed loan program from the U.S. Department of Housing and Urban Development (HUD) to provide housing in Tribal communities. The work of Tribal housing departments involves regulatory authority over financing and implementing the legal obligations imposed by HUD. Additionally, Tribal Nation laws and regulations are necessary to establish tenant and landlord responsibilities and obligations. Within Tribal community areas, Tribal Nation regulatory authority may be exerted for neighborhood quality of life standards such as enforcement of residential waste restrictions or animal control policies.

In conjunction with maintaining Tribal residential areas, Tribal Nations have engaged in community planning efforts and often have delegated authority to land use and planning agencies to zone Tribal land areas for specific uses. Regulations may govern a land use permitting process or utility construction in a newly zoned area. Stewardship of Tribal Nation lands has led to environmental protection legislation and oversight agencies. Tribal environmental departments may have regulations on a wide-variety of environmental standards, such as air quality, emission controls, water quality, instream flow standards for Tribal waterways, ceremonial sites use, and solid waste disposal regulations.

Traditional Tribal activities of hunting, fishing, and gathering or harvesting may require detailed regulations due to negotiations with federal and state governments to continue to exercise treaty reserved rights off-reservation and on-reservation. Tribal fishery and hunting departments manage permit processes for quantity and type of fish or game. Fines and equipment confiscation may be administered by departmental personnel in enforcing regulations. Seasonal limitations may be established in regulations with violators subject to penalties under Tribal Nation law. These types of regulations may be likened to the historic policies of clans tasked with the authority to oversee fishing, hunting, and gathering or harvesting times of the Tribal community.

One more area worth noting that is common to most Tribal Nations as a matter of regulatory authority is the administration of Tribal Nation elections. The general procedures governing Tribal elections may be contained in the Tribal constitution with a provision allowing for the creation of an election board to implement and add to those general directives. Election regulations usually detail candidate eligibility requirements, voter eligibility, availability of absentee voting and under what circumstances, the review of election board determinations, and other aspects related to electing Tribal Nation representatives. Because the election of Tribal leadership is at the heart of Tribal Nation government, it is common for any appeal of an election board determination to be fast-tracked in the Tribal court to meet timing deadlines in the election process.

In sum, Tribal Nation regulatory authority is extensive and covers a wide range of governmental services, processes, and responsibilities. Rule-making in Indian Country is an ongoing activity of Tribal agencies and offices to implement new Tribal Nation standards and laws, to meet federal statutory provisions, and to address areas of concern raised by those residing in the Tribal community. For the safe and effective functioning of Tribal communities, Tribal Nation Councils often delegate rule-making authority to the agencies, boards, and offices directly serving the community as the firsthand experts on the needed regulations.

2. BIA Administration in Indian Country

As part of the federal trust responsibility to Tribal Nations, the U.S. federal agency directly delivering treaty and agreement guaranteed services is the Bureau of Indian Affairs (BIA) within the U.S. Department of the Interior. The regulations created to implement federal Indian programs, policies, and responsibilities are contained in the Code of Federal Regulations in Title 25—Indians Chapter I Bureau of Indian Affairs, Department of the Interior. This extensive set of regulations governs the implementation of federal laws and policies providing processes and standards to be met.

A quick survey of the regulations in 25 C.F.R. Chapter I includes regulations concerning: Indian Country law enforcement (25 C.F.R. § 12); Probates of Indian estates (25 C.F.R. § 15); Federal schools for Indians (25 C.F.R. § 31); Preparation of rolls of Indians (25 C.F.R. § 61); Trust funds for Tribes and individual Indians (25 C.F.R. § 115); and many other subjects of federal administration. Thus, the BIA has numerous regulations in place that affect the daily operation of federal and Tribal services for Tribal Nations and individual Tribal citizens.

Title 25 of the Code of Federal Regulations contains several other chapters that all pertain to federal Indian policy and service delivery. Chapter II provides regulations for the Department of Interior's oversight of the Indian Arts and Crafts Board. Chapter III contains the regulations issued by the National Indian Gaming Commission to implement the Indian Gaming Regulatory Act, 25 U.S.C. § 2701 et seq. In Chapter IV, the regulations are set forth for the specific federal policy carried out by the Navajo and Hopi Relocation Office.

Title 25 Chapter V of the Code of Federal Regulations implements a federal policy known as "Indian self-determination" passed into federal legislation in 1975. Under the Indian Self-Determination and Education Assistance Act, 25 U.S.C. § 5301 et seq., many of the federal programs administered specifically to serve Tribal Nation populations became available for Tribal Nation administration upon entering into a contract between the BIA and the Tribal Nation. These contracts are popularly called "638 contracts" derived from the title of Public Law 93-638, as the bill was known when enacted into federal law. The regulations contained in Chapter V provide the means and processes through which a Tribal Nation applies for administration of a particular federal program, such as a 638 contract for operation of Tribal court services. Tribal Nations must provide detailed documentation of the program operation, performance standards, and budget planning to receive funding and approval of the 638 contract. At regular intervals, the Tribal Nation is responsible for submitting performance and financial reports to the BIA for continuation of the 638 contract.

Title 25 Chapter VI includes the regulations that accompany the amendments to the Indian Self-Determination and Assistance Act. A provision of the Act included an initial pilot project called "Indian Self-Governance." The second set of regulations in Chapter VI implement the full-scale Indian Self-Governance provisions that allow a Tribal Nation to submit a package of programs for contracting and implementation and receive funding for the entire package without adhering to in-depth reporting requirements to the BIA per program. In response to the Indian Self-Governance initiative, the Indian Health Service (IHS), for example, created the Office of Tribal Self-Governance, which is responsible for a national program to provide information and technical assistance to Tribal governments and organizations in support of IHS Self-Governance activities.

The final chapter of Title 25 is Chapter VII containing the regulations derived from the Office of Special Trustee within the Department of the Interior implementing the American Indian Trust Fund Management Reform Act of 1994, 25 U.S.C. § 4001 et seq. These regulations govern technical assistance to Tribal Nations who may wish to participate in the management of trust funds or remove funds from the U.S. government trust accounts process to choose investment options, which remain subject to compliance with federal regulations.

In the daily functioning of Tribal Nation government, the regulations contained in Title 25 of the Code of Federal Regulations have a significant role. In this set of regulations, the appeals processes for BIA determinations that impose important consequences on Tribal Nation action are set forth. The delivery of federally-guaranteed services to Tribal populations and Tribal Nations are regulated within this title of the Code of Federal Regulations. Practitioners in Indian Country working on behalf of Tribal Nations or individual Tribal citizens must have a working knowledge of pertinent regulations contained in Title 25 for many of the land, education, health and welfare issues and programs within Tribal Nation communities.

CHECKPOINTS

- Tribal Nation governance is traditionally based upon clan systems and kinship networks that require adherence to high level standards of conduct. With the influence of the U.S., the majority of Tribal Nation governance systems have shifted toward written law codes and constitutionally based governments.
- Tribal Nation courts resolve disputes involving civil laws. The U.S. Supreme Court has provided that non-members have certain procedural avenues to challenge the civil adjudicatory authority of Tribal courts when actions arise on certain lands within Tribal Nation boundaries.
- Tribal governments have various administrative agencies and offices to carry out civil regulatory functions, such as: tax offices, personnel agencies, and departments of fish and wildlife.

- Many Tribal Nation social services are guaranteed under treaty provisions with the U.S. government. These guaranteed services are administered by federal agencies, but may be contracted and operated by Tribal governments.

CHAPTER 5

Tribal Nation Corporations and Economies

ROADMAP

- Learn about the rich Tribal Nation history of commercial networks that are being resurrected through contemporary markets.
- Learn that Tribal government-owned businesses are the norm in Indian Country. Tribal Nation economic development is a high priority to provide a better quality of life in Tribal communities.
- Understand the primary relationship between Europeans and Tribal Nations was based on commerce. The U.S. Constitution contains the "Indian Commerce clause" placing regulatory authority as a matter of congressional responsibility.
- Understand the types of economic incentive programs enacted in federal Indian law to support Tribal Nation economic development.
- Know the best practices for Tribal Nation commercial practices. Learn about the various types of corporations that exist in Indian Country, including the Alaska Native Corporations.

This chapter addresses Tribal Nation governmental economic development, highlights the federal incentives for Tribal Nation government-owned business, and offers general principles of best commercial practices in Tribal communities. According to the report issued in 2003 by the U.S. Commission on Civil Rights, *A Quiet Crisis: Federal Funding and Unmet Needs in Indian*

Country, Native Americans continue to suffer from intergenerational poverty. From pages 34 and 35 of the report:

> Native Americans have a lower life expectancy—nearly six years less—and higher disease occurrence than other racial/ethnic groups. Roughly 13 percent of Native American deaths occur among those under the age of 25, a rate three times more than that of the total U.S. population. Native American youth are more than twice as likely to commit suicide, and nearly 70 percent of all suicidal acts in Indian Country involve alcohol. Native Americans are 670 percent more likely to die from alcoholism, 650 percent more likely to die from tuberculosis, 318 percent more likely to die from diabetes, and 204 percent more likely to suffer accidental death when compared with other groups. These disparities exist because of disproportionate poverty, poor education, cultural differences, and the absence of adequate health service delivery in most Native communities.

Since that report was issued, the statistics have not improved. In the August 2022 National Vital Statistics Report on *Provisional Life Expectancy Estimates for 2021*, the American Indian/Alaska Native population saw the largest drop in life expectancy, which was already at the lowest rung in the United States. In 2019, the life expectancy for Native Americans was 71.8 years, the lowest of all populations in the U.S. by three to ten years. In 2020, the life expectancy for Native Americans dropped to 67.1 years, the lowest by four to ten years with other U.S. populations. The final set of data provided life expectancy for Native Americans in 2021 as 65.2 years, on par with the total U.S. population in 1944—eighty years ago. The federal Indian Health Service fact sheet on health disparities for American Indians and Alaska Natives, with treaty-guaranteed health services in the United States, reported in October 2019: "The American Indian and Alaska Native people have long experienced lower health status when compared with other Americans. Lower life expectancy and the disproportionate disease burden exist perhaps because of inadequate education, disproportionate poverty, discrimination in the delivery of health services, and cultural differences. These are broad quality of life issues rooted in economic adversity and poor social conditions."

Tribal Nation economic development is a high priority for Tribal leadership to alleviate these disparities occurring in Tribal communities. Economic development is particularly important because Tribal Nation governments do not enjoy the same tax base as federal, state, and other local governments and must find other avenues to support governmental infrastructure.

A. Historical Tribal Trade Practices

Tribal commercial activity has been ongoing since time immemorial. Tribal Nations and Indigenous peoples have established well-traveled trade routes that became the paved highways connecting the United States in mid-North America. Prior to European settlements, Tribal Nations had far-reaching commercial relationships with each other from the tip of North America to the southernmost point of South America. As Europeans expanded into Tribal Nation territories, the first relationships between Tribes and Europeans were centered on commercial exchange, which led to mutual alliances, intermarriage, cross-cultural exchanges, and, at times, warfare.

Historical trading practices between Tribal peoples in mid-North America were based upon a worldview of kinship. Engaging in trade with relatives required fair dealing, quality exchanges, and a sense of obligation beyond the trade transaction. These concepts were carried over to trade relationships with the newcomers to Tribal Nation lands, namely the British, Dutch, French, Spanish, and Russians, depending on geographical location. From the late 1500s until the late 1700s, Europeans established trading posts and colonies in mid-North America under the authority of religious orders and monarchies in Europe. Tribal alliances were sought by the Europeans seeking beneficial trading relationships to export goods back to Europe.

The fur trade for European export and the metal weaponry and metal implement trade for Tribal Nation citizenry formed the basis of initial trading exchanges. The British sought formal agreements to form alliances with large Tribal Nations in the northeastern region of North America. From 1684–1775, the Cherokee Nation entered into at least eight treaties or agreements with British government officers, colonial officers, or traders. This custom of treaty-making was similar to the unions and confederacies frequently entered into between Tribal Nations as part of enlarging alliances and trade networks. Tribal Nations have a long history of treaty-making to govern human and non-human relationships, such as stewardship of particular plant species or animal species. The concept of treaty-making includes regular interactions to confirm kinship and fulfill obligations agreed to.

1. U.S. Policy on Commerce with Tribal Nations

Beginning with the revolt by the British colonies along the eastern seaboard of mid-North America, a permanent settlement of Euro-Americans was established as the newly formed United States of America. As the U.S. government was organized, the importance of commerce with Tribal Nations became incorporated in the Articles of Confederation and, later, in the U.S. Constitution. Article 1, section 8 of the U.S. Constitution empowers the U.S. Congress as follows: "To regulate Commerce with foreign Nations, and among the several States, and with the Indian Tribes." The U.S. Congress implemented legislation to exercise this authority with Tribal Nations soon thereafter.

2. U.S. Trade and Intercourse Acts

In the first set of statutes enacted by the United States, the Trade and Intercourse Act of 1790, 1 stat. 137 (July 22, 1790), was included and is commonly referred to as the "Non-Intercourse Act." As the original Act was set to expire, Congress passed re-enactments. In 1834, the expiration provision was eliminated, so the Act, codified at 25 U.S.C. § 177, remains federal law. The purpose of the Act was to authorize the purchase of Tribal Nation lands exclusively by the U.S. federal government. Any other purchases would be violations of the federal law and subject a violator to a penalty of $1000. By creating a federal law that made the federal government the only legally recognized purchaser of Tribal Nation lands, the threat of land speculators or other countries gaining territory in mid-North America was addressed. This restriction on the right to sell land imposed upon Tribal Nation governments remains in effect. Thus, under present federal Indian law, the U.S. government is the sole entity entitled to purchase land from Tribal Nation governments within the borders of the U.S. This has barred Tribal Nations from entering into the real estate markets of the U.S. when lands are tribally-owned.

3. U.S. Indian Trader Licensing

Regulation of commerce included federal statutes and regulations specifying requirements to license "Indian traders" within Tribal Nation territories. The Commissioner of Indian Affairs in 1876 was empowered to appoint licensed traders governed by federal regulations. 25 U.S.C. § 261. Indian traders may be licensed up to a period of 25 years and must meet the requirements under the federal regulations to conduct business on reservations. 25 C.F.R. § 140.11. Anecdotal accounts have been handed down in many Tribal communities of unethical trading post owners who extended credit to families and then presented a statement of debts to the local Indian agent and thereby received the family's share of treaty payments directly. The federal regulations prohibit such conduct along with the sale of liquor and drugs by Indian traders. 25 C.F.R. §§ 140.23, 140.18, and 140.19.

4. Federal "Buy Indian Act" and the Indian Arts and Crafts Board

The U.S. Congress passed a law in 1908 encouraging the Secretary of the Interior to employ Tribal member labor and purchase products from American Indians and Alaska Native peoples "on the open market" and when "practicable." 25 U.S.C. § 47. This law is known as the "Buy Indian Act." For detailed regulations on the procurement process under the Buy Indian Act, provisions are set forth in 48 C.F.R. Part 1480. In 2003, the Native American Contractors Association was formed to advocate on behalf of Tribal Nations, Alaska Native Corporations, and Native Hawaiian owned businesses in federal contracting. In addition to the Buy Indian Act, another federal statute established the Indian Arts and Craft Board in 1935 within the Department of the Interior to promote the marketing of products created by American Indians and Alaska Natives as beneficial for economic welfare. 25 U.S.C. § 305.

To ensure that the marketplace acknowledged genuinely created art and crafts from Tribal citizens, federal criminal statutes provide penalties for fraudulent claims that items are "Indian-made." Under the Indian Arts and Crafts Act of 1990, offering, displaying for sale, or selling an item and misrepresenting that it is "Indian produced, an Indian product, or the product of a particular Indian or Indian tribe or Indian arts and crafts organization" is unlawful. The law was amended in 2010 to increase penalties for unlawful acts, with misrepresented goods valued at $1000 or less and goods valued at $1000 or more, and increased penalties for subsequent violations. 18 U.S.C. § 1159(b). Both federally recognized and state-recognized Tribal Nations and their members are included in the definitions section of the law. 18 U.S.C. § 1159(c)(3). The penalties under this law increase for subsequent offenses. Individuals and businesses falsely marketing goods as Native American-produced are subject to fines and/or incarceration. 18 U.S.C. § 1159(b). In

Eagle Butte, South Dakota, wall mural. Photo credit: Angelique EagleWoman.

addition, a civil action for monetary damages may be brought by the U.S. Attorney General upon recommendation of the Secretary of the Interior, the Indian Arts and Crafts Board, a Tribal Nation, an individual Tribal artisan, or an association of Tribal artists against a violator of the Indian Arts and Crafts Act. 25 U.S.C. § 305(e). Any amounts recovered from the violator are awarded to the Tribal Nation, Tribal individual, or arts association on whose behalf the action was filed.

These laws are examples of the federal government's role from the early 1900s to the present in promoting American Indian services, products, and arts. Through the Indian Arts and Crafts Act, the U.S. has a responsibility to protect the authenticity of "Indian-made" or Native American products.

B. Contemporary Tribal Nation Commerce

The contemporary growth of Tribal Nation commerce traces back to the policy shift in U.S. Indian affairs by the 1930s. During the late 1800s, few Tribal Nations were able to meet basic sustenance needs for Tribal peoples. Due to the allotment of Tribal Nation lands, the territorial harvesting of wild rice, corn, squash, berries, and other natural foodstuffs was disrupted, with movement limited to small parcels of individually-owned allotments. Hunting and fishing seasons were also severely limited or altogether prohibited by U.S. Indian agents at the same time. As intergenerational poverty set in for Tribal peoples, an outcry from concerned organizations and federal officials led to the ushering in of new federal legislation intended to lessen federal control over Tribal Nation lands and governments.

1. Tribal Constitutions and Federal Loan Funds

As part of the new deal legislation in the 1930s, the Indian Reorganization Act (IRA) of 1934 signaled a return to proactive Tribal Nation government and more autonomy from the Bureau of Indian Affairs. This was particularly true in the business realm for Tribal governments. Specifically, the IRA provided a process for adopting a Tribal Constitution that contained governmental powers to enter into contracts, handle business affairs and interact with the federal government, 25 U.S.C. § 5123(e), which was formerly codified as 25 U.S.C. § 476(e). This portion of the law was originally enacted as section 16 recognizing the authority of Tribal Nation governments to establish Tribal laws to form business corporations. Under 25 U.S.C. § 5124, Tribal Nations had the opportunity to seek a federal charter incorporating a business owned by the Tribal government. The federally chartered Tribal corporations operating under this provision are often referred to as section 17 corporations. After a Tribal Nation corporation receives approval for a federal charter, the charter remains in effect unless revoked by an act of Congress. An excellent resource detailing Tribal corporations and businesses across the country is *Tiller's Guide to Indian Country: Economic Profiles of American Indian Reservations* (BowArrow Publishing, 2015 3rd ed.) by Dr. Veronica Velarde Tiller.

To assist Tribal Nation business entities entering into the U.S. economy, the IRA established a federal revolving loan fund. 25 U.S.C. § 5113. In 1961, the federal law was amended to increase the federal appropriation into the revolving fund from $10 million to $20 million. In 1974, Congress consolidated monies from various federal law provisions and consolidated funds into one general Indian Revolving Loan Fund available to both Tribal Nations and Tribal individuals. 25 U.S.C. § 1461. The Secretary of the Interior is vested with the authority to receive loan applications by Native American organizations, corporations, and individuals, including educational loans for Tribal citizens. 25 U.S.C. § 1462. The two standards under the applicable statute are: (1) "there is a reasonable prospect of repayment" from the loan applicants and (2) the loan applicants are "unable to obtain financing from other sources on reasonable terms and conditions." 25 U.S.C. § 1463. The federal regulations governing direct federal loans to Indian entities and individuals are at 25 C.F.R. Part 101.

2. Tribal Government-Owned Corporations, Alaska Native Corporations, and Native Hawaiian Organizations

Many Tribal Nations have adopted corporation and business entities law provisions or codes. These Tribal laws provide the process for organizing a business entity, registering the business with the Tribal government, and the responsibilities and tax liabilities of the business entity. For example, the Dry Creek Rancheria Band of Pomo Indians Business Code Title 3 Corporations and Tribal Entities established a Tribal Department of Commerce to receive applications for incorporation and to issue certificates of incorporation upon approval of a business entity. Title 3 Section 5(B). The U.S. Bureau of Indian Affairs provides on its website model codes for Tribal business corporations, Tribal limited liability corporations, and for Tribal law on secured transactions in compliance with the Uniform Commercial Code (UCC) Article 9 provisions.

a. Establishment and Features of Tribal Nation-Owned Corporations

When the Tribal Nation establishes a Tribal corporation under Tribal laws, the corporation operates differently than one formed under state law. The Tribal corporation owned by the Tribal government is governed by Tribal legislative acts primarily, although the Tribal Council, or Tribal legislative branch, may appoint a Board of Directors that would report back to the Council on matters relating to the corporation. Typically, no stocks or shares would issue from this type of corporation to individual Tribal citizens. In a few instances, Tribal Nation-owned corporations have issued one share to each member of the Tribal Council during their term of office. Tribal citizens would indirectly influence the corporation's operation through their power to elect those who serve on the Tribal Council. Profits from Tribal Nation corporations are available to return to the Tribal government, to be reinvested in the corporation, or to fund specific programs as determined by the Tribal Council.

Tribal governments may seek to purchase ownership interests in corporations formed under state laws or to establish corporations under state law. Such state law-created business entities do not enjoy Tribal sovereign immunity and are subject to state regulation and taxation. The more common practice is for Tribal Nations to operate corporations formed under Tribal law.

Tribal corporations formed under Tribal Nation authority as recognized in section 16 of the IRA, 25 U.S.C. § 5123(e), enjoy Tribal sovereign immunity unless such immunity is expressly waived by the corporation. This prevents the corporation from being sued without its consent. As a practical matter, Tribal Nation corporations often waive Tribal sovereign immunity to the extent of the contract amount to do business with other entities. This limited waiver is set out in contracts and would include the law and process for dispute resolution and the proper court to resolve litigation that arises from the business interaction.

Section 17, 25 U.S.C. § 5124, Tribal corporations under federal charters must be approved by the Secretary of the Interior. These federal charters may include a "sue and be sued" clause for dispute resolution purposes. At least one state court has interpreted the "sue and be sued" clause of a section 17 corporation as permitting the corporation to be sued to the full extent of the corporate assets, thus excluding the Tribal government's assets. In the *S. Unique, Ltd. v. Gila River Pima-Maricopa Indian Community* case, the Arizona Court of Appeals opined that the section 17 corporate defendant could be sued in Arizona state courts due to the corporate charter's "sue and be sued" clause as a waiver of sovereign immunity, along with the provision that suit could be brought "in courts of competent jurisdiction within the United States," 674 P.2d 1376, 1383 (Ariz. Ct. App. 1983). Since service of process was insufficient in the action, the case was dismissed.

For Tribal Nations in Oklahoma, the Oklahoma Indian Welfare Act (OIWA) of 1936 provided similar key features found in the Indian Reorganization Act. The OIWA contains one section, 25 U.S.C. § 5203, that authorized both adoption of Tribal Constitutions and issuance of federal corporate charters to Oklahoma Tribal Nations. The next section of the OIWA, 25 U.S.C. § 5204, provides for another business structure, the cooperative association. "Any ten or more Indians, as determined by the official tribal rolls, or Indian descendants of such enrolled members, or Indians as defined in the Act of June 18, 1934 [IRA, 25 U.S.C. § 5101 et seq.], who reside within the State of Oklahoma in convenient proximity to each other may receive from the

Secretary of the Interior a charter as a local cooperative association for any one or more of the following purposes: Credit administration, production, marketing, consumers' protection or land management." *Id.* Further, the cooperative association once organized may be dissolved by a majority vote of the membership. An organized cooperative association was held to be available to legal action in state court and any court filings were to also be served on the Secretary of the Interior to allow intervention in the suit or removal to federal court. 25 U.S.C. § 5205.

As a general matter, Tribal Nations enjoy sovereign immunity from lawsuits filed without the consent of the Tribal Nation government. This was upheld in the 1998 U.S. Supreme Court decision, *Kiowa Tribe of Oklahoma v. Manufacturing Technologies, Inc.*, 523 U.S. 751, holding that the Tribe could not be brought into an Oklahoma state court on a loan repayment issue without Tribal Nation consent to the state court's jurisdiction. Following this line of cases from the U.S. Supreme Court, the power of the doctrine of Tribal sovereign immunity for a Tribal Nation's off-reservation business activities was upheld in *Ogden v. Iowa Tribe of Kansas and Nebraska,* 250 S.W.3d 822, 825 (Mo. Ct. App. 2008), when a former employee brought suit against the Tribal government in a Missouri state court. The case was dismissed on sovereign immunity grounds and the Missouri Court of Appeals affirmed.

In 2001 the U.S. Supreme Court broadly interpreted waiver of Tribal Nation sovereign immunity in the decision, *C & L Enterprises, Inc. v. Citizen Band of Potawatomi Indian Tribe of Oklahoma,* 532 U.S. 411. In that case the Tribal Nation entered into a contract that contained a clause authorizing arbitration for dispute resolution and that the arbitration judgment could be filed in "any court having jurisdiction." A dispute went to arbitration with the arbitration judgment filed subsequently in Oklahoma state court and the Citizen Band of Potawatomi Tribe objected on sovereign immunity grounds to the authority of the state court. 532 U.S. at 415. In its decision, the U.S. Supreme Court found that by entering into the contract with the wording contained in the arbitration clause the Tribal Nation had consented to a waiver of sovereign immunity when the arbitration award was filed in state court for enforcement, 532 U.S. at 420. Thus, contract wording is important to put all parties on notice of what form of dispute resolution is agreed upon and, if litigation ensues, what court(s) will have authority to hear the case.

In 2014, the U.S. Supreme Court issued a decision upholding a Tribal Nation's sovereignty immunity when a case was brought by a state government into federal court. In *Michigan v. Bay Mills Indian Community*, 572 U.S. 782

(2014), the state brought suit to halt the Tribal Nation from operating a gaming business on Tribal Nation lands purchased with funds through a federal land settlement located off reservation. The Tribal Nation closed the facility and asserted the civil defense of sovereign immunity in the federal court action. The U.S. Supreme Court noted its precedent in *Kiowa Tribe* that Tribal Nations enjoy broad sovereign immunity for activities both on and off reservation and that the U.S. Congress was the proper authority to impose any types of limitations on Tribal Nation sovereign immunity, which had not occurred. The case was dismissed based on this reasoning that upheld the Tribal Nation's sovereign immunity.

In the context of federal exclusive jurisdiction for bankruptcy actions, the U.S. Supreme Court held in the 2023 decision, *Lac du Flambeau Band of Lake Superior Chippewa Indians v. Coughlin*, that the federal Bankruptcy Act's language on applying to "other foreign or domestic government" should be interpreted to include a waiver of Tribal Nation sovereign immunity within a bankruptcy proceeding. This area of application of Tribal Nation sovereign immunity continues to be under scrutiny as Tribal Nations seek to protect governmental revenues from would-be litigants on a variety of issues.

b. Establishment and Features of Alaska Native Corporations

Pursuant to the passage of the Alaska Native Claims Settlement Act (ANCSA) of 1971, 43 U.S.C. § 1601, et seq., Alaska Native Corporations were authorized to be organized under Alaska state law as the entities receiving monetary and land settlements in exchange for the release of title and aboriginal claims in the state. Thirteen regional Alaska Native Corporations (ANCs) were authorized under the federal law, 43 U.S.C. § 1606, with twelve remaining after the dissolution of the thirteenth regional corporation under state law in 2013. In addition, over 200 Alaska Native Village Corporations were also formed from the original Tribal Nation village communities as economic entities under state law. Under the ANCSA, membership rolls were established by the Secretary of the Interior for eligible Alaska Natives to claim compensation for the extinguishment of aboriginal title. 43 U.S.C. § 1604.

With the establishment of the regional ANCs, federal law provided for an initial issuance of 100 shares of common stock to each Alaska Native eligible in the regional ANC based upon the federal membership rolls. 43 U.S.C. § 1606(g). Amendments to the ANCSA have provided that additional shares could be issued for Alaska Natives who were born after 1971 upon affirmative vote from current shareholders. The ANCSA also places restrictions on selling of the corporate shares. 43 U.S.C. § 1606(h)(1)(B). Finally, shares that are passed from original Alaska Native shareholders to non-Natives do not have voting rights attached. 43 U.S.C. § 1606(h)(2)(C).

Alaska Native Corporations are dissimilar to tribally-owned corporations because ANCs are organized under Alaska state law with all of the state regulations, state taxes, and state requirements attaching to the entities as state businesses. ANCs are specialized under federal law in the shareholder provisions limiting voting rights to eligible Alaska Natives and placing restrictions on alienation as described in the amendments to the ANCSA. 43 U.S.C. § 1629c. Depending on economic strategies of the Alaska Native Corporations, there exists a wide spectrum between maintaining minimum profitability and engaging in multi-million-dollar annual business activities for the ANCs. There should not be an assumption about the level of economic profitability of a particular ANC without reviewing reliable data.

c. Tribal Nation Corporations, ANCs, Native Hawaiian Organizations and the Federal SBA Native 8(a) Program

Under the provisions of Section 16 and 17 of the 1934 Indian Reorganization Act, 25 U.S.C. §§ 5123 and 5124, Tribal Nation-owned corporations were established to provide a foundation for rebuilding Tribal Nation commerce and to provide jobs for Tribal citizens. Prior to formation of Tribal corporations, employment opportunities in Tribal communities had been limited to employment within the Tribal Nation social and governmental services programs, the facilities and maintenance operations for Tribal buildings, elected positions within Tribal government, and employment with local non-Tribal businesses. With the entry of Tribal Nation corporations, employment opportunities for Tribal citizens substantially increased in addition to opportunities for non-Tribal citizens in local communities.

Thus, Tribal Nation corporations serve as engines of commercial growth in economically depressed communities with the profits returning to Tribal government to support the Tribal and local community. Likewise, ANCs are regarded as the economic structures to provide sustainable economic development for many rural Alaska Native communities and surrounding communities. Native Hawaiian Organizations (NHOs) are intended to support community development as well as provide employment opportunities for their membership. All three types of business entities serve as economic drivers in their local and surrounding communities. Through these business structures, a return to the prosperity of former times is slowly building across Indian Country and in Native Hawaiian communities.

A further avenue for strengthening the profitability of Tribal Nation corporations, ANCs, and NHOs occurred with their inclusion in the Small Business Administration's 8(a) federal contracting program for small and disadvantaged businesses. Within the federal law authorizing government contracts for socially and economically disadvantaged businesses, an express provision for economically disadvantaged Tribal Nations was built-in at 15 U.S.C. § 637(a)(4) in 1986. The definition of "Indian tribes" is provided at 15 U.S.C. § 637(a)(9)(F)(13) to include "any Indian tribe, band, nation or other organized group or community of Indians, including any Alaska Native village or regional or village corporation (within the meaning of the Alaska Native Claims Settlement Act)" and has recognition as such by the federal government or a state government. Further, Native Hawaiian Organizations are also eligible for the 8(a) Program as defined at 15 U.S.C. § 637(a)(9)(F)(15).

The Native 8(a) Program is structured as a nine-year program that allows economically disadvantaged Tribal Nation-owned businesses, Alaska Native corporations (ANCs), and NHOs to receive preference when bidding on government contracts, 13 C.F.R. § 124.2. These business entities have exemptions provided for in the Native 8(a) Program that allow for non-capped sole source government contract awards and allow multiple subsidiaries to apply for separate bidding opportunities. 13 C.F.R. § 124.519. The availability of such sole source awards was severely limited, however, following a new provision enacted as part of the National Defense Authorization Act for Fiscal Year 2010 (P.L. 111-84).

The new provision was incorporated as of March 16, 2011, into the Code of Federal Regulations at 48 C.F.R. § 6.303-2(d) and provides that any federal agency prior to awarding a sole source contract under the 8(a) Program for an amount over $20 million must issue a Justification & Approval (J&A). The J&A must be approved in writing by a high level federal procurement officer as set forth in 48 C.F.R. § 6.304. Further, the J&A must be provided publicly. 48 C.F.R. § 6.305. By requiring federal procurement officers to comply with more onerous processes, it is anticipated that this requirement will deter the awarding of the sole source contracts previously only available to Tribal corporations, ANCs and NHOs. The additional provision grew out of negative congressional and media attention on the Native 8(a) Program, which was viewed as unjustified by the Native American Contractors Association since

Native 8(a) contracts compose less than 1% of the annual federal contracts awarded on an annual basis.

The intention for allowing the Native 8(a) exemptions was to provide economic incentives to grow Tribal businesses in some of the most impoverished regions in the U.S. As stated previously, Tribal Nation-owned corporations, ANCs, and NHOs provide benefits for entire communities unlike other for-profit enterprises that are individually-owned. The Native Hawaiian Organizations Association emphasizes that profits derived by NHOs are used to support "youth programs, access to legal defense, leadership development, innovative youth education, specialized job training, health, financial literacy, business development, cultural engagement, community development, and other community needs," according to its website.

On the national level, the Native American Contractors Association (NACA) serves as a consortium for the Native 8(a) Program and actively monitors developments in federal business policy impacting the program. This serves as an example of Tribal Nations continuing to organize as confederacies advancing mutual economic interests in contemporary times.

d. The Tribal Nation Gaming and Tourist Industries

Historically, Native Americans engaged in social gambling activities and later were encouraged to play bingo as a pastime after church services by missionaries settling in Indian Country. From these activities, Tribal Nation governments developed commercial bingo halls and invited customers from on- and off-reservation to participate. The first such commercial bingo operation has been attributed to the Seminole Tribe of Florida opening its enterprise in 1979. In the mid-1980s, state officials sought to close down Tribal bingo operations that provided higher bet limits or jackpots than the state-regulated gaming operations. In Florida and California, litigation ensued that would eventually lead to federal legislation regulating the operation of the Tribal Nation gaming industry.

The U.S. Supreme Court decision in *California v. Cabazon Band of Mission Indians*, 480 U.S. 202, 217–18 (1987), upheld inherent Tribal Nation authority to operate a commercial bingo hall by the Cabazon Band and found that the federal government had encouraged such economic development. In opposition attorneys for the state of California argued that, pursuant to Public Law 280, California criminal laws applied when the Tribal Nation bingo hall operated outside the regulations of state and county gambling ordinances.

480 U.S. at 205. In the Court's decision a distinction was made between activities that were criminal/prohibitory where Public Law 280 jurisdiction was proper for the state and civil/regulatory activities that were exempt from the state's jurisdiction under Public Law 280. 480 U.S. at 208–211. Because California regulated bingo games and did not strictly prohibit gambling within the state, the Court held that Public Law 280 jurisdiction was not available to the state to regulate a Tribal Nation commercial activity on-reservation. 480 U.S. at 212.

Following the *Cabazon* decision in 1987, the U.S. Congress quickly responded with passage of the Indian Gaming and Regulatory Act (IGRA) of 1988, 25 U.S.C. § 2701, et seq. The IGRA provided a new federal regulatory framework for Tribal Nation gaming and established the National Indian Gaming Commission (NIGC) to implement the framework. 25 U.S.C. § 2704–2708. The IGRA divided Tribal Nation gaming into three classes with different types of regulation required per class. Class I gaming was designated within the exclusive regulation of Tribal Nations, 25 U.S.C. § 2710(a)(1), and includes the following types of gaming: "social games solely for prizes of minimal value or traditional forms of Indian gaming engaged in by individuals as a part of, or in connection with, tribal ceremonies or celebrations." 25 U.S.C. § 2703(6).

For Class II gaming, the IGRA regulatory mechanisms are in full force through the National Indian Gaming Commission (NIGC) and the requirements placed on Tribal governments operating such gaming. The IGRA definitional section states that Class II gaming includes: all forms of electronic or manual bingo, certain types of card games that are authorized and not prohibited by state laws, and games not specifically excluded. 25 U.S.C. § 2703(7)(A). The NIGC has published regulations defining the electronic games allowed under the Class II designation at 25 C.F.R. § 502.3. Class II gaming excludes "any banking card games, including baccarat, chemin de fer, or blackjack (21)" or any slot machines. 25 U.S.C. § 2703(7)(B).

The basic requirements a Tribal Nation government must meet to operate Class II gaming on Tribal Nation lands include the requirement that the surrounding state does not prohibit gambling, the NIGC has approved the Tribal Nation laws governing the operation of Class II Tribal gaming, and gaming revenues must be spent in the five ways authorized by the IGRA as demonstrated in an annual audit submitted to the NIGC for review. 25 U.S.C. § 2710. Furthermore, the Tribal Nation government must contribute a percentage of its proceeds from Class II gaming to the operating budget of the National Indian Gaming Commission. 25 U.S.C.§ 2717.

Under the IGRA, Tribal Nation governments can expend net revenues from Class II gaming enterprises for five purposes or be in violation of the federal law. The five authorized uses of these Tribal Nation revenues are: (1) "to fund tribal government operations or programs;" (2) "to provide for the general welfare of the Indian tribe and its members;" (3) "to promote tribal economic development;" (4) "to donate to charitable organizations;" or (5) "to help fund operations of local governments." 25 U.S.C. § 2710(b)(2)(B). Tribal Nation gaming businesses are the only types of non-federally-operated businesses in the United States that are directed to expend their revenues as dictated by federal statute.

In the IGRA, Class III gaming includes any other type of gaming not included in Class I and Class II, or simply all types of casino games. 25 U.S.C. § 2703(8). For a Tribal Nation government to operate a Class III gaming facility, the following requirements must be met: approval of a Tribal Nation gaming ordinance by the NIGC, the surrounding state authorizing some form of gaming within its borders, and a compact between the Tribe and the surrounding state approved by the Secretary of the Interior. 25 U.S.C. § 2710(d).

The Tribal Nation-state compacting process has given rise to litigation in federal courts resulting in a key provision being stricken from the IGRA. In the original text of the IGRA, Tribes were directed to file suit in federal court when a state authorizing gaming refused to negotiate in good faith with the Tribe to enter into a Tribal-state compact. In 1996, the U.S. Supreme Court held in *Seminole Tribe of Florida v. Florida,* 517 U.S. 44, 72–73, that the U.S. Congress lacked the authority to legislate within the IGRA a waiver of state sovereign immunity. Thus, the remedy for Tribes to file suit in federal court when states failed to negotiate in good faith was only available if the state government agreed to waive the sovereign immunity embodied in the U.S. Constitution's Eleventh Amendment.

Tribal Nations continue to negotiate for Class III gaming with surrounding states to operate gaming facilities on Tribal Nation lands. When negotiations are entered into for a Tribal-state gaming compact, the IGRA provides the subjects of such negotiations. 25 U.S.C. § 2710(d)(3)(C). Many states entering into Tribal-state compacts have sought payments from the Tribes labeled as "revenue sharing" provisions. The IGRA expressly forbids states to impose taxes through the compacting process, but payments in lieu of taxes and revenue sharing for exclusivity in operating regions have been approved by the Secretary of the Interior. Under the IGRA, the Secretary of the Interior must approve the compact prior to the Tribal Nation government commencing Class III gaming.

As early as 1985, Tribal Nations organized a national association to further Tribal economic initiatives in the gaming industry. The Indian Gaming Association (IGA) currently has 184 Tribal government members. One of the stated purposes of the IGA is "to advance the lives of Indian peoples economically, socially, and politically. IGA operates as an educational, legislative, and public policy resource for tribal policy makers as well as the public, on issues related to Indian gaming and tribal community development," according to the Association's website. With the devastation of the Covid-19 pandemic on the economy in 2020, the Tribal Nation gaming industry demonstrated a recovery in 2021. The *Indian Gaming Update* October–December 2022 edition reported, "Indian gaming revenues topped $39 billion in 2021; an increase of 40 percent over 2020 and more than 13 percent over the record revenues generated in 2019." The website for the Indian Gaming Association, https://indiangaming.org/, notes that there are 250 plus Tribal Nations engaged in the gaming industry, with 500 plus gaming locations, and those gaming operations employ 1.2 million nationwide.

The Tribal Nation gaming industry has provided Tribal governments across the country with an opportunity to provide employment opportunities, accumulate capital to diversify into other industries, and build commercial relationships in contemporary markets. A small percentage of Tribal governments have experienced huge financial gains by locating gaming operations in close proximity to large urban areas.

As Tribal Nations have gained expertise in the gaming industry, many have expanded into adding resort features to the gaming facility. Tourism has become increasingly important to Tribal Nation economies and attracting tourists on vacation or for events to Tribal entertainment centers has developed over the last decade. Additions to the original casino may include a five star hotel, on-site spa, golf course, a variety of dining options, entertainment facilities for concerts, indoor water parks, and play centers for children. Tribal resorts have full-scale marketing for featured events, such as headliner bands, boxing matches and national poker tournaments. This area of Tribal economic development will likely continue to expand in the coming decades as Tribal Nations highlight Tribal cultural museums and tribally made products unique to their people and provide one-of-a-kind experiences for tourists.

C. Tribal Nation Business Laws, Employment and Taxation

Tribal Nation laws provide for taxation of businesses operating within the Tribal territory. Tribal government legislates the amount of tax to be assessed, the requirements for business licenses and for vendors entering the Tribal Nation domain. Best practices for opening a business in Indian Country begin with contacting the Tribal Nation tax office for information on the current rate schedule for business taxes, on registering to do business in the Tribal jurisdiction, on obtaining a business license, and on complying with Tribal laws. Tribal governments often have delegated authority to a planning or land use department to provide recommendations on Tribal zoning ordinances to provide for effective management of economic development on Tribal Nation lands. Businesses seeking to locate in Indian Country should consult such Tribal governmental departments to adequately comply with the community layout on Tribal Nation lands.

1. Employment Preference for Tribal Members

Tribal Nation governments have followed the U.S. government in creating "Indian preference" statutes to provide priority in the hiring of Tribal citizens for businesses operating in the Tribal Nation territory. The U.S. government, in the Indian Reorganization Act of 1934, legislated a preference for Tribal members to be employed in federal positions related to U.S. Indian affairs. 25 U.S.C. § 472. In 1974, the U.S. Supreme Court held in *Morton v. Mancari,* 417 U.S. 535, 554–555, that the federal Indian preference was based on the Tribal Nation-U.S. political relationship and did not constitute invidious racial discrimination towards non-Indians employed in the Bureau of Indian Affairs. Rather, the Court focused on the goal of furthering Indian self-government by employing American Indians in federal Indian programs as the proper purpose of the statute. 417 U.S. at 554.

Similarly, Tribal governments have enacted employment preferences for Tribal members in the first instance. Private businesses operating within the Tribal jurisdiction and contracting with the Tribal Nation government will be expected to follow the Tribal member or Tribal business preference statutes. Often, Tribal governments will require specific language in business contracts implementing Tribal member or business preference in hiring for construction projects or other business ventures on Tribal Nation lands. The governmental office monitoring the preference statute is commonly referred to as the Tribal Employment Rights Office or "TERO." The goal of Tribal employment preferences is to provide opportunities for Tribal members to have jobs within their home communities, particularly when the Tribal government is engaged in economic activity.

In 1977, the Council for Tribal Employment Rights (CTER) was founded to represent the interests of Tribal Nation and Alaska Native Village governments. In 2022, there were over three hundred Tribal Nations joined together in the CTER across eight regions. The Council provides model codes for workplace safety and training, advice on the best practices for Tribal preference within Tribal lands, and holds an annual conference to share legal and policy developments.

2. Taxation in the Tribal Jurisdiction

Tribal laws establish sales taxes on motor fuels, cigarette purchases, leases, and other transactions in a blanket fashion for all who engage in Tribal commerce. Federal taxation applies to individual income of Tribal members, Tribal employment activities, and Tribal gaming per capita payments under the IGRA, 25 U.S.C. § 2710(b)(3)(D). Tribal member income derived from an allotment is exempt from federal taxation as are payments under treaties, federal settlement acts or other federal laws. I.R.S. Revenue Ruling 67-284. Tribal Nation corporations are not subject to a federal corporate tax. I.R.S. Revenue Ruling 94-16.

In a series of U.S. Supreme Court decisions, the Court has determined that states have concurrent taxing authority for commercial activity of non-members doing business in the Tribal Nation jurisdiction. The U.S. Supreme Court has upheld the general principle that state governments cannot directly tax Tribal Nation governments or Tribal members within Tribal lands. In the 1976 decision of *Moe v. Confederated Salish and Kootenai Tribes of the Flathead Reservation,* 425 U.S. 463, the Court held that the state of Montana could not impose taxes on Tribal lands for cigarette sales to Tribal members, a license fee for Tribal vendors selling cigarettes, or for property taxes on vehicles located on Tribal lands. 425 U.S. at 480–481. As for Montana's imposition of a cigarette sales tax on purchases by non-members at Tribal smoke shops located on Tribal lands, the Court stated "[t]he State requirement that the Indian tribal seller collect a tax validly imposed on non-Indians is a minimal burden designed to avoid the likelihood that in its absence non-Indians purchasing from the tribal seller will avoid payment of a concededly lawful tax." 425 U.S. at 483. Thus, state governments have asserted a right to tax non-Tribal members when they enter reservation boundaries and the U.S. Supreme Court has upheld such taxes.

With the U.S. Supreme Court sanctioning state taxation on purchases by non-Tribal members, Tribal government must weigh the decision to add Tribal Nation taxes to these same purchases. Double taxation of a good available off-reservation subject to only single taxation discourages consumers from making purchases on-reservation. In the interest of offering goods at competitive rates, the Tribal government may choose to not impose a Tribal tax alongside the state tax for non-member purchases. The negative consequence for Tribal Nations is loss of tax revenue to support basic governmental services, such as road maintenance, social service programs, and support for education on Tribal Nation lands.

Collection of state taxes imposed within Tribal Nation jurisdictions has been an area of friction in the last several decades. The U.S. Supreme Court has provided guidance to state governments by upholding pre-collection of taxes prior to taxable goods entering Tribal Nation territories and by upholding imposition of state taxes in the chain of distribution before reaching the Tribal lands. In *Wagnon v. Prairie Band of Potawatomi,* 546 U.S. 95 (2003), the U.S. Supreme Court approved a Kansas tax law imposing a motor fuels tax on the fuel distributor where the fuel was purchased by the Potawatomi Tribe at a purchase price that included the state tax. The Court stated that the legal incidence of the tax fell on the non-Indian distributor and, thus, was not a direct tax on the Tribal Nation fuel station. 546 U.S. at 106–108. This area of regulatory jurisdiction through governmental taxing authority requires a careful and thorough analysis for any business operating in Tribal territories.

D. Best Practices for Business Certainty in Tribal Nation Communities

In general, business flourishes where certainty exists. For Tribal Nations, best practices to encourage and support business on Tribal land include: providing clear Tribal laws and regulations available publicly for potential investors and business owners; providing limited waivers of sovereign immunity for fair dealings in contracting up to the amount of the contract; maintaining a strong Tribal court system to handle disputes and provide fair resolutions; and engaging in zoning for industry, residential, retail, Tribal governmental development, and environmental conservation areas.

For state incorporated businesses seeking to do business in Tribal Nation lands, best practices include: becoming versed in Tribal Nation laws on taxation, licensing, and employment preferences; understanding the Tribal Nation goal of providing employment opportunities for Tribal members; and familiarization with the Tribal court system for dispute resolution. One of the significant benefits of doing business in Indian Country is the ability to partner with and contribute to an entire community.

There is also a growing trend in Indian Country for Tribal Nation businesses to seek contracting opportunities with other Tribal Nation businesses. With Tribal government-owned businesses serving as the economic engine in Tribal communities, private Tribal member businesses are seeking ways in which to provide services to the larger Tribal Nation corporations and industries. In pursuing these Tribal Nation economic networks, the Tribal trade route model is being re-energized across North America.

CHECKPOINTS

- Tribal Nations engaged in trading partnerships and alliances with Europeans prior to the formation of the United States. With the limitations imposed by federal law on Tribal Nation resources and governance, Tribal governments have prioritized economic development.
- Tribally-owned corporations may be established pursuant to a Tribal constitution, through approval of a federal charter or under state law. Tribal government officials determine the structure of the corporate leadership.

- Federal programs, such as Native 8(a), provide incentives to Tribal Nation-owned corporations, Alaska Native Corporations, and Native Hawaiian Organizations to participate in the federal procurement process and federally designated economically depressed areas.
- The Tribal Nation gaming industry operates pursuant to the federal Indian Gaming Regulatory Act (IGRA), which contains many specific requirements that Tribal government licensed gaming facilities must comply with. The National Indian Gaming Commission is the direct federal agency that implements the provisions of the IGRA.
- Tribal Nation entities have sovereign immunity from lawsuits unless expressly waived in a contract. Best commercial practices are to waive sovereign immunity up to the amount of a contract; designate a specific court and body of law to resolve disputes in the contract; and act with good faith in all commercial dealings.
- Taxation is a key component to supporting Tribal governmental services. Tribal Nation tax offices and agencies operate under Tribal law overseeing issuance of business licenses, employment preferences, and calculation of Tribal taxes.

CHAPTER 6

Family Law in Tribal Nation Communities

ROADMAP

- Learn about the historical Tribal restorative justice principles that applied to resolving issues involving family interactions.
- Learn about the impacts of early U.S. Indian policy intended to assimilate American Indian families into a model of Euro-Christian farmers. The assimilation practices implemented during this time period continue to affect Tribal families.
- Understand the development of Tribal courts as upholding Tribal family values in dispute resolution and family law issues.
- Understand the history leading to the enactment of the federal Indian Child Welfare Act, its continued importance in Tribal communities, and current legal challenges to the legislation.

At the heart of every society are the principles that define and shape family life. For Tribal peoples, traditionally the domestic sphere of life was in harmony with the governance structure of clans and the roles of each family member. The immediate and extended family formed a circle of relations around each person born or adopted into the Tribe. In some Indigenous languages, relative terms were employed to identify the speaker and the listener, underscoring a kinship relationship. The kinship worldview permeates the traditional worldviews of Tribal Nation communities. The earth is regarded as a female relative and often referred to as mother and/or grandmother. From this basic kinship relationship flow the reciprocal obligations and expectations for living as a good relative, as well as the strong sense of belonging in the Tribal community. Tribal values of love, generosity, and compassion support the sense of community-orientation and kinship roles.

For thousands of years, Tribal Nations have existed with values, norms, and legal principles embedded in cultural interactions, education through oral teachings, and in governance processes. In contemporary times, Tribal Nations deal with the same issues as other communities: (1) how to ensure a safe environment for children and families and (2) how to define "family" for various legal purposes. Family law as it is understood in contemporary times involves children, juveniles, elders, marriages, domestic relations, and defining "family" for purposes of delegated decision-making in health care, child and elder care, and property distribution. The contemporary term, "Two Spirit," harkens back to traditional community inclusion of all persons in the Tribal community, including those who were third-gendered. With a mixture of reinvigorating traditional legal principles and contemporary legal concepts, Tribal Nations continue to provide legislation and cultural protection to kinship values and domestic relations.

A. Principles of Restorative Justice in Historical Family Law Situations

Historically, family life in Tribal communities included common human disagreements and disruptions followed by efforts at reconciliation and resolution. Certain clans could be designated to provide mediators for disputes or certain wise individuals. Disruption to the social fabric was viewed as requiring a realignment of relationships to bring the society back into balance. Restorative justice principles allowed for families to engage in the resolution process and require actions of the individuals in disharmony to make amends. A common way to conclude a restorative justice event was to provide a feast and dance for the entire community to demonstrate the return to harmony. Traditional harmony practices are integral to the expression of values and social norms within Tribal Nation communities.

Some Tribes were culturally matrilineal with women being the property owner of the family home. In these cultures, at the time of marriage, the man left his family and moved to join the woman's family and lived life surrounded by her siblings and extended family. The maternal uncles were recognized as a father-figure to the children of the marriage. Women could freely marry and divorce at her own choosing. This created a power dynamic where domestic violence was uncommon. Many modern anti-domestic violence campaigns in Indian Country, involving a broad spectrum of Tribal cultures, harness this knowledge with messages that remind community members that violence against women (and children) is not traditional.

From the historical practices of family life to the contemporary, the ability of Tribal Nation communities to positively impact family law has been undermined by U.S. Indian laws and policies. With the attempt to eliminate Tribal Nation cultural, spiritual, and legal existence, U.S. policy and law was enforced with the threat of military violence for over one hundred years against Tribal peoples. In this chapter, the impact of U.S. Indian policy on this aspect of Tribal society will be examined in addition to the role of Tribal judicial systems over the same time period to the present.

B. Impacts of Early U.S. Indian Policy Eras on Tribal Family Life

The devastation to Tribal family life due to early U.S. Indian policies would be difficult to overstate. With the European history of frequent conflicts, the newly formed U.S. engaged in warfare against Tribal communities, leading to the killing of children, mothers, fathers, and families. When the U.S. Indian policy changed to one of removal and reservation containment, Tribal Nation family members died in the hundreds during forced marches, through severe hot weather conditions for some and brutal cold for others, across great expanses of country. The removal policy was intended to open up land areas for the benefit of White land speculators and to encourage White settlement. These forced and coerced removals of American Indians by the U.S. military can be aptly called death marches. Once on reservation areas, starvation often set in as hunting, fishing, and territorial harvesting were forbidden by U.S. Indian agents. Disease, famine, and warfare were the primary features of U.S. Indian policy for most Tribal communities, leading to long term social disruption, deep mourning periods, depression, post-traumatic stress, and a legacy of suicide.

After the removal and reservation eras, U.S. Indian policy switched to one of the worst policy eras, known as the assimilation and allotment era. A major thrust of the assimilation policy was aimed directly at Tribal children. Throughout the late 1800s and up through the mid-1900s, the U.S. Indian policy on education was to remove children from Tribal Nation communities and send them to distant military-style boarding schools to receive educational, vocational, and "civilization" training. The trauma experienced by the Tribal community in having their children taken and the trauma experienced by the children, some as young as four years old, who were taken to a foreign boarding school environment with the intent to erase language, culture, and family ties, was intense and is long lasting. The Bureau of Indian Affairs provided federal funding, often from treaty payments due to Tribes, for either the direct administration of federal boarding schools or to support Christian religious organizations administering boarding schools.

In 1928, the U.S. government authorized a survey on U.S. Indian policy impacts, "The Problem of Indian Administration," commonly known as the "Meriam Report" after the principal author, Lewis Meriam. The Meriam Report reviewed Indian education policy and the conditions at the boarding schools and strongly condemned both under the Indian Service Administration. For example, the low salaries and qualifications of key personnel in the government-run boarding schools were highlighted as follows.

> *Matrons and "Disciplinarians."* One of the best illustrations of the need for better equipped personnel is in the case of such positions as "matron" and "disciplinarian." The very words reflect an erroneous conception of the task that needs to be done; but whatever they are called, the positions need to be filled by people with appropriate training for this work. The matron of an Indian school influences the lives of boys and girls probably more than any other person on the staff. Education is essentially changing human behavior, for good or ill, and the manner in which the matron and disciplinarian handle the children in their care determines very largely the habits and attitudes that will go to make up what the outside world regards as their personality and character.
>
> It seems almost incredible that for a position as matron the educational requirement is only eighth grade—and even this eighth grade standard is comparatively new. (Meriam Report, Chapter 6, 1928).

The strict disciplinarian nature of these mandatory educational institutions, the long distances from Tribal families, and the physical, mental, emotional, and sexual abuse that was experienced by many children have left lasting impacts on American Indian and Alaska Native communities, individuals, and families to this day.

Further, the manner of operating the government-run boarding schools added an additional burden on the children forced to attend. The system was set up as a half-day plan with the children serving as the laborers in every capacity for the other half of the day. The Meriam Report took issue with this entrenched practice.

> At present the half-day plan is felt to be necessary, not because it can be defended on health or educational grounds, for it cannot, but because the small amount of money allowed for food and clothes makes it necessary to use child labor. The official Course of Study for Indian Schools says frankly:
>
> > In our Indian schools a large amount of productive work is necessary. They could not possibly be maintained on the amounts appropriated by Congress for their support were it not for the fact that students [*i.e.*, children] are required to do the washing, ironing, baking, cooking, sewing; to care for the dairy, farm, garden, grounds, buildings, etc.—an amount of labor that has in the aggregate a very appreciable monetary value. (Course of Study for United States Indian Schools, p. 1, 1922.)
>
> The term "child labor" is used advisedly. The labor of children as carried on in Indian boarding schools would, it is believed, constitute a violation of child labor laws in most states. (Meriam Report, Chapter 6, 1928.)

As large numbers of at least four generations of American Indian and Alaska Native children were mandated to boarding schools operated by the federal government and religious organizations, the cultural practices of child-rearing, homemaking, plant stewardship, art techniques, Tribal languages, and hundreds of years of Tribal Nation knowledge were denied to these children as they were brutally punished for exhibiting anything culturally tied to being Native. In the boarding schools and under the Indian agents on reservations, Christianity was imposed as the only acceptable means of spiritual expression. Two Spirit or third-gendered persons were condemned and forced to conform to Christian concepts of socialization. Siblings in boarding schools were unable to offer comfort to each other as any showing of care or compassion would lead to brutal discipline. Boarding school survivors have begun to share their experiences of the inhumane conditions and actions they endured as small children without protection.

On the reservations, the U.S. Indian superintendent reigned with an iron fist. Any parents refusing to allow their children to be taken to the boarding schools would face any number of punishments by this Indian agent. Those labeled insurgents could face starvation as the Indian agents doled out basic subsistence rations and would withhold rations as punishments. This was especially effective due to the labeling of any American Indians who ventured off the reservation as "hostiles" and subject to being shot by settlers or the U.S. military. Thus, off-reservation hunting was not an option for most of the early and mid-1900s following the establishment of the reservations. The Courts of Indian Offenses were also employed in meting out punishments against those who resisted the U.S. government's assimilation policies.

In June 2021, the U.S. Secretary of the Interior, Deb Haaland, a Pueblo of Laguna citizen, implemented the Federal Indian Boarding School Initiative. As part of the initiative, the federal report, "Federal Indian Boarding School Initiative Investigative Report" was released in May 2022. Tribal consultations were announced across Indian Country to allow boarding school survivors to provide their testimony on childhoods within the federally-funded boarding school systems. On page six, the report provided: "The Department found that between 1819 to 1969, the Federal Indian boarding school system consisted of 408 Federal schools across 37 states or then-territories, including 21 schools in Alaska and 7 schools in Hawaii. Some individual Federal Indian boarding schools accounted for multiple sites. The 408 Federal Indian boarding schools accordingly comprised 431 specific sites." In terms of the conditions within these institutions, the report provided the following at page seven:

> The Federal Indian boarding school system deployed systematic militarized and identity-alteration methodologies to attempt to assimilate American Indian, Alaska Native, and Native Hawaiian children through education, including but not limited to the following: (1) renaming Indian children from Indian to English names; (2) cutting hair of Indian children; (3) discouraging or preventing the use of American Indian, Alaska Native, and Native Hawaiian languages, religions, and cultural practices; and (4) organizing Indian and Native Hawaiian children into units to perform military drills.

Recent federal efforts have centered on locating unmarked gravesites at these boarding school properties. Tribal Nations have engaged in federal processes to recover the bodies of deceased children and provide proper burial within the children's homelands in Indian Country in recent times. Survivors have engaged in providing testimony to fully document and understand the impacts of federal schools and federally funded religious orders' mandatory control over Tribal children up through the 1950s.

C. Development and Role of Tribal Courts in Family Law

American Indians were not U.S. citizens unless a specific federal agreement or federal statute provided for the citizenship status. In some treaties and allotment agreements, specific provisions set forth that by accepting an individual tract of land the Indian owner would become a dual citizen with both Tribal Nation citizenship and U.S. citizenship. By virtue of U.S. citizenship, Tribal Nation citizens would also legally become state citizens as well. The citizenship status of American Indians was important because state and federal courts barred those without U.S. citizenship from bringing cases. A famous example of the importance of American Indian classification under U.S. laws was the 1879 case, *Standing Bear v. Crooks*, filed in the U.S. District Court in Omaha, Nebraska, over which Judge Dundy presided. A family matter was at the core of the case.

Ponca leader, Standing Bear, had traveled from the Quapaw Reservation located in Indian Territory, present-day Oklahoma, back to his homelands to bury his deceased son in the lands that had become the state of Nebraska. The conditions of the Ponca Indians since removal from their homelands to Indian Territory had resulted in the deaths of almost one-third of the Tribe. In January of 1879, Standing Bear and a small group began the long arduous trek back to their homelands for the burial of his son, Bear Shield. They arrived at the Omaha Reservation in March of 1879 and were soon thereafter arrested and held at Fort Omaha under orders from General Crook. Local sympathy led to two attorneys advocating for Standing Bear and the Ponca group by filing a habeas corpus suit in federal court questioning the order of General Crooks to detain the group and return them to Indian Territory. A central issue to the case was whether Standing Bear was a person under U.S. law.

The attorney representing the U.S. government in the case, G.M. Lambertson, argued that Standing Bear as an American Indian did not exist legally as a person or as a citizen and could not bring suit against the United States government. Judge Dundy allowed Standing Bear to testify in the courtroom with the help of an interpreter. At the conclusion of the case, Judge Dundy issued his decision finding that an American Indian was a person under U.S. law; the habeas petition was properly brought before the court on behalf of Standing Bear; and that the Ponca group had the right to return and remain in their homelands. As a result, Standing Bear and the other Tribal members were set free from U.S. military custody and carried forward the burial of Bear Shield on the banks of the Niobrara River. This case serves as an example of the legal standing of American Indians prior to the passage of the 1924 Indian Citizenship Act, 43 Stat. 253 Act of June 2, 1924, and demonstrates the lengths Tribal peoples went to in order to properly carry out family obligations.

With the assimilation policies of the late 1800s outlawing Tribal Nation cultural and other practices, forums to resolve disputes through traditional cultural ways were no longer available to most Tribal communities. As discussed in Chapter Three, following the U.S. Supreme Court ruling in *Ex Parte Crow Dog,* 109 U.S. 556 (1883), that the federal courts lacked criminal jurisdiction for Tribal member against Tribal member crime in Indian Country, the U.S. Congress enacted the Major Crimes Act of 1885, 18 U.S.C. § 1153, asserting federal jurisdiction over crimes where the alleged perpetrator was American Indian and the crime was specifically listed in the Act. See Chapter Three, "Criminal Jurisdiction in Indian Country," on how federal criminal jurisdiction has since been expanded on Tribal lands. Also in 1883, the U.S. Indian Service began setting up Courts of Indian Offenses handling both criminal and civil matters on Indian reservations. Funded and operated by the executive branch, these courts may be viewed as legally suspect and another example of federal officials acting outside the scope of U.S. constitutional restraints to control Tribal Nations.

The Code of Indian Offenses enforced by these courts outlawed cultural practices and served as a tool of assimilation for the local U.S. Indian agent. To foster the legitimacy of these early courts in Indian Country, Tribal citizens were commonly selected by the Indian agent to serve as judges. The policies of assimilation through removal of children and converting to Christianity were embedded in these courts. The original 1884 Code of Indian Offenses included a perpetual term of incarceration for any medicine man or spiritual leader until they renounced their spiritual views. In the revised 1892 Code of Indian Offenses, the term was changed to a sentence of between ten to thirty days for the first offense, and subsequent convictions carried a maximum sentence of up to six months for medicine men or spiritual leaders engaging in ceremonial or traditional practices.

Tribal Nation means of dispute resolution resurfaced as U.S. Indian policy shifted to recognition of Tribal constitutional forms of government. As mentioned in Chapter Four, the Bureau of Indian Affairs provided boilerplate language for most Tribal constitutions, with a common provision for the formal recognition of a Tribal court. Tribes that did not adopt Tribal constitutions, such as the Navajo Nation, also set up Tribal court systems during this time period.

Many Tribal constitutions allow for the appointment and removal of judges to be vested in the Tribal Council. Thus, Tribal Councils may have the authority to remove a Tribal judge in the aftermath of an unpopular court decision. Some Tribal constitutions have been amended or contain provisions allowing for the initial appointment of a Tribal judge by the Tribal Council and then subsequent elections to renew employment for the judge. Tribal governments have the ability to choose the process of appointing and/or electing judges to fit the particular needs of the Tribal court. The judicial system is a key component to every modern government and should be insulated from pressure by political bodies to assure parties before the court that they will receive a fair hearing and just resolution.

Best practices for Tribal judge positions may include the establishment of either a Tribal court administrator or a Tribal judiciary board to vet candidates and then submit recommendations for appointment to the Tribal Council for final determination. The election process for Tribal judges may be another best practice that ensures community engagement in the selection of decision-makers for the Tribal court system. Above all, the Tribal judge's position should not be vulnerable to political removal or to influence in the decision-making role of the judge. For the Navajo Nation judicial system, a candidate for a judgeship must be approved by the Navajo Nation President and the Navajo Council to serve a two-year probationary period. Once that period is satisfactorily completed, then the judge is sent through the approval process once more and if approved has a lifetime appointment in the Navajo Nation judicial system. An online resource on Tribal Court formation, structure, and operation is the Tribal Court Clearinghouse project of the Tribal Law and Policy Institute at: http://www.tribal-institute.org/lists/codes.htm.

In addition to providing a forum for a wide array of subject matter, Tribal courts provide a forum for resolution of family law matters and issues arising from the domestic sphere of Tribal life. Federal laws may shape family law procedures when involving cross or multiple jurisdictions. Family law is generally an area where local governments have primacy, including Tribal courts. The formalities involved in marriage, divorce, child custody, child support, familial visitation, adoptions, establishing paternity, and other matters concerning the family are all within the purview of the Tribal court. Tribal courts are ideally suited for resolving family law issues as institutions that are tied to the local community, society and norms. Tribal courts apply Tribal law and Tribal values to resolve disputes, to manage family relations as necessary, to handle the disposition of estates, and to distribute property in probate matters.

One of the continued barriers to full Tribal Nation autonomy lies in the probate arena, where the United States as the legal title holder to Indian/trust lands continues to exert jurisdiction over real property matters at death. As such, Tribal courts may hear personal property matters and other end of life issues but may have to wait for years of federal backlog to have closure on the full range of probate matters relating to real property. Recall the discussion in Chapter Two on the American Indian Probate Reform Act and the federal process over trust land distribution to heirs.

Many Tribal Nations establish and strengthen their judicial systems to ensure a forum is available to accept transfer of state or county cases for Tribal children in need of care or experiencing neglect. For Tribal Nations from Alaska to Florida, the necessity of providing a functioning Tribal court is often focused first on handling child placement in proper foster or adoptive placements. As the next section will detail, Tribal court systems allow for adhering to traditional values and relative placements when children are unable to safely stay in their parental or legal guardian homes.

D. Tribal Children and Contemporary Laws

Tribal children are the ones who will carry forward the Tribal culture, the Tribal lifeways, the Tribal government, and the Tribal existence. Tribal Nations safeguard Tribal children to ensure that the Tribal community continues on into the future. Many Tribal Nation leaders follow the principle of weighing decision-making by considering the consequences for seven generations into the future. This long-term view on Tribal governance encompasses the lives of children yet to be born and contemplates wise decisions for future generations.

Throughout the history of the relationship with the United States, Tribal children have been especially vulnerable to the assimilation policies of federal officials. After the devastating impacts of the mandatory government boarding school policies up to the early 1950s, Tribal children were once again targeted for incorporation into White mainstream society through the process of state court adoptions. This targeting of Tribal children was promoted and funded by the U.S. federal government.

1. The Systematic Adoption of Tribal Nation Children in the 1950s–1970s

Adding to the traumatic experiences of the U.S. Indian boarding school policy, beginning in the late 1950s through the 1970s, an alarming rate of American Indian and Alaska Native children were again removed from their home Tribal communities through a concerted effort of federal, state, and private agencies through foster care and adoptive placements. One such program was the federally supported Indian Adoption Project. From approximately 1958–1967, the Bureau of Indian Affairs and the U.S. Children's Bureau federally funded the Indian Adoption Project, which was implemented by the Child Welfare League of America. The U.S. Children's Bureau was established by the U.S. Congress in 1912 and was part of the Department of Health and Human Services. The Bureau was known for projects aimed at the reduction of infant mortality and addressing child labor concerns.

The Indian Adoption Project specifically sought out American Indian and Alaska Native children from western reservations or Alaska Native Villages and placed them in White homes in midwestern and eastern states. The program was designed to deliberately adopt Tribal children into White placements, breaking cultural lines. Officially, almost 400 American Indian and Alaska Native children were adopted into White families across the United States through the Indian Adoption Project's efforts. This official Project number doesn't represent the full picture of the push for Tribal Nation children's adoptions. In the report of March 15, 1966, by Project Director Arnold Lyslo, survey results indicated that 696 Tribal Nation children had been "adopted out" of Tribal communities in the year 1965 alone by over 90 agencies operating in states with large Tribal populations. On September 13, 2018, *Indian Country Today* published "Native Americans Expose the Adoption Era and Repair Its Devastation" by Stephanie Woodard, which reported that the federal program joined with private adoption organizations and Christian religious groups.

> The Indian Adoption Project was a federal program that acquired Indian children from 1958 to 1967 with the help of the prestigious Child Welfare League of America; a successor organization, the Adoption Resource Exchange of North America, functioned from 1966 until the early 1970s. Churches were also involved. In the Southwest, the Church of Jesus Christ of Latter Day Saints took thousands of Navajo children to live in Mormon homes and work on Mormon farms, and the Catholic Church and other Christian denominations swept many more Indian youngsters into residential institutions they ran nationwide, from which some children were then fostered or adopted out. As many as one third of Indian children were separated from their families between 1941 and 1967, according to a 1976 report by the Association on American Indian Affairs.

This removal of American Indian and Alaska Native children from Tribal communities occurred during the Termination Era of U.S. Indian policy and worked to diminish the number of Tribal Nation members owed treaty rights and other services by the BIA.

State social workers also played a role in the removal of children from Tribal homes during this time period. Using ambiguous characterizations of "neglect" for American Indian and Alaska Native children in their homes, state and county social workers placed the children into mostly White foster care homes and eventually into adoptive placements. The Association on American Indians prepared a report for the U.S. Congress in the 1970s finding that at least 25–35% of American Indian children were in placements outside of their homes. Across the country, Tribal Nation leaders and organizations began a five-year lobbying effort for federal legislation to address the removal of children from their Tribal homes.

Even as the 40th anniversary of the passage of the federal Indian Child Welfare Act of 1978 approached, detailed below, Tribal children were represented in foster care nationally at a rate 2.5 time greater than their presence in the general population. In some states, Tribal Nation children continue to be represented in the state foster-care system as rates as high as 14.8 times their presence in the general population of that state. Thus, the purpose of the Indian Child Welfare Act remains a necessity to ensure Tribal children remain connected to Tribal culture, language, governance, and existence, as this is in the best interest of Tribal children.

2. The Provisions of the Indian Child Welfare Act of 1978

As a result of this dismal history of removal of Tribal Nation children, the U.S. Congress enacted the Indian Child Welfare Act, 25 U.S.C. § 1901 et seq., in 1978. In the first section of the federal law, the congressional findings included the following:

> (3) that there is no resource that is more vital to the continued existence and integrity of Indian tribes than their children and that the United States has a direct interest, as trustee, in protecting Indian children who are members of or are eligible for membership in an Indian tribe;
> (4) that an alarmingly high percentage of Indian families are broken up by the removal, often unwarranted, of their children from them by nontribal public and private agencies and that an alarmingly high percentage of such children are placed in non-Indian foster and adoptive homes and institutions; and
> (5) that the States, exercising their recognized jurisdiction over Indian child custody proceedings through administrative and judicial bodies, have often failed to recognize the essential tribal relations of Indian people and the cultural and social standards prevailing in Indian communities and families. 25 U.S.C. § 1901 (P.L. 95-608, § 2, Nov. 8, 1978, 92 Stat. 3069).

In addressing these alarming past practices by state social workers and state courts, the Indian Child Welfare Act (ICWA) operates as a jurisdictional transfer statute for cases involving the placement of Tribal member children or eligible for Tribal enrollment children outside of their parental homes. The ICWA provides that such cases are to be transferred from a state court to the appropriate Tribal court. 25 U.S.C. § 1911(b). State court transfer of an Indian child placement case may be withheld upon a finding of "good cause to the contrary," an objection by either parent, or declination of the transfer by the Tribal court. 25 U.S.C. § 1911(b). Another provision in the ICWA mandates that the child's Indian custodian or a Tribal representative has the right to intervene in any state court proceeding involving the placement of the Indian child. 25 U.S.C. § 1911(c). Although the Tribal court is the statutorily preferred forum, as a means of putting decisions about the future of Tribal citizens in Tribal court, many cases that originate in state court remain in state court forums. The proceedings in state courts must then comply with the federal minimum requirements specified in the ICWA.

3. Preliminary Core Principles for the Application of the Indian Child Welfare Act

Two preliminary core principles are important in understanding the operation of the ICWA. First is the definition of an Indian child for the law to apply and second is the type of court proceedings where the ICWA becomes operative. The ICWA states the definition of an Indian child as follows: "'Indian child' means any unmarried person who is under age eighteen and is either (a) a member of an Indian tribe or (b) is eligible for membership in an Indian tribe and is the biological child of a member of an Indian tribe." 25 U.S.C. § 1903(4). Thus, the membership criteria set in each Tribe's laws are of great significance in determining whether the ICWA will apply to a child in a state court placement proceeding. As discussed in Chapter One, Tribal citizenship/membership is a matter of Tribal law but is heavily influenced by the federal government. Federal rolls of Tribal citizenship/members are often entrenched in many contemporary Tribal constitutions developed after the Indian Reorganization Act of 1934. As a result, Tribal Nations must revise these original boilerplate membership provisions in Tribal constitutions to reflect contemporary understandings of who is eligible for Tribal membership.

The second preliminary core principle for application of the ICWA is the type of state court proceeding that will involve this federal law. The ICWA applies when an Indian child is the subject of a state court proceeding covered by the ICWA. The ICWA applies to the following child custody proceedings: foster care placement, termination of parental rights, preadoptive placement, and adoptive placement. 25 U.S.C. § 1903(1)(i)–(iv). In short, any placement of an Indian child outside of the parental home or the legal guardian home would involve application of the ICWA. Therefore, the ICWA is not operative in divorce proceedings or custody disputes between a child's parents. If in the course of a divorce proceeding, a judge ruled that neither parent should be awarded custody and a third-party custody placement is to be made, the ICWA would apply to the third-party placement.

4. Exclusive Tribal Jurisdiction and Domicile

Within the ICWA, Tribal court jurisdiction is recognized as exclusive for child placement proceedings where either: (1) the Indian child is the ward of the Tribal court or (2) the Indian child is a resident or domiciled within the reservation of the child's Tribe. 25 U.S.C. § 1911(a). The federal law does not define "resident" or "domicile" in the definitions section. 25 U.S.C. § 1903.

In 1989, the United States Supreme Court in *Mississippi Band of Choctaw v. Holyfield,* 490 U.S. 30, addressed the definition of "domicile" to determine whether the Mississippi Choctaw Tribal Court had exclusive jurisdiction over a voluntary adoption proceeding for twin babies. The case involved unwed parents both of whom were enrolled in the Mississippi Choctaw Tribe and lived on the Mississippi Choctaw reservation, and both of whom signed a consent-to-adoption form for the twins. 490 U.S. at 37–38. The local county court near the hospital where the mother gave birth entered the decree of adoption and did not refer to the Indian Child Welfare Act in the proceeding. Two months after the decree was entered in the county court the Tribal Nation filed a motion to vacate the decree on the ground that exclusive jurisdiction over the infants was in the Tribal court. The county court overruled the motion relying on the fact that the mother was off-reservation when the children were born and, therefore, the children had never resided on the reservation. 490 U.S. at 38–39. On appeal, the Supreme Court of Mississippi affirmed and stated that the Mississippi Band of Choctaw Tribe's argument was creative in asserting that the babies in their mother's womb lived on the reservation. In doing so, the court did not follow state court cases holding that a child's domicile followed that of the child's parents. 490 U.S. at 40.

In the U.S. Supreme Court, the court held that the state courts had failed to correctly apply the ICWA along with the common law principle that children are domiciled where their parents were domiciled. Under the ICWA, the decision stated that the situation was clearly governed by that federal law as the state court proceeding was within the definition of a "child custody proceeding" and the twin babies were "Indian children." 490 U.S. at 42.

Turning to the definition of the word "domicile" as critical to the operation of the federal law, the Court held that Congress did not intend for each state to define the term and give uneven results to the Indian Child Welfare Act. In fact, the Court's opinion pointed out that "the congressional findings that are a part of the statute demonstrate that Congress perceived the States and their courts as partly responsible for the problem it intended to correct." 490 U.S.

at 45. In applying the generally accepted definition of a minor's domicile, the Court's opinion stated the following.

> It is undisputed in this case that the domicile of the mother (as well as the father) has been, at all relevant times, on the Choctaw Reservation. Tr. of Oral Arg. 28–29. Thus, it is clear that at their birth the twin babies were also domiciled on the reservation, even though they themselves had never been there. The statement of the Supreme Court of Mississippi that "[a]t no point in time can it be said the twins ... were domiciled within the territory set aside for the reservation," 511 So.2d, at 921, may be a correct statement of that State's law of domicile, but it is inconsistent with generally accepted doctrine in this country and cannot be what Congress had in mind when it used the term in the ICWA.

490 U.S. at 48–49. Noting that parents cannot defeat the provisions of the ICWA and cut the children's ties with their Tribe and that three years in litigation may have led to bonding with the adoptive parents, the U.S. Supreme Court concluded by upholding the language of the ICWA and finding exclusive jurisdiction in the Tribal court. 490 U.S. at 52–55. In exercising its exclusive jurisdiction, the Mississippi Choctaw Tribal Court then approved the adoption to the non-Indian adoptive parents and required the adoptive parents to maintain contact with the children's Tribal relatives.

5. The ICWA Procedural Safeguards for Involuntary Proceedings in State Courts

If the child custody proceeding does occur in state court, then the ICWA mandates procedural standards to uphold the purposes of the law. The state court is first mandated to send notice by registered mail to the child's Tribal Nation and parent/custodian of any pending proceeding involving the child and of the right of intervention in that proceeding. 25 U.S.C. § 1912(a). The court may not proceed with a placement or a termination of parental rights until at least ten days after the child's Tribal Nation and parent/custodian have received the notice. 25 U.S.C. § 1912(a). Further, after notice is received, an additional twenty days to prepare may be requested by the child's Tribe and/or parent/custodian. 25 U.S.C. § 1912(a). The parent or Indian custodian of the child may be appointed an attorney for any removal, placement, or termination of rights proceeding upon a determination of indigency or financial need by the court. 25 U.S.C. § 1912(b). Finally, the court may appoint an attorney to represent the Tribal child when it would be "in the best interest of the child" in any removal, placement, or termination of parental rights proceeding. 25 U.S.C. § 1912(b).

In 2013, the United States Supreme Court handed down its second decision involving the interpretation of the provisions of the ICWA, *Adoptive Couple v. Baby Girl*, 570 U.S. 637 (2013). The 5–4 decision held that an Indian biological father who did not have physical or legal custody of his daughter was not covered under the protections of § 1912(f). In that case, a father who was a citizen of the Cherokee Nation sought to intervene in South Carolina state court proceedings where the non-Indian unwed birth mother voluntarily placed their daughter born in Oklahoma up for adoption. The majority concluded: "In sum, when, as here, the adoption of an Indian child is voluntarily and lawfully initiated by a non-Indian parent with sole custodial rights, the ICWA's primary goal of preventing the unwarranted removal of Indian children and the dissolution of Indian families is not implicated." 570 U.S. at 649. The Court cited to the BIA Guidelines, 44 Fed. Reg. 67593 (1979), as supportive of this announced requirement of pre-existing custody by the Indian parent prior to application of the ICWA provisions for parental rights termination under § 1912(f) and the provisions for active efforts to rehabilitate the Indian family under § 1912(d). Further, the majority opinion provided that no other alternative party sought adoption of the child and therefore the placement preferences in § 1915(a) did not need to be applied for the Indian child involved. 570 U.S. at 654–656. The case was ultimately remanded back to the highest court in South Carolina to determine proper custody of the Cherokee girl.

During the legal battle, the child had been returned to her Cherokee father in Oklahoma by order of the South Caroline Supreme Court. After the U.S. Supreme Court decision was announced, the father was scheduled to attend a 30 day out-of-state training as part of his U.S. military service. The Cherokee Nation District Court, following an emergency guardianship hearing, ordered that the step-mother and paternal grandparents, which included a Cherokee grandfather, serve as custodians of the child during the father's short military leave. Later the same day, the South Carolina Supreme Court remanded the adoption case back to a lower state court to finalize the adoption to the non-Indian couple and to terminate the Cherokee father's rights, as he was not entitled to the ICWA's parental rights termination protections. The litigation over the custody of this child as a citizen of the Cherokee Nation has involved the highest federal court in the United States, the highest state court in South Carolina, the courts of the state of Oklahoma, and the District Court of the

Cherokee Nation. This is an illustration of the complexity faced by a Tribal Nation citizen and father to seek custody of his daughter due to the intersection of federal, state, and Tribal laws regarding Tribal children and how the interpretation of federal statutory language can result in an outcome depriving a parent of custody of their child.

Before a state court can order foster care placement of an American Indian or an Alaska Native child or termination of parental rights, the state agency must prove to the court that a high level of effort was made to support the Tribal family and keep the family intact. The law expressly states that these efforts must be "active efforts" demonstrating that the Tribal family received "remedial services and rehabilitative programs designed to prevent the breakup of the Indian family and that these efforts have proved unsuccessful." 25 U.S.C. § 1912(d). For a Tribal child to be placed in foster care, the court must determine by the high standard of "clear and convincing evidence" that the placement is necessary to prevent "serious emotional or physical damage" to the child. 25 U.S.C. § 1912(e). When the state court must determine whether parental rights should be terminated, the ICWA asserts a very high standard for such a determination. The state court can only terminate parental rights if there is sufficient evidence to establish beyond a reasonable doubt "that the continued custody of the child by the parent or Indian custodian is likely to result in serious emotional or physical damage to the child." 25 U.S.C. § 1912(f).

If the state court determines that the Tribal child will be placed in foster care, then the ICWA has established placement preferences that are mandatory unless good cause to the contrary is found. 25 U.S.C. § 1915(b). The order for placement of an Indian child in foster care is as follows:

> (i) a member of the Indian child's extended family;
>
> (ii) a foster home licensed, approved, or specified by the Indian child's tribe;
>
> (iii) an Indian foster home licensed or approved by an authorized non-Indian licensing authority; or
>
> (iv) an institution for children approved by an Indian tribe or operated by an Indian organization which has a program suitable to meet the Indian child's needs.

The court is directed to follow a Tribal governmental resolution of the child's Tribal Nation if a different preference order has been designated, as long as the court finds the placement will be "the least restrictive setting appropriate" for the particular child's needs. 25 U.S.C. § 1915(c). For the adoption of a Tribal child under state law, the preference for the adoptive home is: "(1) a member of the child's extended family; (2) other members of the Indian child's tribe; or (3) other Indian families" unless there is good cause to the contrary for following this order of preference. 25 U.S.C. § 1915(a). These same placement preferences will apply to any Tribal child's removal from one foster care placement to another type of placement whether another foster care placement, a preadoptive placement, or an adoptive placement. 25 U.S.C. § 1916(b).

For both foster care and adoption placement, the court is directed to consider the cultural and social standards of the child's Tribal community in meeting the placement preference requirements. The ICWA identifies the appropriate community as "the Indian community in which the parent or extended family resides or with which the parent or extended family members maintain social and cultural ties." 25 U.S.C. § 1915(d). Also, the court shall ensure that the records of the foster care or adoptive placement are maintained by the state and available for review at any time upon the request of the child's Tribal Nation or the Secretary of the Interior. 25 U.S.C. § 1915(e).

Within the federal law, the right to petition for the return of the Tribal child that has been adopted is also provided for in certain situations. If an adoption decree is set aside or vacated for an Indian child, the Indian parent/custodian has the right to petition for the return of custody. Also if the adoptive parents voluntarily agree to terminate their parental rights to the Tribal child, then the child's biological parent or the prior Indian custodian may file a petition requesting the return of the child. 25 U.S.C. § 1916(a). A court receiving the petition will grant such petition except when it would not be in the best interests of the child applying the evidentiary standards set forth in section 1912 of the ICWA. 25 U.S.C. § 1916(a).

6. Voluntary Foster Care Placement or Adoption of a Tribal Child

The Indian Child Welfare Act also governs when the biological parent(s) of the Indian child voluntarily choose(s) to relinquish custody of the child either to foster care placement or the adoption process. This process was at issue in the prior discussion of the U.S. Supreme Court case, *Mississippi Band of Choctaw v. Holyfield,* 490 U.S. 30 (1989). The voluntariness of such an action must meet the strict requirements of the federal law. The consent to terminate parental rights must be in writing, given before a judge and the judge must file along with the consent a certificate verifying "that the terms and consequences of the consent were fully explained in detail and were fully understood by the parent or Indian custodian." 25 U.S.C. § 1913(a). No consent is valid within ten days prior to the birth of a Tribal child or within the ten days following the birth. 25 U.S.C. § 1913(a).

As discussed above in *Adoptive Couple v. Baby Girl*, 570 U.S. 637 (2013), the U.S. Supreme Court's opinion indicated that when a Tribal child has a non-Indian parent with sole custody who enters into a voluntary adoption of the child then the ICWA provisions on termination of parental rights may not apply for the Tribal parent. In other words, an Indian parent's rights are strongest when that parent has had custody of their child. Each fact situation for a voluntary adoption of a Tribal child must be carefully considered as a result of that U.S. Supreme Court opinion and the provisions of the ICWA.

When voluntary consent allows for placement of a Tribal child in foster care, the parent or Indian custodian may withdraw his/her consent "at any time." 25 U.S.C. § 1913(b). The Indian Child Welfare Act provides that once consent is withdrawn the child must be returned. In the situation of voluntary termination of parental rights, the parent may withdraw consent at any time up until the final decree of termination for any reason and the child shall be returned. 25 U.S.C. § 1913(c). When a Tribal child is voluntarily placed for adoption, the parent may again withdraw consent for any reason up until the final decree of adoption and the child shall be returned. 25 U.S.C. § 1913(c). Further, the parent has the right to assert a challenge that his/her voluntary consent was obtained through fraud or duress within two years of an adoption decree. The parent may file a withdrawal of consent and petition the court to vacate the adoption decree for the return of the Tribal child. 25 U.S.C. § 1913(d). If state law provides for a longer time period than two years to assert a challenge, then that will be available to the parent. 25 U.S.C. § 1913(d).

7. The Washington Indian Child Welfare Act and Tribal Court Exclusive Jurisdiction

The state of Washington's actions involving the federal Indian Child Welfare Act provide an example of the complexity and need for clarification that can arise in this area of family law. Under Public Law 280, the federal government delegated its criminal and limited civil forum access for certain matters arising in Indian Country to specific states; see Chapter Three for more information on this federal law. In the Washington state legislation accepting the federal Public Law 280 delegation, the state explicitly asserted jurisdiction over a number of areas involving Indian children, including compulsory school attendance, domestic relations, adoption proceedings, and dependent children. RCW 37.12.010. State courts in Washington and elsewhere exercising such jurisdiction would still be subject to the case transfer provisions of the ICWA under 25 U.S.C. § 1911(b) discussed previously. Further, the intervention rights in any state court child custody proceeding for the Indian parent/custodian and the child's Tribal Nation would continue intact under 25 U.S.C. § 1911(c). The interaction between the ICWA's designation of exclusive Tribal jurisdiction and Washington Public Law 280 jurisdiction involving Tribal children would be decisively clarified in state legislation in 2011.

The state of Washington provides an example of state proactive efforts through its Department of Social and Health Services (DSHS) to better implement the provisions and purpose of the ICWA. Following passage of the ICWA, the DSHS developed a manual on Indian Child Welfare policy for state caseworker practices and entered into specific Tribal-state agreements on procedures. In 2004, Tribal officials and DSHS officials held a summit to discuss solutions to the ongoing problems and differing interpretations of the ICWA in state placement proceedings involving Tribal children. From the summit, efforts turned to introducing state legislation incorporating the provisions of the ICWA and, therefore, domesticating the federal law into state law. After almost seven years of revising draft legislation to meet concerns of legislators, adoption attorneys, foster care organizations, and Tribal officials, the state law became effective July 22, 2011. RCW 13.38.010.

The relationships developed between the state DSHS and Tribal officials provided the basis for incorporation of the ICWA into Washington state law and serves as a model for other state and Tribal governments. By passing this state legislation, state legislators set forth the following intention.

> The legislature finds that the state is committed to protecting the essential tribal relations and best interests of Indian children by promoting practices designed to prevent out-of-home placement of Indian children that is inconsistent with the rights of the parents, the health, safety, or welfare of the children, or the interests of their tribe. Whenever out-of-home placement of an Indian child is necessary in a proceeding subject to the terms of the federal Indian child welfare act and in this chapter, the best interests of the Indian child may be served by placing the Indian child in accordance with the placement priorities expressed in this chapter. The legislature further finds that where placement away from

> the parent or Indian custodian is necessary for the child's safety, the state is committed to a placement that reflects and honors the unique values of the child's tribal culture and is best able to assist the Indian child in establishing, developing, and maintaining a political, cultural, social, and spiritual relationship with the child's tribe and tribal community.
>
> It is the intent of the legislature that this chapter is a step in clarifying existing laws and codifying existing policies and practices. This chapter shall not be construed to reject or eliminate current policies and practices that are not included in its provisions.

RCW 13.38.030, Findings and intent. The state law did provide clarification in many important respects. While other state courts across the country may still be embroiled in controversies over the interpretation of key provisions of the federal ICWA, Washington has straightforward state law to sidestep such controversies when Indian children are involved in placement proceedings.

Within the Washington Indian Child Welfare Act, the definitions section provides clear guidance on terms that had previously been subject to dissimilar treatment depending on the presiding judge or caseworker. For example, an express definition for "active efforts" and the minimum standards necessary to accomplish such efforts in reuniting an American Indian or Alaska Native family where a child is subject to a state placement proceeding is now available at RCW 13.38.040(1). Another significant provision of the state law was to address Tribal exclusive jurisdiction. The state law largely tracks the ICWA provisions set forth at 25 U.S.C. § 1911(a). The following are the provisions from the Washington Indian Child Welfare Act, RCW 13.38.060:

> (1) An Indian tribe shall have exclusive jurisdiction over any child custody proceeding involving an Indian child who resides or is domiciled within the reservation of that tribe, unless the tribe has consented to the state's concurrent jurisdiction, the tribe has expressly declined to exercise its exclusive jurisdiction, or the state is exercising emergency jurisdiction in strict compliance with RCW 13.38.140.
>
> (2) If an Indian child is already a ward of a tribal court at the start of the child custody proceeding, the Indian tribe may retain exclusive jurisdiction, notwithstanding the residence or domicile of the child.

Subsection 1 limits state concurrent jurisdiction assumed under Public Law 280 to instances where a Tribal Nation has expressly consented to the state's concurrent jurisdiction; otherwise the Tribal court will have exclusive jurisdiction over a Tribal child residing or domiciled on the Tribe's reservation. With this clarification, Tribal child placement proceedings no longer require a full analysis of the state's delegated jurisdiction under Public Law 280 to determine whether a Tribal child on their home reservation is subject to a state court proceeding or is under the jurisdiction of the local Tribal court.

Each state may enact its own version of the Indian Child Welfare Act to provide uniform application by state agencies and courts. Washington serves as a recent model of this process. California, West's Ann. Cal. Fam. Code § 170, and Iowa, I.C.A. § 232B.1, have also incorporated provisions of the federal ICWA into state law. It should be noted that problems may still arise in these states interpreting the state law. For example. in the 2008 case, *In the Interest of N.N.E.* 752 N.W.2d 1 (2008), the Iowa Supreme Court held that the Iowa state ICWA's placement provisions were unconstitutional in a voluntary termination of parental rights proceeding by finding that under the federal ICWA the placement preferences could be disregarded on a finding of "good cause" that was not available under the Iowa ICWA. I.C.A. § 232B.9.

Another trend developed in the late 1980s has been to apply a standard known as the "existing Indian family" doctrine to allow state court judges to evaluate whether the parent(s) of the Tribal child met the state judge's definition of an Indian family as a prerequisite for following the ICWA provisions. State court judges finding that the parent(s) did not culturally participate in their Tribal heritage could then rule that there was no concern for the ICWA to address in placing the child in a non-Indian home. This doctrine has been severely criticized for the subjective discretion of state court judges to define "Indian families" and add new requirements to the federal law but may remain active in some state court jurisdictions. There has been another recent trend in some jurisdictions to abandon this doctrine. In 2004, the Oklahoma Supreme Court determined that the doctrine "was no longer viable" for cases involving application of the ICWA in the state court case, *In the Matter of Baby Boy L.*, 103 P.3d 1099. Kansas state courts were the first to develop the doctrine and in 2009 the Kansas Supreme Court expressly rejected its further application in the case, *In re A.J.S.*, 204 P.3d 543.

Further, many states have passed laws known as "Safe Haven Acts," which give immunity from criminal prosecution to any parent(s) or legal guardian who abandons a child to a state agency or medical facility. The standard provisions under these state laws provide that no identifying information can be required from the parent about the child. Without identifying information, the provisions of the ICWA can be easily circumvented when the abandoned child is a Tribal child. Resolving the intersection between state safe haven laws and the federal mandates of the ICWA will require ongoing communication between state, Tribal, and federal agencies.

8. The Bureau of Indian Affairs Guidelines in the C.F.R. on the Indian Child Welfare Act

On the federal level, the Bureau of Indian Affairs (BIA) has published guidelines as direction to state courts on the application of the ICWA. These original guidelines were published in 67584 Federal Register Vol. 44 No. 228 on Monday, November 28, 1979, as "The Bureau of Indian Affairs, Guidelines for State Courts; Indian Custody Proceedings" (hereinafter, BIA Guidelines) and continue to be relevant and referenced in state court decisions. The BIA Guidelines were relied upon by the U.S. Supreme Court in the *Adoptive Couple v. Baby Girl* 2013 decision interpreting the parental rights termination provisions of the ICWA. The BIA Guidelines expand on some of the provisions of the ICWA and provide the federal agency's interpretation on some key terms of the federal law.

In December 2016, the Bureau of Indian Affairs issued new guidelines and supplemental regulations for the implementation of the ICWA. 25 C.F.R. part 23. Although not binding, the BIA Guidelines and regulations provide the agency's suggested best practices. In Section A.3 of the BIA Guidelines, states are encouraged to allow non-attorneys to represent the Tribal Nation in state court proceedings as a way to eliminate or minimize barriers to Tribal participation. For example, "[m]any tribes have limited funds to hire local counsel. The Department encourages all State courts to permit Tribal representatives to present before the court in ICWA proceedings regardless of whether they are attorneys or attorneys licensed in the State, as a number of State courts have already done." Due to resource constraints, Tribal governments may need to deputize a Tribal representative who is not licensed to practice law, such as a Tribal social worker or other representative, to appear in a proceeding and represent the Tribe's interest. The 2016 BIA Guidelines, in Section B.1. also highlight the importance of due diligence to determine the impacted Tribe and due diligence on whether a child is an American Indian or Alaska Native, regardless of whether other family members are Tribal members. Prompt and proper notice to the Tribal Nation is critical to make sure that proceedings do not go on for long periods of time without Tribal participation. Finally, the BIA Guidelines in B.2 confirm that state courts are prohibited from considering the "existing Indian family exception," a judicially created exception to the application of the ICWA mentioned above.

By implementing regulations in 2016 in 25 C.F.R. Part 23, the federal agency has also exercised its regulatory authority to fill in gaps in interpretation for the ICWA. For example, the Indian Child Welfare Act does not address the situation where a Tribal child is enrolled in one Tribe and eligible for enrollment in another Tribe or where the child is not enrolled in any Tribe, but is eligible for enrollment in several Tribes. 25 C.F.R. § 23.109 provides direction to contact only the Tribe where the child is an enrolled member in the first situation and, in the second, directs that all Tribes where the child is eligible for enrollment receive notice of the placement proceedings for an agreement between the Tribes on where the child should be enrolled. Finally, the regulation provides that if no agreement is reached between the Tribes, only then may the state recommend enrollment in a particular Tribe taking into consideration the child's contacts with the Tribe and preference of the parent(s) among other factors.

One of the most important interpretations provided in the BIA Guidelines and 2016 regulations concerns the term "good cause" as applied to determine that "good cause" exists to halt transfer of the child placement proceeding from state to Tribal court. The Indian Child Welfare Act does not define what is "good cause"—the standard necessary to prevent the child's case from being transferred to the child's Tribal court, 25 U.S.C. § 1911(b). In 25 C.F.R. § 23.118(c), state courts *must not consider* the following in determining whether there is good cause to deny transfer of the proceedings to the relevant Tribal court.

> (c) In determining whether good cause exists, the court must not consider:
>
> (1) Whether the foster-care or termination-of-parental-rights proceeding is at an advanced stage if the Indian child's parent, Indian custodian, or Tribe did not receive notice of the child-custody proceeding until an advanced stage;
>
> (2) Whether there have been prior proceedings involving the child for which no petition to transfer was filed;
>
> (3) Whether transfer could affect the placement of the child;
>
> (4) The Indian child's cultural connections with the Tribe or its reservation; or

> (5) Socioeconomic conditions or any negative perception of Tribal or BIA social services or judicial systems.

Thus, the 2016 regulations ensure a thorough review prior to a state court denying a transfer of the proceeding for the child to the child's home Tribal court.

Another provision of the BIA Guidelines establishes a right for an adult adoptee eighteen years or older to request from the state court the person's Tribal affiliations, as stated in 25 C.F.R. § 23.138: "Upon application by an Indian who has reached age 18 who was the subject of an adoptive placement, the court that entered the final decree of adoption must inform such individual of the Tribal affiliations, if any, of the individual's biological parents and provide such other information necessary to protect any rights, which may include Tribal membership, resulting from the individual's Tribal relationship." These provisions support the return to Tribal communities of Tribal members adopted out of their homes pursuant to state court proceedings.

9. The Continuing Necessity of the Indian Child Welfare Act

The National Indian Child Welfare Association (NICWA) serves as a national resource center for training and information to promote the protection of American Indian and Alaska Native children. The NICWA website confirms the ongoing need for the Indian Child Welfare Act.

> Although progress has been made as a result of [the] ICWA, out-of-home placement still occurs more frequently for Native children than it does for the general population. In fact, recent research on systemic bias in the child welfare system yielded shocking results. Native families are four times more likely to have their children removed and placed in foster care than their White counterparts. So in spite of the advances achieved since 1978, [the] ICWA's protections are still needed.

In recent years, non-Native adoptive parents, a subset of the adoption industry, and the Goldwater Institute have launched a legal and media campaign to set aside the ICWA. Part of the strategy has been to engage in litigation around the constitutionality of the federal law. On June 15, 2023, in *Haaland v. Brackeen*, 599 U.S. 255 (2023), the United States Supreme Court 7–2 soundly rejected a variety of such arguments and held that prior decisions articulated the U.S. Congress as exercising plenary authority in Indian affairs. 599 U.S. at

272–273. The opinion grounded the power in the U.S. Constitution, article I, § 8, clause 3 (the Indian Commerce Clause); the U.S. Constitution, article II, § 2, clause 2 (the Treaty Clause); in governmental preconstitutional powers of diplomacy and war; and as part of the federal government's trust relationship toward Tribal Nations. 599 U.S. at 273–275. "In sum, Congress's power to legislate with respect to Indians is well established and broad." 599 U.S. at 275. The Court rejected three other arguments that the ICWA's requirements involving state courts amounted to commandeering by the federal government. 599 U.S. at 280–291. Further, the Court stated that the individual petitioners' alleged injury and right to relief against the federal government would be an advisory opinion, which was prohibited under Article III of the U.S. Constitution. 599 U.S. at 294. Finally, the Court held that the state of Texas as one of the petitioners lacked standing to assert an equal protection argument as a government and not an individual. 599 U.S. at 294–296. The 2023 *Brackeen* decision is the third U.S. Supreme Court opinion regarding the Indian Child Welfare Act since its enactment in 1978.

The work to train state and county courts, social workers, and family law lawyers on the provisions of the Indian Child Welfare Act continues and some states have been proactive in adopting and updating state law to embody the purposes of the ICWA. As the Indian Child Welfare Act has heightened standards in the field of child protection, some family law practitioners refer to the federal law as a gold standard due to the active efforts to rehabilitate the family and the high threshold prior to termination of parental rights.

E. Tribal Law and Tribal Families

Tribal governments may enact Tribal laws on a wide variety of subjects that support Tribal families and Tribal values. The Tribal value of gaining knowledge and wisdom is supported by Tribal laws requiring children to attend school and holding parents responsible for truancy or excessive absences during the school year. Child protection and juvenile codes serve to translate Tribal values into the societal norms enforceable in Tribal Nation communities to guide and protect the Tribe's youth.

1. Tribal Law and Domestic Relations

Social cohesion as a Tribal value is enhanced with Tribal laws that recognize legal unions in marriage. Marriage licenses are issued by Tribal courts and marriage ceremonies take place in Tribal courts. Tribal courts are employed to handle marriage dissolutions, child custody matters in the event of divorce or death of the child's parents, and property distribution as a result of a divorce. Domestic relations is a broad category and involves human interactions as relatives in the Tribal community. Over hundreds of years, Tribal Nations have followed values, norms, and legal principles on harmonious relationships within families and extended families. As Tribal communities heal from the intergenerational traumas from U.S. Indian policy eras, human relationships and families can face crises that require legal solutions.

a. Tribal Communities and Domestic Violence

In support of healthy Tribal families, Tribal codes include provisions to address, appropriately punish, and rehabilitate those engaging in the abuse of family members. Domestic violence laws may apply to any family member or may be written in separate codes to address particular family relationships. Spousal abuse and intimate relationship partner abuse are often the focus of Tribal domestic violence protection laws. Elder abuse laws may also be enacted to protect the senior members of families from injury and harm. A Tribal legislature may broadly define those protected by domestic violence provisions as simply "household members."

A victim of domestic violence in a Tribal community may seek a temporary protection order by filing a petition with the Tribal court on an emergency basis. The temporary order will be enforceable by Tribal law enforcement on Tribal lands against a Tribal member defendant named in the order. The Tribal court will schedule a hearing on the temporary order to allow for the alleged victim and defendant to each present testimony and evidence on whether the order should become a permanent protection order or should be dismissed. The hearing will often lead to other family law filings if the parties are married or have children together. Violation of a civil protection order may result in criminal prosecution if the Tribal law provides for this in the criminal domestic violence laws.

Tribal Nations are increasingly dedicating funding and prioritization to domestic violence shelters for victims, counseling services for those involved in domestic violence, and rehabilitative services for perpetrators. Intertwined with issues of domestic violence may be substance abuse issues, lack of anger

Northern Cheyenne Tribal Health. Photo credit: Angelique EagleWoman.

management skills, mental health issues, and other issues. Tribal courts are in a position to order a wide variety of program attendance and community service engagement for Tribal members to resolve domestic violence situations in a holistic manner. In some instances, Tribal Healing and Wellness Courts have been established to bring community services into the lives of Tribal members dealing with a host of issues.

As discussed in Chapter Three, "Criminal Jurisdiction in Indian Country," creating safe Tribal communities often involves navigating jurisdictional issues for the proper law enforcement and court authority to address the actions of an alleged perpetrator. When the alleged perpetrator is non-Native committing domestic violence, then Tribal courts may seek to qualify for Special Tribal Criminal Jurisdiction under the 2022 reauthorization of the Violence Against Women Act for specific types of crimes listed in 25 U.S.C. § 1304(5): "The term 'covered crime' means—(A) assault of Tribal justice personnel; (B) child violence; (C) dating violence; (D) domestic violence; (E) obstruction of justice; (F) sexual violence; (G) sex trafficking; (H) stalking; and (I) a violation of a protection order." Tribal Nation courts must meet federal standards and be authorized to carry out the Special Tribal Criminal Jurisdiction set forth in federal law.

Tribal courts may order civil sanctions to a non-Native perpetrator such as exclusion from Tribal lands, civil fines, or participation in rehabilitative service programs. Due to the limitations on Tribal criminal prosecution of non-Indians, cooperation with state law enforcement and courts may be necessary to fully resolve such situations and hold accountable a non-Native person committing domestic violence acts against a Tribal citizen on Tribal lands and/or in Tribal communities. In meeting these challenges, some Tribal government officials have entered into agreements with local state officials to provide for recognition of Tribal protection and other orders in state courts and vice versa.

b. Mental Health and Substance Abuse Issues in Tribal Communities

In dealing with the changing eras of U.S. Indian policies, the vast majority of Tribal families have experienced intergenerational poverty, dealt with racism, and experienced severe cultural transition and trauma. As Tribal governments have rebuilt community infrastructure through social services and Tribal courts, a priority has been to assist family members with mental health issues and/or assist those who suffer from the effects of substance abuse. Many Tribal Nations have developed a Tribal drug court program and/or a Tribal wellness court program that is available to address many of the issues arising when a family is in crisis through ordering family members to attend substance abuse programs or mental health counseling programs. Often these services become necessary after a child neglect or abuse proceeding has been brought against parents in crisis.

Tribal programs can be structured around the traditional Tribal values that re-align families with the parenting and lifestyle practices known prior to the government boarding school era. Thus, these types of individual and family services can provide healing over generations and a return to wellness in Tribal family life. Tribal Healing and Wellness Courts require consent from the participant to engage in a plan with coordinated steps to address multiple issues the participant may be facing, such as homelessness, lack of job training, substance abuse, underdeveloped parenting skills, lack of anger management responses, and other issues. The successful participation in the plan may involve mentors in the Tribal community, involvement in Tribal ceremonial practices, reconnection to Tribal language and teachings, and other milestones to uplift the individual to fully recover from the crisis that brought the individual into legal proceedings.

There are limited options for Tribal members experiencing ongoing mental health issues in most Tribal communities. Many Tribal Nations are enacting adult guardianship codes to allow relatives to provide oversight and assistance for adults who are unable to fully function on a daily basis. Few assisted living residential centers exist in Tribal communities, requiring partnerships and funding agreements with state funded centers. As the reality of the lived experiences of boarding school survivors becomes more well known, the need for Tribal facilities focused on traditional values and healing processes is evident. This is an important area that may continue to be a focus for Tribal domestic law.

c. Same-Sex Marriage

Although same-sex marriages are not recognized in some Tribal Nations, the traditions of same-sex marriage have been passed into official Tribal law in several Tribal communities. The Coquille Tribe of Oregon legalized same-sex marriage in May 2009 and the Suquamish Tribe of Washington in August 2011. In many pre-Christian Tribal communities, same-sex couples were viewed as an important part of the community. The transgender, third-gendered and/or intersex individual was referred to in some Tribal traditions as a "Two Spirit" person with special spiritual gifts to assist the Tribal community.

The United States Supreme Court decision in *Obergefell v. Hodges*, 576 U.S. 644 (2015), did not legalize same-sex marriage throughout Indian Country because the United States Constitution does not apply to the actions or inactions of Tribal governments. See discussion of *Talton v. Mayes*, 163 U.S. 376 (1896), in Chapter Three.

The laws of each Tribal Nation will determine how marriage is defined and regulated in each jurisdiction. Although Tribes may differ in their cultural and religious acceptance or rejection of same-sex marriages, contemporary Tribal governments are addressing the issue through Tribal legislation and Tribal court decisions. On one end of the spectrum are Tribes that have legislatively prohibited same-sex marriages under Tribal law and refuse to recognize and enforce marriages from other jurisdictions. On the other end of the spectrum are Tribes that affirmatively legalized same-sex marriage by Tribal legislation in the years before same-sex marriage was legalized throughout the United States.

2. Traditional Legal Principles and Tribal Domestic Law

Increasingly, Tribal Nations are revising their laws to include traditional legal principles, especially for domestic law matters. Tribal Nations with a common language and historical, traditional principles may share traditional legal concepts and codify those concepts for Tribal courts to follow. Each Tribal Nation has its own authority and interpretation of traditional legal principles and practitioners should have familiarity with the Tribal Nation laws in which they practice. The establishment of Tribal Healing and Wellness Courts have developed along with embracing traditional legal and societal practices of rehabilitation and compassion for those dealing with difficulties leading to societal repercussions. As traditional and customary laws are revitalized in Tribal Nations, there is a harmony restored in resolving domestic law issues and providing a pathway for individuals to find balance in their lives.

CHECKPOINTS

- The domestic sphere of Tribal law is an area where Tribal values, culture, and wisdom form the core. Tribal courts generally have exclusive authority in handling domestic issues occurring on Tribal lands involving their citizens.
- Due to the U.S. Indian policy of assimilation, Tribal members have suffered from the removal of children from Tribal homes and federal strategies to alter or eliminate Tribal culture and lifeways. Many Tribal Nations have prioritized protection of Tribal languages, Tribal knowledge, and Tribal education systems to remedy the traumas from that policy era.
- The federal Indian Child Welfare Act (ICWA) was enacted to remedy cross-cultural misunderstandings of state agencies towards Tribal families and provide a transfer process for cases involving placement of Tribal children from state courts to Tribal courts. Some states have passed their own state laws to further implement the provisions of the ICWA.
- Tribal family law continues to develop to address contemporary needs of Tribal families. Tribal Healing and Wellness Courts have developed to address family issues in a holistic manner.

CHAPTER 7

Natural Resources in Indian Country

ROADMAP

- Understand the reciprocal and respectful relationship of Tribal Nations in terms of natural resources, including the earth, air, water and fire.
- Learn about the extensive role of the U.S. Department of the Interior in the management and leasing of Tribal lands to utilize surface and subsurface resources.
- Learn about the engagement in environmental protection policies for water, air, and land by Tribal Nations in collaboration with the U.S. Environmental Protection Agency and the impacts of climate change on some Tribal Nations.
- Understand the foundational Tribal Nations and United States treaties, which often include perpetual treaty hunting, fishing, and gathering rights for Tribal citizens in off-reservation ceded lands.
- Understand the impact of the energy industry in Indian Country and the federal laws that support the industry.

From time immemorial, Tribal Nations have stewarded natural resources in a reciprocal relationship with the physical world. Many Tribal traditions refer to the earth as Mother Earth or Grandmother Earth. This reference to maternal relations signifies the nurturing and sustaining of human life from the earth. Likewise, many Tribal Nations view elements of the natural world as imbued with spiritual essence and in relationship with human beings. Through respect for water spirits, there is a contemporary water protectors' movement in Indian Country. Tribal Nations employed controlled burning techniques to prevent large-scale wildfires in their forests. This also contributed to high air quality. Tribal legal principles and societal values have imposed restraints on human activity to curb over-utilization, waste, or contamination of natural resources. These Tribal legal principles are connected to the respect for and interdependence with other living beings, such as birds, deer, and fish.

Tribal peoples sustainably engaged with the natural world for human life and society. The use of natural resources was necessary for Tribal Nations and communities to construct reliable housing due to geography and weather conditions. Forests continue to provide a wealth of materials, in timber, plants, animals, and other resources. Understanding the interrelationships of living beings in various geographical locations is often referred to as traditional ecological knowledge in contemporary times. The close relationship between Tribal Nations and specific geographies has resulted in expertise on balancing human consumption of resources with retention of resources to flourish and increase.

There are vast natural resource holdings throughout Indian Country from land, water, and timber to a variety of subsurface estates with known and potential economic development viability. Because these resources are located within the land base retained by Tribes, there may be significant environmental and ecological concerns. With these natural resources located within or adjacent to treaty protected or other types of Tribal lands, stewardship principles applied by Tribal Nations may involve cooperation with the federal and state governments. In applying Tribal legal principles and values of conservation and protection over natural resources, many Tribal Nations and Tribal members are engaged in resisting efforts for energy resource extraction and pipeline transport on or adjacent to Tribal permanent homelands or on lands with historical, ceremonial, or spiritual significance for Tribal communities.

This chapter will cover Tribal Nation natural resource development, management, and issues. For a full understanding of the material, readers should cross-reference this discussion with Chapter Two, "Native American Property Law"; Chapter Four, "Tribal Government, Civil Jurisdiction and Regulation"; and Chapter Nine, "Sacred Sites and Cultural Property Protection," as there is significant overlap in these areas. To understand the current landscape of Tribal Nation relationship with natural resources, it is necessary to examine the assertion of the trustee relationship by the United States over Tribal Nations' lands and resources.

A. United States as Trustee for Tribal Nation Natural Resources

The federal government's allocation and reallocation of land and natural resources has shaped much of federal Indian law and policy. In some eras, the federal government has actively terminated Tribal property rights or limited Tribal holdings to smaller and smaller territories. On the other hand, the federal government has played an active role in protecting Tribal natural resources from acquisitions by third parties, including the implementation of federal restraints on alienation that have ensured unencumbered Tribal property interests. As a result of federal restraints on alienation, state taxation and regulation of Tribal natural resources is generally prohibited.

The development of natural resources inside Indian Country is generally a matter of federal law because the United States has asserted the status of legal title holder over Tribal natural resource estates. Therefore, the United States acts as a trustee for the beneficiary Tribal Nation or beneficiary individual Tribal citizen. Although property interests have been taken from Tribes without their consent and redistributed to third parties, as with the Surplus Lands Acts of the late 1800s and early 1900s, most forms of natural resources reallocations have been implemented in a more subtle fashion.

As the trustee of Tribal lands and natural resources, the United States has long exercised leasing power over both the surface and subsurface holdings of Tribes. The United States has exercised the power to approve oil and gas and other mineral production with or without Tribal consent. This power also includes the authority of the federal government to grant easements across Tribal land for highways, roads, pipeline construction and maintenance, utilities, and other projects. While the trustee is theoretically charged with always acting in the best interest of the beneficiary, there is considerable room for abuse and lack of accountability that creates a precarious relationship among Tribes, individual Tribal members, and the United States in this arena. This relationship is, without a doubt, one of the more contentious aspects of the modern government-to-government relationship between Tribal Nations and the United States Department of Interior, which is charged in most instances with administrative control in this area. Federal action at the Tribal level involves the area Bureau of Indian Affairs offices administered by the U.S. Department of the Interior.

When a natural resource is determined available for development, the United States, as the trustee, negotiates the terms of the development agreement, including bonus payments, royalty rates, and other compensation. In many instances, the compensation that has been negotiated for Tribal Nations by the United States has resulted in rates of return well below the competitive market values, or at times lower than federal public land rates, for the same natural resources. Criticism of the undervaluation in BIA leasing of Tribal natural resources focuses on the lower rates for U.S. private industry to exploit Tribal resources and the consequent low rate of return to Tribal Nations and Tribal members under these types of leases. Legal scholars have commented that leasing Tribal Nations' resources at lower-than-normal rates are a type of subsidizing of the U.S. private industry allowed by the U.S. as trustee.

Although there is a trend in modern federal legislation and regulations to return more control to Tribal decision-makers, including the power for Tribal Nations to be the business entities in their own natural resource development and marketing, the federal government continues to play a significant role in leasing and in the collection of royalties and other compensation. Depending on the natural resource at issue, the United States plays a daily role in the management and administration of Tribal natural resources as a duty under federal law, most notably timber, oil, and gas.

Although the Tribal natural resources arena is an area with many documented federal abuses, it is also an area where the federal government has been more aggressive in ensuring Tribal autonomy than in some other areas. The federal Environmental Protection Agency (EPA), for example, is one of the few federal agencies that has recognized Tribal governmental authority, similar to that of state governments, for regulations governing pollution control. The federal EPA views Indian Country to be a marker of territorial jurisdiction and does not limit its view of Tribal Nation regulatory power as limited to only those lands that are owned by the Tribe or its citizens/members. By its very nature, environmental regulation cannot be effective if regulation is treated as a checkerboard of land tenure patterns with the Tribe regulating one tract of land and the state, perhaps with less stringent environmental controls, regulating the adjacent parcel of land. Under federal laws such as the Clean Water Act, Clean Air Act, and Safe Drinking Water Act, Tribal Nations may enjoy the benefits of participating in federal environmental programs as the local regulatory body in much the same manner as states agencies charged with environmental protection.

1. Leasing of Tribal Lands

The Secretary of the Interior is charged with approving the leasing of Tribal lands, both in the case of lands held by the Tribal government as the owner and allotted lands, provided the lands are held in federal trust status. 25 U.S.C. § 415. Extensive regulations operate depending on the type of lease sought. 25 C.F.R. Part 162.00. The maximum period for a lease is controlled by federal statutes and regulations, and will depend largely upon the type of natural resource at issue.

The Secretary's approval of a lease is a federal action that implicates the National Environmental Policy Act (NEPA) and requires a study of environmental consequences of the federal action. Although such review is typically advantageous to the Tribes to ensure sustainability of resources and minimize environmental degradation, the NEPA is often viewed by the Tribes as an undue bureaucratic obstacle to development. When Tribal Nations are considering whether to retain a tract of land in fee status, or request that that federal government take the land into trust, NEPA considerations and the time delay often associated with such review is a critical factor in making that decision. If the Tribe retains fee title to the land, the Tribe is free to lease its land on its own initiative, without federal approval. Once land use or natural resources are leased on trust lands with the requisite federal approval, the Department of Interior takes an active role in lease management. The federal government, as trustee, has the duty to ensure lease compliance, which includes ensuring that the lease terms are complied with by all third parties.

In recent years, national attention has focused on Tribal challenges to the Dakota Access Pipeline and other energy transport pipelines as they relate to federal permits for pipelines in or near Indian Country. Although pipeline challenges implicating other communities are also common, the Indian Country challenges are of fundamental importance to Tribal Nations given the unique history and the fact that reservations are designed to be permanent homelands with the guarantees of Tribal self-governance. Potential leaks that could cause damage to lands, water, sacred sites, and cultural resources of importance to the Tribes threaten treaty-reserved rights. Tribal Nations in government-to-government relationships with the federal government expect proper consultation and actions consistent with the United States' role as a trustee for Tribal Nation and Tribal member resources as described below.

2. Duties of the Federal Trustee

As the trustee, the United States has the power to foreclose a lease for failure to make payments and the duty to collect payments, including the duty to account for the natural resources removed according to the terms of the lease. As the trustee, the United States owes a fiduciary obligation to the Tribal Nations or individual Tribal member property owners and may be held accountable for damages for violation of the trust responsibility.

Enforcement claims in breach of trust cases are brought against the executive branch, typically the Secretary of the Interior, over the conduct of the Bureau of Indian Affairs. The origin of the trust responsibility is multifaceted and either comes from the contractual relationship between the Tribal Nation and United States in treaties, from an implicit understanding of the guardian-ward/fiduciary relationship the United States declared to implement over the Tribal Nations, or it derives expressly from provisions of federal statutes or regulations.

Tribal Nations are frequently frustrated with the lack of clarity with respect to the trust responsibility and conflicting language in federal court cases that declare that the United States, as a trustee, does not have the same duty one may expect from a trustee in the private sector, such as a bank. For instance, the United States is said to have only a "limited" trust relationship with Tribal allottees following the General Allotment Act, whereby the United States required the division of Tribal property to individual Tribal members subject to a trust status under the federal law. Numerous federal laws begin with preambles and findings that the United States as trustee owes unique obligations to Tribal Nations and Tribal members. Yet, these provisions have not been held to a "complete" trust standard. According to U.S. Supreme Court decisions, the "complete" trust duty of the United States arises only when a specific statute or regulation affirmatively requires the federal government to take action, and then the United States can be held accountable for failing to affirmatively act.

In the management of timber, specific duties are assigned that would invoke an enforceable trust, such as the management of sustainable yields. This was held to be true in the *United States v. Mitchell* (463 U.S. 206 (1983) (*Mitchell II*)) decision where the U.S. Supreme Court upheld a Tribal claim for breach of the trust responsibility in failing to properly manage the timber on the Quinault Indian Reservation. In that case, the Court held that it was significant that the U.S. role was almost daily supervision of every aspect of the Tribal timber operations, thereby creating an enforceable trust duty subject to monetary damages for a breach of that duty. The fact that the United States approves a lease, however, does not necessarily mean that the United States could be held accountable for breach of trust if the price for the lease is below market value.

The most notorious breach of trust lawsuit against the United States, *Cobell v. Salazar*, 573 F.3d 808 (D.C. Cir. 2009) (*Cobell XXII*), was a class action lawsuit that led to a $3.4 billion settlement regarding the administration of assets from natural resource development and management of Tribal trust lands on behalf of individual Tribal member owners. The settlement called for a comprehensive evaluation of federal trust administration of Indian resources, both hard assets and the funds that are administered from appropriation of natural resources. As a result of the lawsuit and settlement agreement, reform recommendations have been called for. In *Cobell*, the federal government had been the repository of funds collected on behalf of the individual allottees, from mineral leasing and other land use sources. After collecting the funds on behalf of the allottees, the United States was unable to provide a reliable accounting to the individual account holders and the settlement represented an estimate of monies owed. *Cobell* provides the classic example of how individual Tribal landowners are tied to a system that, to date, fails to meet their needs. Lands are held by the United States, and consequently monies from the sale, lease, and development of natural resources are administered by the federal government down to the collection, withdrawal, and oversight of funds. Although opportunities for Tribal Nation control at the local level are available, and more and more Tribes have taken on the role of natural resources and property management by opening Tribal realty offices, the Tribes are limited in carrying out the necessary federal functions by delegation. A Tribe is not free to create a free-standing and more efficient administrative office because the United States continues to be the legal title holder, absent legislative reform to the contrary. Further, absent legislative mechanisms that ensure that the lands and natural resources will not become subject to state taxation and regulations, Tribes are reluctant to support a system whereby the United States could simply walk away from the current broken system and escape accountability as a trustee.

B. Water Rights, Air Regulation, and Climate Change

The ability to ensure an adequate water supply, both in terms of quality and quantity, is critical to Tribal community sustainability. Tribal Nation water rights have their origin in the time immemorial use of water, the creation of the reservation systems, and other scenarios where the United States, either by treaty, executive order or statute, recognized Tribal permanent homelands. This federal recognition has been viewed by federal courts as the U.S. government process of a "set aside" to a Tribal Nation and as a recognized Tribal territory under federal law. Although rights to water were typically not expressly reserved, federal courts have ruled that it would have been inconceivable that Tribal Nations would have been able to maintain a community, including domestic activities, resources development, and agricultural pursuits, without sufficient water to support those needs. Therefore, the implied reservation of water rights accompanies Tribal Nation rights to land and territory. In the West, where water can be scarce, a Tribe's water rights are preserved as to the dates of time immemorial use for hunting and fishing rights acknowledged in treaties. In the U.S. Supreme Court case, *United States v. Winans*, 198 U.S. 371 (1905), the Court stated that Tribal Nations reserve all rights not expressly waived or relinquished in treaties. In the water rights context, this translates to reserving water used for hunting and fishing purposes since time immemorial.

For most other purposes, the creation of the reservation sets the date for the Tribal Nation water rights as set forth in the U.S. Supreme Court case, *Winters v. United States*, 207 U.S. 564 (1908). In the western system of prior appropriation that prioritizes water rights in order of "first in time, first in right," the *Winters* doctrine established Tribes as among the most senior, and therefore prioritized, water rights holders in a given area. Should the Tribe have sufficient water to meet its own needs, Tribal water rights may be leased to individuals, including non-Indians or nonmembers, provided the United States, as trustee, approves and manages such leases.

In terms of environmental viability, Tribal regulation of water has been upheld and supported by the federal government through the Clean Water Act. 33 U.S.C. § 1377. The Clean Water Act was amended to include a provision for Tribal Nations to be treated as states, referred to as "TAS" status, in terms of setting water quality standards within Tribal boundaries or on Tribal lands. Many Tribes maintain their own Tribal environmental protection of-

White Stone Lake. Photo credit: Angelique EagleWoman.

fices that regulate water within the Tribe's territory, including the issuance of permits and establishment of Tribal water quality standards. This is one area where Tribal regulatory power can have off-reservation reach. If the Tribe sets water quality standards that are higher than a state or municipality located upstream, the other jurisdictions may have to adopt more stringent water quality standards to ensure that the water meets the Tribal standards when the stream enters the Tribal jurisdiction. Similar to the Clean Water Act, the federal Safe Drinking Water Act, 42 U.S.C. § 300j-11(b), includes the ability of Tribes to be treated as states to set safe drinking water quality standards within Tribal boundaries and on Tribal lands.

Conflicts over the extent of Tribal Nation water rights, although federal in nature, are adjudicated in state courts because the United States has consented to this forum pursuant to the 1952 McCarran Amendment, codified at 43 U.S.C. § 666. Water rights adjudications typically take years to resolve and have been the source of some conflict between Tribal Nations and the United States as the trustee. As the trustee, the federal government is the party representing the Tribal governments in the enforcement of water rights, but the federal government may have competing interests. These competing interests may occur from sub-agencies within the Department of the Interior or from the United States representing the interests of other Tribes or owners within the same litigation. A national online e-repository of Native American Water Settlements is maintained jointly by the University of Idaho College of Law and the Utton Center at the University of New Mexico School of Law. Documents from these types of settlements are available at: http://repository.unm.edu/handle/1928/21727.

Next, the federal Clean Air Act, 42 U.S.C. § 7401 et seq., has the strongest delegation of federal environmental regulatory authority to Tribal governments. Under 42 U.S.C. § 7601(d), Tribal Nations may establish and enforce EPA-approved Tribal implementation plans ("TIPs") for air quality within Tribal boundaries and on Tribal lands. Within the federal legislation is a process for Tribal governments and state governments to resolve issues that may arise in re-designating air quality across regions. 42 U.S.C. § 7474(e). Air as a natural resource is becoming increasingly protected by Tribal Nations as a result of the opportunity for the federal regulatory delegation under the Clean Air Act.

The federal law dealing with the regulation of solid waste and dump sites is the Resource Conservation and Recovery Act (RCRA), 42 U.S.C. § 6901 et seq. While other federal environmental statutes have been amended to allow the Tribes-as-states designation, the RCRA does not include this provision. The default authority for environmental regulation under the RCRA is the federal government on Tribal lands and within Tribal boundaries. Tribes may collaborate and seek grants from the EPA for specific programs on handling and providing cleanup of solid waste on Tribal lands.

As Tribal Nations experience the impacts of climate change, there is an increasing urgency in establishing sustainable practices and engaging in conservation measures. The use of fossil fuels is linked to the warming of the planet and the attendant climate crisis emerging in contemporary times. Energy pipelines from fossil fuel companies have led to confrontations with Tribal members and movements when those pipelines run through or adjacent to Tribal lands. Federal and state energy permitting authorities have not regularly engaged in consultations with Tribal Nations to investigate potential negative impacts on treaty resources or Tribal subsistence needs.

For some Alaska Native Villages, the rising levels of bodies of water has presented a crisis requiring the complete relocation of the Tribal community to higher ground further inland. These impacts have also been felt by Tribal Nations in the Louisiana area where flooding has caused entire Tribal communities to lose access to resource rich islands and complicated fishing traditions. Other Tribal Nations have been impacted by uncontrolled wildfires as well as the air pollution of smoke-filled air infiltrating Tribal communities. The loss of permanent homelands from climate change and its effects is a devastating consequence for those Tribal Nations bearing the brunt of U.S. industries' resource exploitation practices.

Tribal Nations, Tribal organizations, and Tribal citizens are often at the forefront of protesting energy expansion on federal public lands, which were ceded under treaties or agreements to the United States. With a view of interdependence between human beings and the natural world, Tribal Nations are often cognizant of the consequences of human activity. For example, the emphasis on renewable energy through electric vehicles creates dependence on lithium batteries to alleviate dependence on fossil fuel-powered vehicles. When lithium mining is allowed on federal public lands that are significant culturally and spiritually to Tribal Nations, the result is further degradation of Tribal stewardship and protection of significant off-reservation lands.

Tying energy development and use to climate change and increasingly negative environmental consequences, Tribal Nations offer legal principles, values, and traditional environmental knowledge based on a reciprocal relationship with the earth. This reciprocal relationship requires human activity to be limited at the point when that activity, such as energy development, has a negative impact on the natural resource or on the human environment. As Tribal Nations assert greater control of their natural resources and engage in cooperative management agreements with the U.S., the influence of Tribal legal principles of reciprocal relationships with the natural world may be incorporated into federal and state environmental regulatory practices.

C. Hunting, Fishing, and Gathering/Harvesting Rights

Similar to water rights, it is presumed that Tribal territorial rights included the implied right to sustainability for the continued exercise of hunting, fishing, and gathering/harvesting rights. It would have been inconceivable that Tribes would have agreed to a smaller and fixed territory without the right to use the resources within the territory, and to make use of the resources without the infringement of outside regulations, particularly regulation from the states. Tribal leadership exercised foresight in the negotiation of treaties and agreements to ensure perpetual hunting, fishing, and harvesting rights on lands sold or ceded to the United States. Tribal hunting and fishing rights have been protected to such a great extent that federal courts recognized continued treaty rights in individual Indians even after the United States no longer recognized the political existence of a Tribe as a federally recognized Tribal entity. For example, in the *Menominee Tribe of Indians v. United States* case, 391 U.S. 404 (1968), the U.S. Supreme Court held that treaty hunting and fishing rights survived for the Tribal members after the federal termination of the Menominee Tribe. It should be noted that the Menominee Tribe was fully restored to federal recognition in 1973.

Outside of a Tribe's current territory, it is possible that these use rights continue, even if the Tribe has expressly waived other rights in subsequent treaties. Tribal Nations have successfully asserted use rights, even on private third-party lands, where treaties preserved the rights for Tribal members to hunt and fish in the places that they traditionally used for such purposes prior to removal. In these instances, it becomes a fact question, through the development of the historical record, whether the lands at issue were lands where the Tribal Nation exercised such rights. A good example of a contemporary decision upholding off-reservation or "usufructuary" treaty rights is *Minnesota v. Mille Lacs Band of Chippewa Indians*, 562 U.S. 172 (1999). The U.S. Supreme Court interpreted the 1837 Treaty with the Mille Lacs Band, and other related Tribes, and concluded that no subsequent actions on the part of the federal government had abolished the off-reservation treaty rights to hunt, fish, and gather on the lands ceded by the Tribe. Therefore, the treaty rights continued unhampered.

Modern conflicts have centered not around the right to access lands for such purposes, but whether, based on a treaty right, how Tribal hunting and fishing is to be construed against competing hunting and fishing rights. In turn, what entity has the right to regulate hunting and fishing through the requirements of licensing or regulation of seasons or quantity restrictions become significant for the exercise of Tribal treaty rights.

Tribal governments maintain the exclusive right to regulate hunting, fishing, and gathering on tribally owned lands, and to condition the entry upon such lands by Tribal licensing requirements or other such regulations. Tribal power in this instance applies to both Tribal members and non-members. Where Tribes no longer maintain the right to exclude, however, Tribal power to regulate non-member hunting and fishing will not be exclusively recognized. For example, in *Montana v. United States*, 450 U.S. 544 (1981), the U.S.

Supreme Court held that the Crow Tribe did not have the authority to ban all hunting by non-Indians on privately owned fee lands within the Crow Reservation's boundaries. Thus, states and local non-Tribal governments typically require licensing and apply seasonal limits on fee lands, even if inside Tribal territorial boundaries.

Specific treaty provisions are worth mentioning to demonstrate the ongoing enforcement of treaty rights. As the United States sought to expand westward, Isaac Stevens was appointed territorial governor of Washington, which included the position of Superintendent of Indian Affairs. As territorial governor, Stevens negotiated many treaties to provide for non-Indian settlement in the region. One feature of the so-called "Stevens Treaties" was the insistence of various Tribes in the Northwest to include the right of fishing "at all usual and accustomed grounds." In the Stevens Treaties, these fishing rights were to be exercised "in common with all citizens of the Territory." The U.S. Supreme Court interpreted this treaty language in *Washington v. Washington State Commercial Passenger Fishing Vessel Association*, 443 U.S. 658 (1979), and found that the Tribal Nation parties retained a maximum of 50 percent allocation of the annual fish harvest to allow Tribal member fishers a moderate living standard.

For off-reservation regulatory matters of the fish runs, the states are to consult with treaty Tribes prior to adversely impacting treaty rights. The states continue to exercise regulatory powers for conservation purposes over Tribal members and non-Indians alike. If a state regulation is not necessary for conservation purposes, and the regulation would otherwise be inconsistent with treaty-based rights, the state powers would be preempted in favor of the treaty right. In extreme circumstances, state powers could potentially result in a complete ban relative to a certain species, if proven necessary and regulation was imposed in the least restrictive means. Tribes have increasingly developed scientific expertise in the areas of the country where they exert off-reservation treaty rights to engage in such conservation decisions. Two prominent collaborations for Tribal Nation regulatory authority are the Columbia River Inter-Tribal Fish Commission (CRITFC) and the Great Lakes Indian Fish & Wildlife Consortium (GLIFWC).

D. Energy and Resource Development

Consistent with the economic development discussion in Chapter Five, "Tribal Nation Corporations and Economies," Tribes have viewed the development of their natural resources as an economic priority and necessity, but also as a decision that is complex for each community. In addition to the numerous federal law requirements that address leasing and development of various resources on Tribal land, Tribal Nations are becoming increasingly sophisticated in how they manage development as a matter of Tribal law. Many Tribes, in addition to Tribal environmental protection offices, maintain departments of natural resources, forestry, hunting and fishing agencies, and Tribal agriculture departments that not only administer Tribal programs aimed at promoting the Tribal economy, but also serve as the regulatory body of first contact with federal and private partners. Further, since taxation of natural resources is an important part of the Tribal tax base, Tribal governments often create Tribal tax commissions charged with overseeing severance taxes that are accessed from many energy development activities.

The evolution of federal statutory schemes in Indian Country, regardless of the natural resources at issue, typically started with a general statute such as the Mineral Leasing Act of 1920, which granted authority for the Department of the Interior to oversee development operations on federal public lands. Specific to Indian Country, the Indian Mineral Leasing Act of 1938, 25 U.S.C. §§ 396a–396g, was intended to extend greater authority to Tribal governments in line with the Indian Reorganization Act of 1934, 25 U.S.C. § 5101 et seq. Beginning in the 1970s, statutory reforms continued a strong federal presence in the development of Tribal resources and added a modern policy of protection of the environment. Some of these federal law reforms provided more flexibility in private and Tribal business enterprise collaborations, increasing options for Tribes, and creating more of an open market for federal leasing, including agreements for Tribes to have more control over long-term planning. The Indian Mineral Development Act of 1982, 25 U.S.C. §§ 2101–2108, included greater flexibility for Tribal governments to act as partners with third parties or engage in other arrangements, rather than straight leasing agreements. These federal regulatory schemes continued to expand to include not only the traditional oil, gas, and coal leases, but also geothermal, wind, and developing technologies. As an active partner in natural resource development, Tribal Nations are more likely to receive a substantial rate of return on development of Tribal natural resources, may impose sustainability limits on resource extractions, and are poised to gain business acumen in the energy industry.

Under the Energy Policy Act of 2005, the Indian Tribal Energy Development and Self-Determination Act was enacted, allowing for a Tribal Nation to submit an energy development plan for overall project approval to the Department of the Interior. Once approved, the Tribal government would have the authority to negotiate all related agreements to implement the energy development project. This was viewed as a far more efficient and superior process to the past practices of interrelated leases for a project, with each proceeding through a lengthy approval process. The Department of the Interior is required to create processes to encourage increased Tribal autonomy, including the above-mentioned Tribal energy resource agreements (TERAs) in which the Tribal Nations approve and manage their own leases and agreements for energy development. It is the continuing trend in federal policy to loosen restrictions or clarify processes for more meaningful self-determination by Tribal Nations in the energy development area.

The Department of Interior has implemented the Helping Expedite and Advance Responsible Tribal Homeownership (HEARTH) Act of 2012, which removes U.S. approval authority and authorizes Tribal Nations to lease lands restricted from alienation and/or in trust status. Although the legislation's applicability is limited to surface rights, it is another step toward recognizing Tribal Nation autonomy to develop Tribal leasing regulations. The Tribe's leasing regulations, however, are not self-executing under the Act and cannot be fully implemented until approved by the Secretary of the Interior.

In the U.S. policy era of Indian self-determination, federal legislation regarding Tribal natural resources has loosened some federal restrictions and processes for Tribal Nations to assert greater managerial authority and decision-making in this field. In recent years, the Department of the Interior has consulted regarding co-management plans with Tribal Nations over natural resources, rivers within Tribal boundaries, and protection of Tribal treaty resource areas off-reservation. One of the responsibilities of the U.S. as trustee is to conserve Tribal resources and this duty is best carried out through consultation and cooperation with Tribal Nations.

In meeting the advancing technologies and opportunities over natural resource development, conservation, and protection, Tribal Nations are moving forward blending traditional ecological knowledge with technological, scientific, and legal skills and expertise to implement Tribal stewardship and sustainable use in these areas.

CHECKPOINTS

- Tribal Nations since time immemorial have developed expertise on reciprocal relationships with the natural world for human quality of life. Tribal stewardship and natural resource use are informed by traditional legal principles and values.
- Tribal natural resources on trust lands are under the management authority of the U.S. Department of the Interior. An extensive body of federal regulations has been created on the leasing, extraction, and approval processes for commercial use of Tribal natural resources.
- The federal trust responsibility to Tribal Nations governments and individuals provides guidance on federal decision-making regarding Tribal natural resource extraction and usage.
- A strong relationship of collaboration has been maintained between many Tribal Nations and the U.S. Environmental Protection Agency (EPA). Several major federal environmental protection statutes have been amended and implemented by the EPA recognizing Tribes as similar to states for federal programs and processes.
- Tribal governments have invested heavily in the protection of treaty hunting, fishing, and gathering rights. Tribal natural resource departments supply scientific expertise to Tribal conservation efforts. Tribal Nations are experiencing some consequences of the climate change crisis and are seeking to respond for the protection of Tribal communities.
- Recent federal laws have supported the U.S. Indian policy of Indian self-determination by providing for greater Tribal Nation authority over natural resource and energy development.

CHAPTER 8

Tribal Nation-State Government Relations

ROADMAP

- Know that the primary relationship was established between Tribal Nations and the U.S. federal government through diplomatic relations resulting in treaty relations and agreements on shared resources and territory.
- Learn about the history of relations between Tribal Nations and state governments as states were established expanding the U.S. territory.
- Understand there are important common areas of concern shared by Tribal Nations and state governments, allowing for diplomatic and cooperative relations.
- Learn that, increasingly, Tribal Nations and state governments are entering into agreements and compacts to address practical needs in local communities.
- Understand the designation of state-recognized Tribes as different than federal recognition.

Tribal Nations have a long history of entering into alliances with others. The many histories of Tribal Nations' relations with the United States are the foundation for the interactions of Tribal Nations and state governments. The primacy of federal authority is set forth in the *Worcester v. Georgia* decision, 31 U.S. (6 Pet.) 515 (1832), as preempting state law in "Indian affairs" and Tribal Nation relationships. As state governments were incorporated into the

United States, the Tribal Nations' perspective is that state governments will honor the federal policies and laws upholding the federal obligations and treaty terms with Tribal Nations. Under the U.S. Constitution, the Supremacy Clause contained in article VI provides the following. "This Constitution, and the Laws of the United States which shall be made in Pursuance thereof; and all Treaties made, or which shall be made, under the Authority of the United States, shall be the supreme Law of the Land; and the Judges in every State shall be bound thereby, any Thing in the Constitution or Laws of any State to the Contrary notwithstanding."

Further, under the U.S. Constitution, individual states were eligible to seek admission to the federal union pursuant to article IV, section 3, after organizing as territories. The territories were formed after treaties were entered into by U.S. federal officials with Tribal Nations to allow for settlement in lands ceded or purchased under the treaties. Thus, the states created after the original thirteen in the United States often were required to recognize in the federal admission act that the newly established governing body would not interfere with reserved Tribal Nation lands or rights.

An example of this language in an act of admission from the Kansas-Nebraska Act of 1854 was as follows:[1]

> ... *Provided further*, That nothing in this act contained shall construed to impair the rights of person or property now pertaining the Indians in said Territory' so long as such rights shall remain unextinguished by treaty between the United States and such Indians, or include any territory which, by treaty with any Indian tribe, is not, without the consent of said tribe, to be included within the territorial line or jurisdiction of any State or Territory; but all such territory shall excepted out of the boundaries, and constitute no part of the Territory of Nebraska, until said tribe shall signify their assent to the President of the United States to be included within the said Territory of Nebraska. or to affect the authority of the government of the United States make any regulations respecting such Indians, their lands, property, or other rights, by treaty, law, or otherwise, which it would have been competent to the government to make if this act had never passed.

10 Stat. 277, Section 1. This same boilerplate language was included in section 19 of the Kansas-Nebraska Act for the limitations on the admission of Kansas

1. https://www.archives.gov/milestone-documents/kansas-nebraska-act.

to the United States. Other examples of the reserved rights of Tribal Nations can be found in the enabling acts of many of the states joining the union throughout the West. The enabling act to organize the states of Montana, North Dakota, South Dakota, and Washington, 25 Stat. 676, February 22, 1889, contained numerous provisions limiting state authority to tax Tribal members or Tribal lands as well as similar language to the Kansas-Nebraska Act explicitly recognizing Tribal Nation treaty rights and lands as under the authority of federal law.

Over time, tensions arose when state government officials failed to respect reserved Tribal Nation territories within the designated state boundaries. These tensions have been exacerbated at times by federal legislation pitting state and Tribal governmental control against each other, such as through the passage of the General Allotment Act of 1887, codified at 25 U.S.C. § 331 (repealed), whereby Tribal Nation lands were re-designated as "surplus" and purchased as federal lands. Some of these lands were then sold to settlers under state government jurisdiction within the boundaries of Tribal Nation reservations. Throughout this history, federal and state governmental tensions have also become highlighted in the area of federal Indian law, with Tribal Nations seeking enforcement of agreements and treaties with each of these levels of the United States, the federal level and the state level.

Tribal Nation interactions with state governments occur on a variety of jurisdictional contexts. Chapter Two sets forth a fuller discussion of the allotment policy and the tensions created from new land tenure patterns that may allow some forms of state taxation inside Indian Country. Chapter Three discusses the positive nature of Tribal-state cross-deputization agreements for addressing challenges in law enforcement. Chapter Six highlights the history of state-Tribal Nation conflict over foster care and adoptive placements involving Tribal member children. This chapter will review historical governmental relations and opportunities for contemporary collaborations between state governments and Tribal Nations.

A. Historical Tribal Nation-State Government Relations

The foundational federal Indian law cases of the 1800s interpreting treaties and the U.S. Constitution's Commerce Clause provide the basis for the doctrine that the federal government preempts state government policy and law in Indian affairs. The U.S. Supreme Court expressly held in *Worcester v. Georgia,* 31 U.S. (6 Pet.) 515 (1832), that the treaties entered into between the federal government and the Cherokee Nation preempted the laws of the state of Georgia within the territory of the Cherokee Nation where those state laws seized Tribal lands, sought to nullify Tribal laws, and required a state license for non-Indians to reside within the Tribal territory. In the opinion, Chief Justice Marshall stated:

> The acts of the legislature of Georgia interfere forcibly with the relations established between the United States and the Cherokee nation, the regulation of which, according to the settled principles of our constitution, is committed exclusively to the government of the union.

31 U.S. at 520. Thus, under federal Indian law as set forth by the U.S. Constitution and as interpreted by the U.S. Supreme Court, relations with Tribal Nations are within the primary authority of the federal government and not the individual state governments in the United States.

As a practical matter, the state governments are in frequent relations with Tribal governments due to territorial proximity and the interrelationship with Tribal citizens, who are also citizens of the United States and state governments. With passage of the 1924 Indian Citizenship Act, 43 Stat. 253 (June 2, 1924), any American Indian or Alaska Native who had not become a citizen of the United States by a prior law did so with presumed state citizenship; both were then attached to the preexisting Tribal citizenship. Tribal Nation-state government relations run the spectrum from friendly cooperation from state governments to aggressive attempts to negate Tribal Nation sovereignty and assert state governmental control. Greater levels of cooperation in Tribal Nation-state government relations may be reached where interests converge on both sides.

One of the most well-known statements on Tribal Nation-state government relations was contained in the U.S. Supreme Court opinion, *U.S. v. Kagama,* 118 U.S. 375 (1886), where American Indians were characterized in a very negative light along with the attitudes of state citizens and governments toward American Indians.

> These Indian tribes *are* the wards of the nation. They are communities *dependent* on the United States,—dependent largely for their daily food; dependent for their political rights. They owe no allegiance to the states, and receive from them no protection. Because of the local ill feeling, the people of the states where they are found are often their deadliest enemies.

118 U.S. at 383–384 (emphasis in the original). This Court opinion was written prior to the Indian Citizenship Act of 1924 and does not fully reflect Tribal Nation-state government relations that have evolved since the late 1800s. The language does signal tensions where state governments are infected with local negative feeling towards Tribal Nations.

B. Contemporary Tribal-State Governmental Relations

In this chapter, the development of Tribal Nation-state government relations will be explored in the key areas of: (1) state governmental Indian affairs commissions and Tribal liaisons; (2) Tribal Nation-state government relations and law enforcement; (3) Tribal Nation-state government revenue agreements and collaborative measures on specific industries; and (4) Tribal Nation-state government co-management agreements. Other areas of mutual interest exist beyond these key areas, such as family law matters, including implementing the provisions of the federal Indian Child Welfare Act in state court proceedings involving Tribal Nation children or those eligible for enrollment in a Tribal Nation, and implementing the federal Temporary Assistance to Needy Families (TANF) provisions under state law formulas. The interaction between Tribal Nation sovereignty and state governmental authority continues to call for refined approaches, with the call at times bringing governments together and at times falling on deaf ears.

Tribal governments operate from a sovereignty that pre-dates the establishment of the United States. With the formation of the United States and its component state governments, new governmental relations became necessary between local, state, and federal governments and Tribal governments. Tribal governments must maintain relations with all of these levels of the United States government and seek acceptable agreements for matters that impact the Tribal Nation territory, Tribal citizenry, and Tribal Nation interests.

1. State Governmental Indian Affairs Commissions and Tribal Liaisons

Due to the many points of contact between state governments and Tribal Nations, many state legislatures and governors have established formal commissions and Tribal Nation liaison positions to promote cooperation between the particular state and area Tribal Nations. For example, the state of California has an Office of Tribal Affairs and Governor Gavin Newsom has issued two notable policy statements on issues impacting Tribal Nations. In Executive Order N-15-19, the government of California has apologized for the history of "violence, exploitation, dispossession and the attempted destruction of tribal communities" and reaffirms the government-to-government basis for collaboration with the more than one hundred Tribal Nations in the state boundaries. On September 25, 2020, the California Governor declared an administrative policy for "every State agency, department, board and commission (collectively, 'entities') subject to my executive control to seek opportunities to support California tribes' co-management of and access to natural lands that are within a California tribe's ancestral land and under the ownership or control of the State of California, and to work cooperatively with California tribes that are interested in acquiring natural lands in excess of State needs."

Another step toward better intergovernmental relations is the creation of a liaison position between state government and Tribal government(s). State governors may also appoint a cabinet-level official in this role who has experience working with or in Tribal communities. Within state governmental departments, Tribal Nation liaison positions facilitate cooperation between state government and Tribal Nation(s) to apply for federal funding for projects that will benefit both state and Tribal communities. Within the state of Minnesota, the Minnesota American Indian Affairs Commission (MIAC) was established in 1963 with the eleven Tribal Nation leaders to provide input to the governor, legislature, and state agencies. An annual summit is held between the MIAC and the governor based on an agenda proposed by the MIAC. The Washington Governor's Office of Indian Affairs includes three positions to consult with the twenty-nine federally recognized Tribal Nations in the state. Both Minnesota and Washington mandate that state agencies appoint a Tribal government liaison and post the information publicly. In South Dakota, the governor's administration includes the position of secretary for the South Dakota Department of Tribal Relations as the Tribal Nation liaison with the nine Tribal Nations in the state. These Tribal Nation liaison positions within state governments are actively promoting beneficial relations with area Tribal governments.

Many states have a history of dedicating an office or commission to liaison and consult with Tribal Nations, such as Alabama, Arizona, Colorado, Georgia, Kentucky, Maryland, Massachusetts, North Carolina, and Vermont, to name a few. Many states have identified a specific purpose for establishing Tribal Nation relations commissions. For example, Georgia has established by state law the Georgia Council on American Indian Concerns with a primary purpose of protecting Indian burial sites and archaeological sites and promoting economic development. Kentucky has established the Kentucky Native American Heritage Commission for the following purposes according to the Commission's website: "All Kentuckians will recognize, appreciate and understand the significant contributions Native Americans have made to Kentucky's rich cultural heritage. Through education and increased awareness, the people of Kentucky will understand the histories, cultures and matters of concern to Native American peoples." Another example is the Vermont Commission on Native American Affairs. This state commission "is charged by law to recognize the historic and cultural contributions of Native Americans in Vermont, to protect and strengthen Native American heritage, and to address needs in state policy, programs, and actions."

In addition, state agencies and programs may incorporate Tribal Nation liaison positions in a variety of governmental areas. State environmental protection programs often incorporate Tribal Nation liaison positions and boards to foster intergovernmental environmental protection plans. Michigan, New York, and Wisconsin incorporate Native American affairs positions within their departments of family services. The state of Arizona has an extensive number of Tribal Nation liaisons working with various departments of state government, with 40 such positions listed in the state's Tribal Nation liaison directory. The areas of government where common interests emerge for Tribal Nations and state governments are extensive and evolving as evidenced by the well-established practice of state positions for Tribal Nation liaisons.

In New Mexico, the state Indian Affairs Department (IAD) was founded in 2004 as the successor to the Office of Indian Affairs established in 1953. The mission of the IAD includes the following three goals: "Advocating for tribal interests at state and federal levels through policy and legislative work;

Supporting tribes with access to resources, technical assistance and funding opportunities; and Connecting tribes with the executive branch, other tribes and with the tools and resources they need to be self-governing and self-sufficient." There are 23 federally recognized Pueblos and Tribes in New Mexico interacting with the state IAD.

2. Tribal-State Relations and Law Enforcement

As discussed in Chapter Three, "Criminal Jurisdiction in Indian Country," Tribal Nations have primary criminal jurisdiction in the Tribal territory with the exception of criminal activity perpetrated by non-Indians. Concurrent jurisdiction will exist either with the federal government by federal law or with state governments when there has been a federal delegation, such as in the Public Law 280 states. Federal delegation of criminal authority to state governments for alleged Indian/Tribal member criminal activity within Indian Country has had a significant impact on Tribal Nation-state governmental relations where those delegations are in effect. The interaction between state law enforcement and Tribal Nation citizenry has necessarily increased with the delegations. State law enforcement will also have authority in Indian Country where criminal activity involves non-Indian on non-Indian crimes as exclusively state criminal jurisdiction. State law enforcement has concurrent criminal jurisdiction with the federal government for non-Indian on Indian/Tribal member crimes per the U.S. Supreme Court's decision in *Oklahoma v. Castro-Huerta*, 597 U.S. 629 (2022).

In recent years, there has been a reported epidemic of violence perpetrated against Native American women. Those studying this epidemic have highlighted a perceived lack of state and federal prosecution of non-Indians committing violence within Indian Country, thus imposing no consequences on non-Native perpetrators. Tribal law enforcement officers lack authority over non-Indian perpetrators according to the U.S. Supreme Court decision in *Oliphant v. Suquamish Tribe,* 435 U.S. 191 (1978). With the passage of the 2010 Tribal Law and Order Act (TLOA), the offices of the U.S. Attorney General across the nation are to work more closely with Tribal Nation law enforcement and report on decisions to decline prosecutions for those investigated for possible criminal activity on reservations. 25 U.S.C. § 2809. In every federal district, the TLOA requires that at least one assistant United States Attorney will be appointed as the Tribal liaison for the district. 25 U.S.C. § 2810.

Further, the TLOA encouraged cooperation among state, Tribal, and local law enforcement under 25 U.S.C. § 2815 by authorizing the U.S. Attorney General to provide assistance when cooperative agreements are entered into at those governmental levels. The cooperative agreements may relate to topics of "mutual aid, hot pursuit of suspects, and cross-deputization."

In addition, the 2022 VAWA amendments found in the Indian Civil Rights Act with provisions for "special Tribal criminal jurisdiction" may be an avenue for Tribal Nations to assert authority over non-Indians committing one of the listed crimes against Indians on Tribal lands.

> (5) Covered crime
>
> The term "covered crime" means—
>
> (A) assault of Tribal justice personnel;
> (B) child violence;
> (C) dating violence;
> (D) domestic violence;
> (E) obstruction of justice;
> (F) sexual violence;
> (G) sex trafficking;
> (H) stalking; and
> (I) a violation of a protection order.

25 U.S.C. 1304(5). For this authorization by federal law, "[t]he exercise of special Tribal criminal jurisdiction by a participating tribe shall be concurrent with the jurisdiction of the United States, of a State, or of both." 25 U.S.C. § 1304(b)(2). This is further discussed in Chapter Three, "Criminal Jurisdiction in Indian Country."

Currently, state and county levels of coordination with Tribal law enforcement vary from very collaborative to completely uncooperative. Due to the history of hostility expressed in the *Kagama* decision mentioned previously, both Tribal citizens and state citizens may resist officers from the other's community enforcing laws and making arrests in their neighborhoods. However, the positives to be gained from joint law enforcement efforts can be very beneficial to the safety and protection of both Tribal Nation and state citizens. Examples of collaborative practices between Tribal and state law enforcement include the development of cooperative agreements and cross-deputization agreements. The National Indian Law Library (NILL) website contains some examples, found through the search engine term Tribal Compacts, of state law enforcement agreements entered into with Tribal Nation law enforcement departments.

The operation of Class III gaming in Tribal communities under Tribal Nation-state government compacts has provided another opportunity for mutual law enforcement activities. The Indian Gaming Regulatory Act (IGRA) provides that gaming compacts may include express provisions on the prosecution of criminal activity in Tribal gaming enterprises and on what criminal laws will apply in the gaming enterprise. 25 U.S.C. § 2710(d)(3)(C). By reaching an agreement, uncertainty and delay in response time by appropriate law enforcement personnel to handle immediate situations may be significantly decreased. In order for Tribal Nations to effectively operate businesses, law enforcement must be responsive to protect the patronage, enforce the applicable laws at the establishment, and have authority to handle any criminal situation that may arise.

In a variety of contexts, law enforcement authorities at the Tribal, state, and local levels are engaging in mutual efforts to prevent harbors for criminal activity when jurisdictional lines are crossed. By allowing for cross-deputization agreements in Tribal territories, Tribal police officers can arrest and transfer non-Indians to the local state court system for prosecution and, in turn, state and county officers can arrest and transfer Tribal members to the local Tribal court system for prosecution. Cross-deputization agreements can assist in eliminating fugitive situations where perpetrators seek to hide from a particular jurisdiction, for instance where a warrant has been issued, by traveling to another jurisdiction. With proper training and shared interests in community safety, Tribal and state law enforcement can work collaboratively for the good of Tribal members and non-Indians/nonmembers in areas where both live.

3. Tribal-State Revenue Agreements

Taxes and governmental income are the usual primary sources of operational revenue for any government in the United States. State governments can acquire taxes and revenue from transactions occurring on Tribal Nation lands due to U.S. Supreme Court decisions on state taxation of non-Tribal members doing business on Tribal lands; federal laws on extraction of resources from Tribal Nation lands that include state taxation provisions; and the Tribal-state compacting process under the Indian Gaming Regulatory Act (IGRA) when revenue sharing is included. Some state governments have engaged in aggressive raids of Tribal Nation smoke shops, for instance, to seize cigarettes at the heart of tobacco tax disputes. In other instances, some state officials have applied strong-arm bargaining tactics when pursuing revenue-sharing agreements with Tribal Nations seeking Class III gaming, which is only permitted when a Tribal-state gaming compact is entered into. In response, many Tribal governments have preferred to go to the bargaining table and enter into a taxation or revenue-sharing agreement rather than have violence erupt from state law enforcement raids in Tribal Nation communities or fighting contentious, expensive legal battles in federal courts with often adverse consequences to Tribal sovereignty as a result.

a. Tribal-State Taxation Agreements

Since the late 1970s, U.S. Supreme Court decisions have allowed state governments concurrent taxing authority for goods purchased by non-members in Tribal communities. These court decisions have arisen from the development of Tribal businesses offering tobacco products and motor fuels, which were frequented by non-Indians and Indians/Tribal members within Tribal communities. For individual purchasers in Montana, the U.S. Supreme Court held in *Moe v. Confederated Salish and Kootenai Tribes,* 425 U.S. 463, 483 (1976), that "[t]he State's requirement that the Indian tribal seller collect a tax validly imposed on non-Indians is a minimal burden designed to avoid the likelihood that in its absence non-Indians purchasing from the tribal seller will avoid payment of a concededly lawful tax." Unlike other governmental jurisdictions with taxes that apply straight across the board to all purchasers, Tribal governments must determine the citizenship status of the purchaser to manage this concurrent state taxation scheme. As for state taxation on fuel sales to Tribal Nation-owned gas stations, the U.S. Supreme Court in *Wagnon v. Prairie Band Potawatomi,* 546 U.S. 95 (2003), held that a Kansas state tax with the legal incidence falling on a non-Tribal-member motor fuels distributor was validly applied when the distributor sold to the Tribal government-owned gas station operating on Tribal lands.

One of the difficulties resulting from this line of federal cases is that, generally, state government has no ability to collect taxes on Tribal Nation lands without the cooperation of Tribal government and Tribal businesses. In *Oklahoma Tax Commission v. Citizen Band of Potawatomi Indian Tribe,* 498 U.S. 505, 514, the U.S. Supreme Court informed state governments that the options they may pursue to collect state taxes for cigarette sales to non-Tribal members on Tribal Nation lands include: holding Tribal officers liable for money damages in federal court, seizing unstamped cigarettes off the reservation, assessing state taxes before the cigarettes reach the reservation, seeking federal authorizing legislation to enter Tribal lands to collect taxes, or entering into tax agreements with Tribal governments. When Tribal Nations resist the collection of state taxes on goods purchased on Tribal lands, some states sent in state troopers to seize cigarettes and arrest Tribal business owners and employees. Federal officers have also raided tobacco shops on Tribal Nation lands under federal warrants for failure to apply state taxes. As of 2013, there had been many state and federal raids on Tribal tobacco shops over the previous 10 years in New York, Oklahoma, Oregon, Washington, and other states.

A well-known example occurred on July 14, 2003, when Rhode Island state troopers executed a state warrant on a Tribal Nation smoke shop operated by the Narragansett Tribe. The shop had been open for two days when state law enforcement descended to seize cigarettes being sold without state taxes applied. In the violent clash that ensued, Tribal leaders were arrested as local television news crews reported on the situation. Instead of resorting to a civil lawsuit, the state leadership sent in "51 police officers, including a SWAT team and a police dog, to enforce tobacco laws," according to testimony in the state cases seeking prosecution of seven Tribal members for resisting arrest as reported in the national newspaper USA Today on February 29, 2008. Ultimately, the federal Court of Appeals upheld the right of the state to collect taxes on cigarette sales to non-Tribal members by executing the state warrant based upon the Rhode Island Indian Claims Settlement Act of 1978 in the *Narragansett Indian Tribe v. Rhode Island,* 449 F.3d 16 (1st Cir. 2006), decision. Furthermore, seven prosecutions were brought against Tribal members with four acquitted of all charges and three convicted of disorderly conduct or assault charges in the aftermath of the state police raid.

As state laws provide for medicinal and recreational use of cannabis, Tribal Nations are entering into agreements regarding taxes on sales of cannabis products. In 2023, the state of Minnesota enacted a legal framework to regulate recreational cannabis sales beginning on July 1, 2023. The legislation specifically exempts the eleven Tribal Nations in the state from state taxation of cannabis sales by a Tribal Nation licensed vendor on Tribal Nation lands. The Minnesota Office of Cannabis Management website on Tribal Nations in Minnesota states, "Minnesota's cannabis law is among the strongest in the nation to honor and recognize tribal sovereignty and the authority of Tribal Nations to make decisions about cannabis sales on tribal land." The state of Washington has legislation requiring Tribal Nations to enter compacts and charge the same rate of Tribal tax on recreational cannabis products as the state and local cannabis taxes. "Twenty-two of the 29 federally recognized Tribes have compacts with the state to grow, process, and/or sell cannabis. Some of the remaining seven Tribes are in the process of negotiating compacts to grow, process, and/or sell cannabis," according to the Washington State Liquor and Cannabis Board website.

To avoid the protracted litigation and prosecution of Tribal citizens that may result from resistance to the imposition of concurrent taxing authority by state governments, Tribal governments have negotiated tax agreements, particularly for tobacco sales and motor fuel sales. The Montana Department of Revenue maintains a web page listing Tribal Nation-state government tax agreements for alcoholic beverages sales and tobacco sales with the eight Tribal governments in the state. Taxation issues between Tribal governments and state governments continue to be an area of controversy, litigation, and negotiation. Attorneys working on both sides of the bargaining table must fully understand the contours of Tribal sovereignty, Tribal Nation-state government relations, and the field of taxation under federal Indian law to effectively practice in this politically charged legal area.

b. Tribal-State Revenue Sharing under Gaming Compacts

Another potential for controversy exists in the revenue-sharing provisions of Tribal-state gaming compacts for Class III gaming under the Indian Gaming Regulatory Act (IGRA), 25 U.S.C. § 2701. With the *Seminole Tribe of Florida v. Florida,* 517 U.S. 44 (1996), decision by the U.S. Supreme Court, the provisions of the IGRA permitting a Tribal Nation to file suit in federal court when a state government failed to negotiate a Class III gaming compact in good faith were effectively stricken from the law. In the aftermath, some state governments have inserted revenue-sharing provisions into Tribal-state gaming compacts. The IGRA prohibits state officials from imposing "any tax, fee, charge or other assessment upon an Indian tribe or upon any other person or entity authorized by an Indian tribe to engage in a class III activity." 25 U.S.C. § 2710(d)(4). Further, state officials cannot condition negotiations for Class III gaming compacts upon assessing any of the above. The IGRA does provide that a state official may negotiate costs for state regulation or enforcement of state civil and criminal laws under a Class III compact. 25 U.S.C. § 2710(d)(3)(C)(iii).

The Secretary of the Interior has final approval authority on all Tribal-state compacts and has taken the informal position that revenue sharing is allowed either to cover regulatory costs of the state under the gaming compact or where the Tribal Nation is receiving a particular exclusivity benefit not available to other gaming operations from the state in the bargaining process. On the U.S. Department of the Interior Gaming Compacts website, a searchable database by Tribal Nation or state government for Tribal-state gaming compacts is available. In California, revenue-sharing provisions have become standard in gaming compacts with payments made directly to the state's general fund and to a special distribution fund that is divided among the non-gaming Tribal governments in the state. The ratified compacts are available on the California Gambling Control Commission website. Some states have entered into Tribal-state gaming compacts in perpetuity with no end date, such as Colorado, Connecticut, Idaho, Kansas, Minnesota, Nebraska, Nevada, New York, Oregon, Washington and Wisconsin; such compacts may end by mutual agreement.

Many of the federal land claims settlement acts for Tribal Nations on the east coast include specific provisions that impact Tribal Nation gaming opportunities. For example, the 1980 Maine Indian Claims Settlement Act provides that any general federal legislation for Tribes will not apply to those in Maine unless specifically mentioned in the federal law. 25 U.S.C. § 1735(b). In *Passamaquoddy Tribe v. Maine,* 75 F.3d 784 (1st Cir. 1996), the federal court of appeals held that the 1988 Indian Gaming Regulatory Act did not apply to the Tribes in Maine due to the above provision in the Maine Indian Lands Claims Settlement Act. In 1987, the Maine legislature did pass state laws authorizing issuance of licenses to the three Tribal Nations in the state to operate "high-stakes bingo." Me. Stat. Ann. Rev. 17 § 314-A. In recent years, attempts by Tribal Nations have failed to garner enough votes in Maine through state referendums to authorize an expansion of Tribal Nation gaming to Class III gaming.

Successful gaming Tribes in the United States include the Mashantucket Pequot Tribal Nation and the Mohegan Tribe in Connecticut. According to the Connecticut Consumer Protection web page under Tribal statistics, the amount received by the state from January 1, 2022, to Dec. 31, 2022, was reported to be over $88 million from the Foxwoods Resort Casino and the Mohegan Sun Casino during the same time period generated the state over $120 million. This high percentage of revenue going straight to state coffers has motivated other state governments across the country to seek to engage in Tribal-state gaming compacts.

Sisseton Wahpeton College Four Direction Drummers. Photo credit: Stephen L. Jackson, Jr.

4. Tribal-State Co-Management Agreements

Opportunities exist for Tribal Nation-state government cooperation on many issues common to both governments. For example, Tribal colleges and universities (TCUs) and state colleges may enter into articulation agreements to allow for students to transfer between degree programs from on-reservation educational institutions to off-reservation state schools. The American Indian Higher Education Consortium (AIHEC) maintains a listing of TCUs with descriptions of articulation agreements entered into with area state educational institutions on its web page. Promoting education is a common goal of both Tribal Nations and state governments that allows for the negotiation of articulation agreements.

Many other potential areas for collaboration exist. Tribal governments and state governments can enter into agreements regarding human services, child care services, environmental protection, and wildlife management, among other common interests. Federal agencies administer funding for many cooperative efforts between Tribes and state governments. For example, in 2005 the U.S. Department of Health and Human Services published *Tribes and States Working Together: A Guide to Tribal-State Child Care Coordination*. For eligibility to receive funding from the federal Child Care and Development Fund (CCDF), "[b]oth States and Tribes are required by Federal statute and CCDF regulations to describe within their CCDF two-year plans how they are coordinating with each other to provide child care services within their boundaries," according to page one of the *Guide*.

C. State-Recognition Status for Tribes

Some state governments provide a process under state law for a Tribe to become a state-recognized Tribe. The National Conference of State Legislatures website provides the following information. "There are 63 state-recognized tribes in 11 states—Alabama, Connecticut, Georgia, Louisiana, Maryland, Massachusetts, New York, North Carolina, South Carolina, Vermont and Virginia. Since 2010, at least 20 states have considered legislation that would adopt a formal process for recognizing tribes." For example, the Vermont Commission on Indian Affairs provides on its website that it "shall assist Native American Indian tribes recognized by the state to secure assistance for social services, education, employment opportunities, health care, and housing; and develop and market Vermont Native American fine and performing arts, craft work, and cultural events." Federal funding opportunities for social services may exist under federal law for state-recognized Tribes. The Native American Programs Act (NAPA) of 1974 authorizes federal financial assistance to Tribes on state reservations. See 42 U.S.C. § 2991b(a).

Some state-recognized Tribes also seek federal recognition, which is a status providing access to other types of federal financial assistance, technical assistance from federal agencies, and the U.S.-Tribal Nation trust relationship. Within the U.S. Department of the Interior, the Office of Federal Acknowledgement implements the Procedures for Federal Acknowledgment of Indian Tribes set forth at 25 C.F.R. Part 83. The process is often a multiyear review requiring substantial historical, genealogical, governmental, and rigorous evaluation to meet the requirements for federal recognition. An example of a state-recognized Tribe that gained federal recognition is the Little Shell Band of Chippewa Indians of Montana which gained Montana state recognition in 2003 and federal recognition in 2019.

In sum, Tribal Nations and state governments are increasingly collaborating in areas of common interest and with the financial assistance of federal agencies. Jurisdictional and revenue issues continue to be hot topics with governmental sovereignty in the balance. As permanent neighbors with citizens of both governments in their jurisdictions, Tribes and state governments have a vested interest in cooperative relations.

CHECKPOINTS

- The primary governmental relationship is between the Tribal Nations and the federal government. Due to the proximity between Tribes and state governments, significant areas of collaboration around common concerns have developed in contemporary times.
- Tribal citizens have dual citizenship as citizens of the United States, which incorporates state citizenship. Both Tribal Nations and state governments serve Tribal members through governmental services.
- State governments have increasingly sought to tax activities within Tribal Nation territories. While there is no direct enforcement mechanism for such state taxation, the trend has been to enter into Tribal Nation-state government tax agreements to satisfy the legal standards set forth by the U.S. Supreme Court. Federal law mandates Tribal-state gaming compacts for Class III types of gaming on Tribal Nation lands.
- State governments may provide a process to grant the status of state recognition for an area Tribe. This state recognition may be a step in the process for a Tribe to meet federal recognition requirements.

CHAPTER 9

Sacred Sites, Cultural Property Protection, and Repatriation

ROADMAP

- Learn that Tribal Nations' cultures have a strong relationship with the stewardship of sacred sites and incorporate a geographically based sense of spirituality.
- Know that Tribal Nations have traditional legal principles governing this area of law and many are implementing codified legal codes.
- Understand that due to the land loss by Tribal Nations, many sacred sites are now located on federal public lands and are under the management authority of federal agencies.
- Understand that the U.S. Constitution has been interpreted by the U.S. Supreme Court to prioritize property ownership rights over spiritually based geographical Tribal Nation stewardship.
- Know that federal laws have been enacted to protect the human remains and funerary objects of Tribal peoples and to provide support for Tribal Nation cultural protection offices.

This chapter presents the issues faced by Tribal Nations and Indigenous peoples in the United States when seeking legal protection for sacred sites and cultural property. Law is necessarily the outgrowth of societal standards and concerns. Tribal Nation traditional legal principles are robust on the responsibilities to sacred sites and the proper stewardship of cultural property. The concept of traditional knowledge for Native Americans includes a broad of array of songs, stories, accounts, intellectual concepts, cultural understandings, all manner of art expressions, plant knowledge, medicinal knowledge, traditional ecological knowledge, star knowledge, dispute resolution knowledge, and numerous other types of knowledge. Within Tribal legal traditions, there were protocols on sharing knowledge that could involve recounting certain knowledge at certain times of the year and by only those individuals who were designated keepers of such knowledge. The same rules exist for various cultural items or medicinal salves or teas. With songs, there are often purposes for singing specific songs and some songs were known as only available to be sung with the permission of a particular family.

The Native American worldview on sacred sites is dissimilar in important respects from the worldview protected under U.S. property law and religious freedom. U.S. law is based on an Anglo or European worldview and provides protection for religious freedom as understood from those perspectives. Any use of cultural property under U.S. law as a commercial resource is at odds with the Native American view of cultural items and expression. Tribal laws are necessary to afford protection to sacred sites and to cultural property, as will be discussed further in this chapter. With increased government-to-government consultation between Tribal Nations and federal agencies, greater protections are developing as Tribal peoples defend cultural property and sacred geographical places.

A. Lack of Protection of Sacred Sites and Limited Protection of Cultural Property under U.S. Law

The spirituality of many American Indian and Alaska Native cultures and ceremonial practices is a geographical-based sense of stewardship and reverence at specific sacred sites as contrasted with the European historical sense of religion that may be "practiced" at any location. This difference in perspective has led to a lack of legal protection in United States law for the continuation of Native spirituality at a sacred site where land ownership has changed hands. With the land loss through the removal and allotment eras in the late 1800s, discussed in Chapters One and Two, many of the sacred sites stewarded by Tribal Nations for thousands of years became separated from Tribal communities through transfer of ownership of the underlying lands pursuant to U.S.

property laws. Millions of acres of lands that were important to the Tribal Nation cycle of life and had been maintained for spiritual purposes suddenly had fences erected around them or subjected Tribal members to trespassing charges for visiting those places.

Some of the medicine men, women, and persons across the country continued to practice and pass on Indigenous beliefs and ceremonies throughout the assimilation period and up to contemporary times. The journeys to sacred sites occurred under cover of darkness when possible. Tribal people had secretly gathered and held ceremonial events even when such practices were outlawed by the U.S. government. With the momentum of the civil rights movements in the late 1960s and the 1970s, Tribal peoples began to seek rights of access and protection of sacred sites under U.S. laws to help restore traditional religious and spiritual practices at sacred sites located on lands outside of Tribal ownership.

1. Tribal Nation Efforts to Protect Sacred Sites

A tension exists in most Tribal Nation traditions between the confidentiality required to steward sacred sites and the disclosure of sacred site locations to assert cultural property protection under U.S. law. Often when the sacred site is in danger of desecration, Tribes and Native organizations will come forward to reveal the sacredness of the endangered place and seek to protect the site for its spiritual purpose. In this section, three persistent efforts to protect sacred sites by Tribal Nations and peoples will be discussed—the Chimney Rock area in northern California, Bear's Lodge in the Black Hills of South Dakota and Wyoming (referred to as "Devils Tower" by the U.S. National Park Service), and the sacred mountain north of Flagstaff, Arizona (referred to by the U.S. Forest Service as the San Francisco Peaks, composed of Humphrey Peak, Agassiz Peak, and Fremont Peak). The sacred mountain is known and used by many of the area Tribal Nations and is called the Abalone Shell Mountain by the Navajo Nation; the Place of Snow on the Very Top by the Hopi Nation; and the Big Rock Mountain by the Havasupai Nation.

a. Litigation to Protect the Chimney Rock Area in Northern California

In 1982, the U.S. Forest Service in northern California adopted a plan to construct a paved road to allow timber harvesting in the Chimney Rock area of the Six Rivers National Forest, where Tribal ceremonies had been performed for centuries. The Yurok, Karok, Tolowa, and other Native Americans had engaged in ceremonies at this sacred place and the Hoopa Valley Indian Reservation was adjacent to the national forest area. Litigation was initiated to halt the construction of the road in conjunction with the timber harvesting plan. Eventually, the issue was decided as a matter of federal law by the U.S. Supreme Court in *Lyng v. Northwest Indian Cemetery Protective Association*, 485 U.S. 439 (1988).

According to the U.S. Supreme Court opinion, a study in 1979 commissioned by the U.S. Forest Service found that the Chimney Rock area was "significant as an integral and indispensable part of Indian religious conceptualization and practice." 485 U.S. at 442. This study recommended that the road not be constructed because it would "cause serious and irreparable damage to the sacred areas which are an integral and necessary part of the belief systems and lifeway of the Northwest California Indian peoples." *Id.* Rejecting the recommendation, the U.S. Forest Service chose a construction route for the road with protective zones around the identified sacred sites along with approving a timber harvesting plan in the area. Tribal governments, Tribal individuals, the National Congress of American Indians, conservation groups, civil rights organizations, and the state of California filed suit in federal district court seeking a permanent injunction against the construction of the road and the timber harvesting plan.

After a permanent injunction was issued by the federal district court, the Ninth Circuit Court of Appeals affirmed the injunction in part and an appeal was taken to the U.S. Supreme Court. The U.S. Supreme Court based its ruling upon the question of whether the Free Exercise Clause of the First Amendment to the U.S. Constitution was violated by the proposed road and timber harvesting plan. Under previous decisions by the Court, if there is a showing that government action places a burden on the exercise of religious practice in violation of the Free Exercise Clause, then the governmental action can go forward only if a compelling need is demonstrated. 485 U.S. at 447.

In the U.S. Supreme Court majority opinion authored by Justice Sandra Day O'Connor, the Court stated the following as central to its decision reversing the injunction:

> The Constitution does not permit government to discriminate against religions that treat particular physical sites as sacred, and a law prohibiting the Indian respondents from visiting the Chimney Rock area would raise a different set of constitutional questions. Whatever rights the Indi-

> ans may have to the use of the area, however, those rights do not divest the Government of its right to use what is, after all, *its* land.

485 U.S. at 453 (emphasis in the original). In the Court's opinion, the Tribal peoples were not being deprived of their right to religious freedom, but instead were seeking to interfere with governmental action on governmental lands.

Further, the U.S. Supreme Court opinion reviewed the 1978 American Indian Religious Freedom Act (AIRFA), 42 U.S.C. § 1996, and concluded that the AIRFA did not authorize any right to bring a case against the U.S. government. Rather, the AIRFA was simply a statement of policy and an obligation to consult with Tribal Nation leaders culminating in a 1979 report. 485 U.S. at 455.

In sum, the *Lyng* case stands for the U.S. Supreme Court holding that adverse governmental action to sacred sites on governmental lands does not violate the U.S. Constitution's Free Exercise Clause. This holding can be understood as the ordering of U.S. property rights above the spiritual rights of Native Americans when sacred site locations are no longer on lands owned by Tribal Nations or Tribal peoples. As a practical matter, the road at issue in the case was never constructed because part of the federal district court's injunction remained intact concerning noncompliance with federal laws prior to construction. As a legal precedent, the *Lyng* case leaves little hope for protection of a sacred site on federal lands for Tribes under the U.S. Constitution, based in part on the concern that Tribal Nations may influence federal actions due to treaty rights perceived as "special rights" not enjoyed by other religious groups.

b. Litigation to Preserve Bear's Lodge in the Black Hills

For the Dakota, Lakota, and Nakota peoples (commonly known as the "Sioux" Nation) and for many other Tribal Nations of the Plains, the Black Hills area is a sacred landscape and is a spiritual center for ceremonial activities, burials, social gatherings, medicine harvesting, and other spiritual activities. The natural earth features of the Black Hills correspond to constellations in the sky, contain a seasonal calendar for territorial movement on the Great Plains, and reflect the historical accounts of events that form the worldview and spiritual philosophy for many of the Plains Tribal Nations. One of these natural features is "Bear's Lodge," which was formed in a sacred manner according to oral traditions. The Arapaho called it "Bear's Tipi"; the Crow referred to it as "Bear's House"; and the Kiowa named it "Tree Rock." In contemporary times, it is called in the English language "Devils Tower" by the

Bear's Lodge. Photo credit: Angelique EagleWoman.

U.S. National Park Service, and is located within the U.S. Black Hills National Forest in Wyoming.

The U.S. claims title to the Black Hills National Forest in violation of the Fort Laramie Treaties of 1851 and 1868. In 1980, the U.S. Supreme Court held in *United States v. Sioux Nation of Indians*, 448 U.S. 371 (1980), that the U.S. government had wrongfully taken the Black Hills from the Sioux Nation and owed just compensation under the Fifth Amendment of the U.S. Constitution. The multimillion dollar amount has never been claimed by the Tribal Nations or Tribal peoples in the lawsuit based upon spiritual principles and beliefs that the Black Hills are sacred lands that could not be purchased by the United States government.

As managed by the U.S. National Park Service (NPS), the sacred site known as Bear's Lodge became a popular destination for recreational rock climbers in the mid-1900s. Tribal peoples continued the historical ceremonial practices at Bear's Lodge in spite of the disruption by tourists and climbers at the site. When the NPS issued a mandatory ban on climbing the monument during the month of June in recognition of the ceremonial activities taking place at the sacred site, a group of recreational climbers successfully challenged the ban as violative of the Establishment Clause of the U.S. Constitution in *Bear Lodge Multiple Use Association v. Babbitt*, No. 96-CV-063-D (D. Wyo. Jun. 8, 1996) slip opinion. Under the Establishment Clause, the U.S. government is prohibited from giving preferential treatment to specific religious organizations. The Department of the Interior thereafter amended the NPS management plan and withdrew the mandatory climbing ban provision.

Subsequently, the NPS enforced the "Final Climbing Management Plan" (FCMP) as amended, which provided that no new bolts or fixed pitons be hammered into the Devils Tower monument, required camouflage climbing equipment, seasonally closed climbing routes near raptor nests, and stated a voluntary ban on climbing for the month of June in recognition of Tribal ceremonies at the sacred site. A nonprofit organization representing recreational climbers and individual climbers brought suit a second time against the Secretary of the Interior in *Bear Lodge Multiple Use Association v. Babbitt*, 2 F. Supp. 2d 1448 (1998). The second case challenged the FCMP as violative of the Establishment Clause with the voluntary June ban on climbing, challenged the NPS cultural interpretative program about Tribal Nation cultural and spiritual beliefs at the monument, and challenged the placement of NPS signs encouraging visitors to stay on the trails. 2 F. Supp. 2d at 1451. The Cheyenne River Sioux Tribe, Tribal spiritual leaders, and individuals intervened in the lawsuit to add a firsthand account on the significance of Bear's Lodge. In addition, national Tribal organizations and religious freedom groups submitted briefs in support of the National Park Service's FCMP.

The federal district court reviewed the challenges to the interpretative program and the signs by the NPS and concluded that the climbers had not provided any evidence of actual harm. While the climbers argued that the cultural program served as a form of indoctrination to children visiting the monument, none of the climbers claimed to be parents of any such children, and thus they could not demonstrate the injury required to pursue a claim in court against the NPS. For this reason, the federal court held that the climbers lacked standing to bring a challenge to the cultural program. 2 F. Supp. 2d at 1453. Similarly, the federal court found no injury to the climbers by the placement of the signs and no evidence was submitted that the signs actually stopped the climbers from leaving the trails.

As for the climbing ban in the month of June, the climbers asserted that the NPS be enjoined from ever imposing a mandatory ban and that both the voluntary and mandatory bans were violative of the Establishment Clause of the U.S. Constitution. The federal district court stated that the mandatory ban on commercial climbing was mooted since it had been withdrawn and suggested it would be unwise for it to be reinstated. 2 F. Supp. 2d at 1452.

In analyzing the voluntary ban, the federal district court drew upon the test developed in the *Lemon v. Kurtzman* case, 403 U.S. 602 (1971). The U.S. Supreme Court has set forth the principles to prevent governmental preference of religion or entanglement with religion under the *Lemon* test as follows: "a governmental action does not offend the Establishment Clause if it (1) has a secular purpose, (2) does not have the principal or primary effect of advancing or inhibiting religion, and (3) does not foster an excessive entanglement with religion." 2 F. Supp. 2d at 1454. Applying this test to the voluntary climbing ban in the month of June at Devils Tower, the federal district court found that the NPS was accommodating Tribal religious worship, which served a legitimate secular purpose by removing barriers due to the public ownership of the sacred site. 2 F. Supp. 2d at 1455. The court noted that the accommodation did not deprive the climbers of their legitimate use of the public lands and that there was no excessive entanglement by the NPS in monitoring the voluntary ban. 2 F. Supp. 2d at 1456.

On appeal to the Tenth Circuit, the approval of the FCMP was upheld in *Bear Lodge Multiple Use Association v. Babbitt*, 175 F.3d 814 (10th Cir. 1999). The Tenth Circuit noted that the number of climbers on Devils Tower had increased substantially from 1973 with 312 climbers to an annual number of more than 6,000 climbers. 175 F.3d at 818. In addition, the Court of Appeals highlighted that "[t]he named individual recreational climbers whose climbing activities have been undeterred by the FCMP have established no injury in fact and therefore do not have standing." 175 F.3d at 821. Likewise, no economic harm was asserted by the commercial guide who brought the case along with the climbers. Finding a lack of standing by the parties who brought the federal lawsuit, the Tenth Circuit affirmed the district court's opinion.

In conclusion, Tribes and Tribal organizations helped educate the National Park Service officials in the Black Hills National Forest who attempted to accommodate and recognize the use of a sacred site. This was challenged and, under the U.S. Constitution, the NPS could only recommend that others voluntarily refrain from climbing on and disrupting the sacred site, Bear's Lodge, during ceremonial activities in the month of June. The National Park Service maintains a website on the Tower that includes "First Stories" and summarizes the sacred narratives on the monument from the Arapahoe, Cheyenne, Crow, Kiowa, and Lakota peoples and Tribes. The NPS website has language on the voluntary June ban on climbing: "The National Park Service advocates this closure to promote understanding and encourage respect for the culture of American Indian tribes associated with the Tower. June is a culturally significant time when many (but not all) Indian ceremonies occur. Although voluntary, this closure has been very successful—resulting in a significant reduction in the number of climbers during June."

c. Litigation over Recreational Activities and Artificial Snow on the San Francisco Peaks

The San Francisco Peaks, as they are now called by the U.S. Forest Service, are sacred mountains to many of the southwest Tribal Nations. In the desert terrain of the southwest, the Peaks are revered as home to spirit guardians who accept prayers and in turn form clouds with life-giving rain. Medicinal plants and special soils are gathered from the Peaks by Tribal peoples in respectful ways to cure those below who are suffering from all manner of ailments. The Tribal Nations stewarding and utilizing the Peaks are numerous and include: the Navajo, Hopi, Havasupai, White Mountain Apache, Hualapai, and Yavapai-Apache Nations. The San Francisco Peaks are composed of: Humphrey's Peak, Agassiz Peak, and Fremont Peak. Humphrey Peak is the highest of the three and is within the Coconino National Forest in northern Arizona.

Since the 1930s, the U.S. Forest Service has permitted downhill skiing and other recreational activities on Humphrey's Peak within 777 acres known as the Snowbowl. The southwest Tribal Nations have persistently asserted stewardship and challenged the actions of the U.S. Forest Service in expanding recreational activities at the Snowbowl, such as installing new lifts, slopes, and facilities in the 1980s. In *Wilson v. Block*, 708 F.2d 735, 739 (D.C. Cir. 1983), various Tribal Nations and Tribal organizations brought suit against the U.S. Forest Service and the U.S. Department of Agriculture when the agencies granted a permit to a private contractor operating the Snowbowl for expansion of the road to the facilities, construction of three additional lifts, clearing 50 acres of forest for new ski runs, and construction of a new day lodge. The lawsuit asserted violations of the American Indian Religious Freedom Act (AIRFA), the fiduciary responsibilities of the U.S. government to American Indians, the National Environmental Policy Act (NEPA), and the Endangered Species Act, among other laws. The Tribal Nation plaintiffs also asserted that their rights under the U.S. Constitution's First Amendment Free Exercise Clause and Establishment Clause were violated.

The Court of Appeals for the D.C. Circuit agreed with the lower court that the Tribal Nation plaintiffs' religious rights were not burdened by expansion of the Snowbowl facilities because "the government had not denied the Indians access to the Peaks or impaired their ability to gather sacred objects and conduct ceremonies, and thus had not burdened their beliefs or religious practices." 708 F.2d at 740. Furthermore, the D.C. Circuit Court found it convincing that the Tribal plaintiffs had continued their religious practices while the Snowbowl had been in operation for the previous 50 years, and thus the expansion could co-exist with the religious practices. 708 F.2d at 745. Taking each federal law argument in turn, the D.C. Circuit Court did not find any relief for the Tribal plaintiffs to halt the expansion permit. In terms of the National Historic Preservation Act, the Chief Forester at the Peaks had complied with the district court's mandate to conduct a review and had concluded that the Peaks were ineligible for listing as a national historic site. 708 F.2d at 753–54. At the end of this lawsuit, the expansion was permitted against the strong opposition of the Tribal Nations and Tribal peoples in the area.

Then in February 2005, the Forest Supervisor at the Peaks approved the proposal of the Snowbowl's private contractor to use recycled wastewater to make artificial snow to maintain the ski resort. After an administrative appeal to reverse the approval was denied, Tribal Nations, Tribal organizations, Tribal members, and others again filed suit in federal court, in *Navajo Nation v. U.S. Forest Service*, 408 F. Supp. 2d 866 (D. Ariz. 2006). The case wound its way up from the federal district court, which denied all of the plaintiffs' claims, to the Ninth Circuit Court of Appeals, which partially granted relief under the Religious Freedom and Restoration Act of 1993 (RFRA), 42 U.S.C. § 2000bb et seq., in *Navajo Nation v. U.S. Forest Service*, 479 F.3d 1024 (9th Cir. 2007), only to be heard again by a full panel of the Ninth Circuit to deny all of the Tribal Nation and organization plaintiffs' claims. The initial lawsuit was filed in June 2005 and the final decision by the en banc panel of the Ninth Circuit was issued on August 8, 2008—*Navajo Nation v. U.S. Forest Service*, 535 F.3d 1058 (9th Cir. 2008).

In the final decision by the full panel of the Ninth Circuit, the RFRA claim was analyzed to determine whether the Tribal Nation and other plaintiffs had presented evidence that the use of the recycled wastewater to make artificial snow constituted a substantial burden on their free exercise of religion. 535 F.3d at 1068. The Ninth Circuit stated that if such evidence was presented, then the burden would shift to the federal government agency to demonstrate a compelling interest to go forward with the permit for the artificial snow. 535 F.3d at 1069. In determining whether a substantial burden would occur, the Ninth Circuit made the following findings.

> The only effect of the proposed upgrades is on the Plaintiffs' subjective, emotional religious experience. That is, the presence of recycled wastewater on the Peaks is offensive to the Plaintiffs' religious sensibilities. To plaintiffs, it will spiritually desecrate a sacred mountain and will decrease the spiritual fulfillment they get from practicing their religion on the mountain. Nevertheless, under Supreme Court precedent, the diminishment of spiritual fulfillment—serious though it may be—is not a "substantial burden" on the free exercise of religion.

535 F.3d at 1070. Further, the Circuit Court held that the Religious Land Use and Institutionalized Persons Act of 2000 (RLUIPA) did not apply in the case when the government acted in a management capacity over its own land. 535 F.3d at 1077. In conclusion, the en banc panel of the Ninth Circuit affirmed the original decision by the federal district court denying relief to those bringing the lawsuit.

The Tribal Nation and other plaintiffs had brought the case due to finding offensive the proposal for spraying up to 1.5 million gallons of artificial snow on the sacred mountain made from raw sewage from the "waste discharged into Flagstaff's sewers by households, businesses, hospitals and industries" and then sent through a water treatment facility. 535 F.3d at 1083 (dissenting opinion). After the water treatment, the Arizona Department of Environmental Quality had issued a precaution that such treated sewage effluent should not be ingested by humans. *Id.* (dissenting opinion). In the dissenting opinion, much of the testimony by the religious leaders of the southwestern Tribes was excerpted to demonstrate the depth of desecration that would be felt as a result of spraying sewage water on the holy mountain. The testimony discussed the sewage water from mortuaries, hospitals, and restrooms as contaminating the mountain and the ceremonies that relied on the water and medicines from the Peaks:

> Foster, Nez, and Navajo practitioner Steven Begay testified that because they believe the mountain is an indivisible living entity, the entire mountain would be contaminated even if the millions of gallons of treated sewage effluent are put onto only one area of the Peaks. According to Foster, Nez, and Begay, there would be contamination even on those parts of the Peaks where the effluent would not come into physical contact with particular plants or ceremonial areas. To them, the contamination is not literal in the sense that a scientist would use the term. Rather, the contamination represents the poisoning of a living being. In Foster's words, '[I]f someone were to get a prick or whatever from a contaminated needle, it doesn't matter what the percentage is, your whole body would then become contaminated. And that's what would happen to the mountain.' In Nez's words, 'All of it is holy. It is like a body. It is like our body. Every part of it is holy and sacred.' In Begay's words, 'All things that occur on the mountain are a part of the mountain, and so they will have connection to it. We don't separate the mountain.'

535 F.3d at 1104 (dissenting opinion). After the final decision by the Ninth Circuit, the U.S. Supreme Court denied review of the decision and thus it stands to permit the proposal for artificial snowmaking from treated sewage effluent to be used at the Snowbowl for recreational skiers.

In reviewing these efforts by Tribal Nations and Tribal peoples to protect sacred sites on lands that they no longer have legal ownership over, the observation can be made that legal protections for religious freedom in U.S. law do not value Tribal Nations' religious views and do not provide sacred site protections for the religions of Tribal Nations. The fundamental cultural difference in viewing sacred land areas as living, holy beings under Tribal beliefs and U.S. property law based upon exploitation of land for commercial profit are fundamentally at odds when Tribal Nations and Tribal members assert religious freedom claims based upon stewardship of sacred land areas. For further information on the Tribal Nation perspective of sacred site protection, the documentary *In the Light of Reverence* (Bullfrog Films 2001), visually depicts Tribal Nation efforts to protect several sacred land areas in the United States.

2. Federal Efforts to Protect Sacred Sites

With the location of sacred sites on lands claimed by the United States through treaties, agreements, and executive orders or by force, Tribal Nations have sought to engage at every level of the U.S. government to provide protection for sacred sites. This has led to several major developments in the executive branch to engage in government-to-government consultation on the issues arising from the location of geographical spiritual places on lands under the control of federal agencies. In 2021, the historic appointment of the first Native American for the position of U.S. Secretary of the Interior, Deb Haaland, Pueblo of Laguna, was celebrated when the Biden Administration responded to widespread efforts by grassroots Tribal activists and Native organizations. Under her leadership, the U.S. Department of the Interior has taken significant steps to increase coordination of consultation between Tribal Nations and federal agencies. Later that same year, another first occurred when Charles F. Sams III, Cayuse and Walla Walla of the Confederated Tribes of the Umatilla Reservation, was sworn in as Director of the National Park Service.

a. Three Executive Orders on Sacred Sites, Tribal Consultation, and the White House Council on Native American Affairs

On May 24, 1996, U.S. President Clinton signed into law Executive Order No. 13007: Indian Sacred Sites. The executive order was directed to all federal agencies and provided a policy of accommodation and consultation regarding sacred sites. The key provisions of the order are as follows.

> Section 1. *Accommodation of Sacred Sites.* (a) In managing Federal lands, each executive branch agency with statutory or administrative responsibility for the management of Federal lands shall, to the extent practicable, permitted by law, and not clearly inconsistent with essential agency functions, (1) accommodate access to and ceremonial use of Indian sacred sites by Indian religious practitioners and (2) avoid adversely affecting the physical integrity of such sacred sites. Where appropriate, agencies shall maintain the confidentiality of sacred sites.

Thus, Executive Order No. 13007 supports access and ceremonial use of sacred sites on federal lands. The order also provided that federal agencies actively preserve sacred sites and maintain the confidentiality of those spiritually important places. Further, the order directed federal agencies to develop policies in line with those provisions within one year of the issuance of the order.

The second executive order in this series sought to mandate the development of consultation protocols throughout the federal government. On November 6, 2000, U.S. President Clinton signed into law Executive Order No. 13175: Consultation and Coordination With Indian Tribal Governments. This executive order sets forth the following three fundamental principles.

> (a) The United States has a unique legal relationship with Indian tribal governments as set forth in the Constitution of the United States, treaties, statutes, Executive Orders, and court decisions. Since the formation of the Union, the United States has recognized Indian tribes as domestic dependent nations under its protection. The Federal Government has enacted numerous statutes and promulgated numerous regulations that establish and define a trust relationship with Indian tribes.
>
> (b) Our Nation, under the law of the United States, in accordance with treaties, statutes, Executive Orders, and judicial decisions, has recognized the right of Indian tribes to self-government. As domestic dependent nations, Indian tribes exercise inherent sovereign powers over their members and territory. The United States continues to work with Indian tribes on a government-to-government basis to address issues concerning Indian tribal self-government, tribal trust resources, and Indian tribal treaty and other rights.
>
> (c) The United States recognizes the right of Indian tribes to self-government and supports tribal sovereignty and self-determination.

Executive Order No. 13175 charges federal agencies and departments with developing consultation and coordination policies for federal action impacting Tribal Nations through proposed legislation, regulations, policies, or other actions.

A third executive order issued on June 26, 2013, by U.S. President Obama focused on the establishment of the White House Council on Native American Affairs in Executive Order No. 13647. A primary purpose of this executive order was to structure coordination within the federal government with the Secretary of Interior as the chair of the new Council on Native American Affairs to "improve coordination of Federal programs and the use of resources available to tribal communities." Subsequent U.S. presidential administrations have issued memorandums of implementation of these executive orders. For example, U.S. President Biden issued the Tribal Consultation and Strengthening Nation-to-Nation Relationships Memorandum to all heads of executive departments and agencies on January 26, 2021, to further affirm and implement the coordination with his administration, all federal departments and agencies, and Tribal Nations.

b. 2023 USDA Forest Service Action Plan on Tribal Consultation

In February of 2023, the United States Department of Agriculture Forest Service released *Strengthening Tribal Consultations and Nation-to-Nation Relationships: A USDA Forest Service Action Plan* (Action Plan). On page 1 of the Action Plan, the USDA Forest Service views Tribal consultations broadly: "In addition to strengthening government-to-government relations with federally recognized Indian Tribes and Alaska Native corporations (ANCs), the U.S. Department of Agriculture (USDA), Forest Service also encourages engagement with non-federally recognized Tribes and Native Hawaiians, as well as American Indian, Alaska Native, and other Indigenous individuals, communities, inter-Tribal organizations, enterprises, and educational institutions." The four focus areas of the Action Plan are set forth on page three as: (1) Strengthen Relationships Between Indian Tribes and the USDA Forest Service, (2) Fulfill Trust and Treaty Obligations, (3) Enhance Co-Stewardship of the Nation's Forests and Grasslands, and (4) Advance Tribal Relations Within the USDA Forest Service.

Within the Action Plan, the Forest Service Office of Tribal Relations coordinates with other units, from the USDA Office of Congressional Relations to the Indigenous Knowledge Implementation Team to local deputy units of the Forest Service, to update and revise federal policy, laws, and processes to better implement Tribal Nation and Native American organization consultations and input.

c. U.S. Cabinet-Level Departments MOU to Protect Sacred Sites

In November 2021, the U.S. Departments of the Interior, Agriculture, Transportation, Environmental Protection Agency, the White House Council on Environmental Quality, the Advisory Council on Historic Preservation, and the Tennessee Valley Authority joined as signatory participating agencies the *Memorandum of Understanding Regarding Interagency Coordination and Collaboration for the Protection of Indigenous Sacred Sites* (MOU). The MOU established an interagency working group with monthly meetings to implement federal laws, policies, and executive orders on protection of Tribal Nation and Native Hawaiian sacred sites.

Participating Agencies will review, at a minimum, the following authorities and their implementing regulations to determine whether additional inter-agency measures may be warranted to better protect sacred sites.

- Executive Order 13007: Indian Sacred Sites
- National Historic Preservation Act
- National Environmental Policy Act
- Native American Graves Protection and Repatriation Act
- Archaeological Resources Protection Act
- American Indian Religious Freedom Act
- Religious Freedom Restoration Act
- Executive Order 13175: Consultation and Coordination with Indian Tribal Governments

The list of federal laws and executive orders is provided on page three of the MOU. Within the MOU, there is an acknowledgement that the United States has affirmed the UN Declaration on the Rights of Indigenous Peoples and includes, on page three, the federal agency responsibility "to recognize, respect, and consider Tribal interpretations of their own treaty and reserved rights." One of the charges under the MOU is an annual report on significant issues raised by Tribal Nations, Native Hawaiian organizations, and spiritual leaders on protection of sacred sites.

B. Protection of Tribal Human Remains and Cultural Property

Along with the loss of stewardship to protect off-reservation sacred sites, a portion of the U.S. military, the scientific community, Indian hobbyists, and artifact collectors for museums have engaged in looting Tribal burial grounds. For example, the U.S. Surgeon General issued Circular No. 2 in 1867 to those interested in the "progress of medical science" to gather "typical crania of Indian tribes, specimens of their arms, dress, implements, rare articles of their diet, medicines, etc." and send them to the Army Medical Museum. One of the frequent complaints from Tribal Nations and Tribal communities has been the extraction of Indian artifacts and remains from Tribal gravesites on and off reservations dating back to the 1800s with no recourse for Tribal families and governments.

1. Archaeological Resources Protection Act

In 1988, the Archaeological Resources Protection Act was amended to include a new section, 16 U.S.C. § 470ii(c), *Federal land managers' public awareness program of archaeological resources on public lands and Indian lands*. The provision provided: "Each federal land manager shall establish a program to increase public awareness of the significance of the archaeological resources located on public lands and Indian lands and the need to protect such resources." In addition, the law requires notice to any affected Tribal Nation regarding an area of cultural or religious significance prior to a permit for excavation being issued if destruction or damage to the site may occur. 16 U.S.C. 470cc(c).

2. Native American Graves Protection and Repatriation Act

Tribal Nations and Tribal groups also took a proactive role in lobbying for the passage of the 1990 federal Native American Graves Protection and Repatriation Act (NAGPRA), 25 U.S.C. § 3001 et seq., to stop the looting and removal of funerary and human remains on federal and Tribal lands. The associated regulations to implement the NAGPRA are found at 45 C.F.R. § 10. Under the NAGPRA, federal agencies and museums receiving federal funding are required to document and publish notices of inventory regarding Native American human remains, funerary objects, sacred objects, and other objects of cultural patrimony. The inventory should include the geographical and cultural affiliation of each item to the extent possible. 25 U.S.C. § 3003. Tribal Nations and Native Hawaiian organizations are to be notified of relevant inventories and may request additional information about listed items or remains. 25 U.S.C. § 3003(b)(2) and (d). The NAGPRA provides that expeditious repatriation of inventoried items or remains shall occur in consultation with the Tribal Nation, lineal descendant, or Native Hawaiian organization that has established cultural affiliation. 25 U.S.C. § 3005(a). If the inventory does not establish cultural affiliation, then the claimant of the item or remains must "show cultural affiliation by a preponderance of the evidence based upon geographical, kinship, biological, archaeological, anthropological, linguistic, folkloric, oral traditional, historical, or other relevant information or expert opinion" to have the item or remains repatriated. 25 U.S.C. § 3005(a)(4).

Under the NAGPRA, a formal Review Committee was established with membership appointed by the Secretary of the Interior. 25 U.S.C. § 3006.

According to the U.S. Department of the Interior's website dedicated to the National NAGPRA, the duties of the Review Committee involve facilitating the resolution of repatriation disputes and consideration of "requests for the disposition of culturally unidentifiable human remains." Additionally, the NAGPRA includes civil penalty provisions for any museum failing to comply with the inventory and repatriation directives. 25 U.S.C. § 3007(a). The Secretary of the Interior has discretion over issuing such penalties and factors under the NAGPRA for the amount to be assessed. 25 U.S.C. § 3007(b). The civil penalties may be increased to provide deterrence and keep pace with inflation. 45 C.F.R. § 10.12. In January 2024, the Department of the Interior issued updated regulations to clarify provisions of the NAGPRA in 45 C.F.R. Part 10.

One notable exception to the reach of the NAGPRA's provisions is the Smithsonian Institution, which was specifically exempted from the legislation. 25 U.S.C. § 3001(4). Rather, a separate federal law was enacted when the National Museum of the American Indian was created as a subsidiary of the Smithsonian. Under 20 U.S.C. § 80q-9(a) and (c), the Secretary of the Smithsonian Institution was directed to inventory Indian human remains and funerary objects in its collections for return to the Tribal descendants or Tribal government with cultural affiliation established by a preponderance of the evidence standard.

The United States Government Accountability Office (GAO) has released a series of reports in 2010, 2018, 2019, 2021, and 2023 recommending 55 actions by responsible agencies and museums with 47 recommendations resolved and 8 recommendations remaining. The 2023 GAO-24-106870 snapshot report, *Native American Priorities: Protection and Repatriation of Human Remains and Other Cultural Items,* found that 52% of identified Native American human remains have not been repatriated and neither had 29% of related funerary items in the thirty years since the 1990 enactment of the NAGPRA. On page two of the snapshot report, the GAO found: "While federal agencies have made some progress, such as making annual data on the status of federal agencies' repatriation progress readily available, challenges remain with implementing and enforcing NAGPRA. In particular, more work is needed to repatriate the hundreds of thousands of Native American cultural items that are still in the possession of federal agencies and museums."

Another GAO Report, dated May 2011 and involving the return of Tribal items and human remains, was *Smithsonian Institution—Much Work Still Needed to Identify and Repatriate Indian Human Remains and Objects* (GAO-

11-515). In reviewing the slow process implemented by the Smithsonian for detailed case studies prior to repatriating funerary objects and human remains, the GAO concluded on the introductory summary page of the report that "it could take several more decades to complete this process." Since the enactment of federal repatriation legislation for the Smithsonian, the Institution had "offered to repatriate over 5,000 human remains, which account for approximately one-third of the total estimated human remains in its collections." The number of funerary objects subject to repatriation was unknown since "the Smithsonian has no reliable estimate of the total number of such objects in its collections," the report further stated. Much work has yet to be done in this area of repatriation and legal practitioners will continue to have a role to play in ensuring the return of Tribal remains, artifacts, and cultural property.

In 2020, the National Museum of the American Indian, which was established by federal law in 1998, released *A Step-by-Step Guide through the Repatriation Process: National Museum of the American Indian* (Guide). The Guide on page 5 identified the National Museum of the American Indian (NMAI) within the Smithsonian Museum Institution as one of two museums subject to federal repatriation legislation, the other being the National Museum of Natural History. According to the Guide, the NMAI is the repository for the former George Heye collection where he "amassed some 800,000 objects from indigenous cultures throughout North, Central, and South America, creating what is still considered one of the most impressive collections of Native American objects in the world." The Guide provides a five-step process for Tribal Nations or lineal descendants to initiate repatriation of such items.

To further provide protection for wrongfully seized Tribal Nation cultural items, the Safeguard Tribal Objects of Patrimony (STOP) Act of 2021 was passed. 25 U.S.C. § 3071 et seq. The purpose of the STOP Act is "to prevent the international export of cultural items prohibited from trafficking under the Native American Graves Protection and Repatriation Act (NAGPRA) and the Archeological Resources Protection Act (ARPA)" according to the U.S. Department of the Interior Indian Affairs website.

In recent years, the U.S. Department of the Interior issued the May 11, 2022, report *Federal Indian Boarding School Initiative Investigative Report*, which included a section on "Marked and Unmarked Burial Sites Across the Federal Indian Boarding School System." On page 85 of the report, the plan to continue to investigate and possibly repatriate the human remains of American Indian, Alaska Native, and Native Hawaiian children to their home communities is stated as follows:

> The Federal Indian Boarding School Initiative investigation includes identifying the location of marked and unmarked burial sites across the Federal Indian boarding school system, which may later be used to assist in locating unidentified remains of American Indian, Alaska Native, and Native Hawaiian children. This investigation component will provide a basis for the Department to plan future sitework, including protection of burial sites and potential repatriation or disinterment of remains of children, under Federal law, including NAGPRA, and in coordination with sister Federal agencies as relevant.

Several Tribal Nations have successfully coordinated the return of their relatives buried in federal Indian boarding schools. The Native American Rights Fund (NARF) assisted some of these Tribal Nations in coordinating with the U.S. Army Corps of Engineers regarding children interred on the grounds of the Carlisle Indian Boarding School in Pennsylvania.

> On September 17, 2023, Spirit Lake Tribe (SLT) and Sisseton Wahpeton Oyate (SWO) arrived at Carlisle Barracks Post Cemetery to bring two of their children, Amos LaFromboise and Edward Upright, home. On the morning of their arrival, as the Tribes sang their honor songs for the first time on Carlisle's grounds, the rain began to pour. Two days after their arrival, the Tribes carefully wrapped the boys' remains in buffalo robes and prepared for the long journey home. After nearly 150 years, the Tribes were finally bringing their boys home to lay them to rest next to each other at the Tribes repatriation grounds.
>
> A week before, the two Tribes finalized a first-of-its-kind signed Plan of Action (Plan) with the U.S. Army for the return of their children's remains. The Plan was established to provide a robust set of terms to ensure a manageable and culturally appropriate process for the disinterment and return of the remains. The predictability and assurance the Plan provided was invaluable after the Tribes spent nearly seven years working to have their children's remains returned to them.

In the 2022 Department of Interior report previously mentioned, "the Department investigation has identified approximately 53 marked or unmarked burial sites. As the investigation continues, the Department expects the number of sites to increase." Thus, the work of Tribal Nations and Native Hawaiian organizations to repatriate and bring home the children who died at the federal Indian boarding schools will continue.

C. Tribal Cultural Protection Laws and Tribal Historic Preservation Offices

In response to the lack of cultural understanding and legal protection of Tribal human remains, gravesites, sacred sites, and cultural property, Tribal Nations have partnered with the National Park Service (NPS) to establish Tribal Historic Preservation Officers (THPO) through receipt of grant funds. The former National Historic Preservation Act (NHPA) was repealed and replaced in 2014 as part of the National Park Service and Related Programs support to Tribal sovereignty in establishing Tribal Nation operated preservation offices. The Standing Rock Sioux Tribe enacted the first Tribal Nation preservation program in August 1996. The National Park Service maintains a comprehensive compilation of U.S. Cultural Laws on its website.

The National Association of Tribal Historic Preservation Officers (NATHPO) offers technical assistance and forums for THPOs to share best practices and consult on their collective and individual efforts. As of 2023, there were 221 National Park Service-recognized Tribal Historic Preservation Officers. According to the NATHPO website, the "NATHPO's mission is to provide guidance to preservation officials, elected representatives, and the public about national historic preservation legislation, policies, and regulations. We promote tribal sovereignty, develop partnerships, and advocate for Tribes in governmental activities on preservation issues."

In addition to the development of formal Tribal Historic Preservation Officers, Tribes have been proactive in passing Tribal laws on cultural property protection, sacred sites, Tribal gravesites, the protection of cultural resources, the protection of intellectual property, and protocols on research conducted on Tribal lands and/or Tribal members. According to research findings reported by Professor Angela Riley in the 2022 article, *The Ascension of Indigenous Cultural Property Law*, in 2020 there were approximately 134 Tribal laws on cultural property protection.

> Eighty-one tribes have laws that protect Burial Sites, Funerary Objects, and Repatriation. Of these, thirty-one explicitly reference NAGPRA. Eighty-nine tribes have passed tribal laws that safeguard Sacred Sites and Ceremonial Places. Forty-eight tribes have enacted laws to protect Intangible Property, with seven explicitly referencing the Copyright Act or including a tribal variation of copyright law, four referencing trademark law, two including patent law, and three referencing or producing

> their own version of the Indian Arts and Crafts Act. And today, there are forty-nine tribes with laws focused on data sovereignty.

121 *Michigan Law Review* at 33. Since the publication of the above referenced article, it is likely the numbers of Tribal laws will increase with more focus on the importance of establishing Tribal law standards for identification and protocols for the return and protection of Tribal Nation cultural items, repatriation of Tribal members, and the protection of many types of traditional knowledge.

Tribal laws and THPOs are serving to protect Tribal Nation cultural resources and, in the process, provide cultural education to the agencies of the U.S. government and to U.S. citizens about the Tribal worldview on sacred sites, Tribal stewardship views, and intercultural dialogue on cultural significance. This is an evolving area of law that will continue to develop and will require competent legal practitioners to serve on the forefront of articulating legal protections applicable to Tribal Nations and Indigenous communities.

CHECKPOINTS

- American Indian and Alaska Native spiritual principles connected to sacred sites are not commonly understood or protected in U.S. law. Cross-cultural understanding is necessary to provide greater legal protections.
- Tribal Nations continue to assert legal arguments and seek federal policy changes to protect spiritually, culturally and historically important geographical sites.
- With the enactment of the Native American Graves Protection and Repatriation Act (NAGPRA), the looting of Tribal cemeteries and the unauthorized collection of ancestral remains are federal offenses on Tribal Nation and federal lands. Federally-funded museums have obligations under the law to inventory Tribal items and respond to requests for repatriation of Tribal cultural patrimonial items.
- Tribal Historic Preservation Officers are operating to ensure that Tribal cultural property is recognized and preserved. Tribes are developing and implementing laws on cultural resource protection, the repatriation of Tribal members, and the protection of various types of traditional knowledge, and are seeking to educate other governments on proper processes.

CHAPTER 10

International Indigenous Rights and Tribal Nations

ROADMAP

- Learn about the international underpinnings of the relationship between Tribal Nations and the United States.
- Learn about the early efforts to join international organizations by Tribal Nation leaders for the purpose of sharing the Indigenous viewpoint on global affairs.
- Understand the development in the United States of the American Indian Movement and the connection to international Indigenous collaborations.
- Know the major international documents that support Indigenous collective human rights, including recent developments.

In this chapter, the history of the interaction between Indigenous peoples, particularly from North America, and the world organizations of nation-states will be discussed. The Tribal Nations and Tribal peoples in the United States have often taken a leadership role in advancing global Indigenous rights. As greater means of communication become available, Indigenous peoples around the world are sharing common issues of land stewardship, survival from assimilation policies, protection of cultural resources, assertion of human rights, and adaptation to changing economics. A basic worldview principle shared by Indigenous peoples is the interconnectedness of life and through this interconnection Indigenous leaders continue to assert traditional guidance on how human beings live and interact with the environment, both on Turtle Island and globally throughout Mother Earth.

A. Early Efforts to Join World Organizations

From time immemorial, trade routes and seasonal gatherings connected Indigenous peoples from the top of the Western Hemisphere to the southernmost point. Connections between cultures from other parts of the world also occurred with less regularity. Evidence is currently being studied in Newfoundland, Canada, on interactions between Indigenous peoples and Norsemen dated from 1000 A.D. Many Indigenous peoples in North America challenge the Bering Strait theory as Natives to the Western Hemisphere who have accounts of interactions with foreigners coming to these shores. There were the circumpolar northern Indigenous peoples who traversed areas in the far north in cyclical movements and had seasonal gatherings. Indigenous peoples of Polynesian cultures journeyed throughout the islands in the Pacific Ocean. Cultural interactions and linkages continued to grow into the 1300s and 1400s.

From 1492, when the Spaniards began colonizing in the Central and South American region, to the early 1700s, a large influx of European men who established trading posts and claimed territory commenced in both North and South America. Commerce and political alliances were initially formed, but were soon followed by the western civilization mode of subjugation and draining the resources of Native inhabitants. In 1776, with the establishment of the United States, the new nation-state began to assert military control over all Tribal Nations, whether engaged in diplomatic relations or not.

As Tribal Nations in the United States experienced severe oppression and economic devastation in the late 1800s and early 1900s, many Tribal Nation leaders continued to assert Tribal sovereignty and advocate from the legal agreements entered into with the United States. Around the globe, Indigenous leaders shared this same experience in asserting their rights in dealing with Great Britain and its governmental offspring. For example, the Maori of New Zealand entered into the Treaty of Waitangi in 1840 with officials from Britain. Where legal agreements were not entered into, warfare ensued as Indigenous peoples sought to protect their homes, families, lands, and ways of life from

European invasion in Africa, Australia, the Philippines, North America, and South America.

Two documented accounts of Indigenous leaders seeking to be heard at the League of Nations in the early 1920s attest to the tenacity of asserting nation-state status by Indigenous peoples. A leader and advocate for the Haudenosaunee Nation, also known as the Iroquois Confederacy of the Six Nations, Deskaheh Levi General traveled to Geneva, Switzerland, in 1923 and spent a year seeking an audience and relief on behalf of his people in response to the actions of Canada and the British monarchy. He was blocked from presenting his case to the League of Nations by those nation-states. Another attempt to gain access to the League of Nations was made by the Maori leader T.W. Ratana in 1925. He also was denied access to protest violations of the Treaty of Waitangi. These early efforts demonstrate the firm belief that Indigenous peoples refused to surrender to outside forces and maintained their rightful sense of entitlement to participate on the global level.

B. Contemporary Indigenous Rights Movements

With the civil rights movements occurring in the United States in the late 1960s and the 1970s, groups that had experienced political and economic exclusion were engaging in civil disobedience and leading protest marches. American Indians raised in urban areas as a result of the 1950s BIA Relocation Program became aware of these strategies to voice feelings of being oppressed and disempowered. One of the most well-known political groups emerging from this sense of urban unrest was known as the American Indian Movement (AIM). Engaging in violent confrontations as well as organizing long-distance peaceful walks, AIM brought media and public attention to the issues facing Tribal members on reservations and throughout the country.

1. The American Indian Movement's Impact on Collective Rights

AIM provided a way for urban and reservation Tribal members to stand together to voice disagreement over U.S. Indian policy and the lack of economic opportunity for Native American people. In 1973, the American Indian Movement gathered together at the village of Wounded Knee on the Pine Ridge Reservation to serve as protection against the local Tribal law enforcement. The U.S. government sent in officers of the Federal Bureau of Investigation (FBI) and the U.S. Marshals Service to surround those gathered together. After more than 70 days, the AIM occupation of Wounded Knee ended, but the group had held off more than 300 armed federal troops, state troops, and antagonistic Tribal officers. Wounded Knee was the historic site of the massacre on December 29, 1890, of unarmed men, women, and children trying to reach the safety of the Pine Ridge Reservation only to be gunned down by U.S. cavalry. The 1973 occupation of Wounded Knee was a reminder that the U.S. government had failed to fulfill its promises in treaties, had failed to provide the necessary assistance to Native Americans, and had continued to view Native Americans as the enemy, rather than the ally.

2. Formation of the International Indian Treaty Council and NGO Status

Following the occupation, the Standing Rock Sioux Tribal Council called together a conference on enforcement of the treaties entered into between Tribal Nations and the United States. Leading international law scholars were invited and met with Tribal peoples from across the country at the conference. From this event, the International Indian Treaty Council (IITC) was formed and a declaration adopted, "Declaration of Continuing Independence by the First International Indian Treaty Council at Standing Rock Indian Country June 1974." The first order of business for the IITC was to attain Non-Government Organization (NGO) status with the United Nations to begin presenting the issues faced by Tribal Nations and peoples to the international community.

The IITC successfully attained NGO status to the United Nations Economic and Social Council (ECOSOC) in 1977. To garner attention on Indigenous people's issues, the IITC organized a conference in Geneva, Switzerland, titled "International NGO Conference on Discrimination Against Indigenous Populations in the Americas—1977." The focus was on the poor economic, political, legal, and social conditions for the Indigenous peoples of the Western Hemisphere due to European invasion and subsequent establishment of settler governments. More than 100 Indigenous delegates attended to provide testimony before the UN officials present. A co-sponsor of the conference was the ECOSOC Sub-Committee on Racism, Racial Discrimination, Apartheid, and Decolonization of the Special Committee on Human Rights. The four-day conference from Sept. 20–23, 1977, culminated in a report that included a Final Resolution and a Declaration by those in attendance. In the Final Resolution on page 22 of the report, the attendance at the conference was reported as follows:

> For the first time, the widest and most united representation of Indigenous nations and peoples, from the Northern to the most Southern tip and from the far West to the East of the Americas took part in the Conference. They included representatives of more than 60 Nations and peoples, from fifteen countries (Argentina, Bolivia, Canada, Chile, Costa Rica, Guatemala, Ecuador, Mexico, Nicaragua, Panama, Paraguay, Peru, Surinam, United States of America, Venezuela).
>
> It is regretted that some delegates were prevented by their governments from attending.

At the center of this historic meeting was a declaration on the human, environmental, legal, political, and social rights being asserted by Indigenous populations.

The work of the Geneva conference continued pursuant to the ECOSOC Resolution 1982/34 establishing the Working Group on Indigenous Populations under the Sub-Commission on the Promotion and Protection of Human Rights. On the website of the Working Group, its two primary mandates were: "to review developments pertaining to the promotion and protection of human rights and fundamental freedoms of Indigenous peoples" and "to give attention to the evolution of international standards concerning Indigenous rights."

C. Significant International Indigenous Human Rights Instruments and Developments

The international landscape for Indigenous human rights has changed considerably in the last several decades due to the increased vocalization from Indigenous peoples on the conditions they face. From the Western Hemisphere, efforts have been made by Indigenous peoples to rejoin the international community of nations on an equal basis. For Tribal Nations in mid-North America, the options are: to work through organizations with NGO status within the UN; to work in collaboration with the United States of America to present issues on an international scale; or to seek partnerships with others recognized within the United Nations nation-state structure to raise issues.

As the UN Working Group on Indigenous Populations continued to document and research the status of Indigenous peoples around the world, four major developments occurred within the UN structure to support inclusion of Native Americans. One was the revision and work on a declaration embodying the human rights to be accorded Indigenous peoples; the second was the establishment of the UN Permanent Forum on Indigenous Issues; the third was the appointment of a Special Rapporteur on the rights of Indigenous peoples by the Commission on Human Rights; and the fourth was the creation of the Expert Mechanism on the Rights of Indigenous Peoples. As Indigenous organizations and Tribal Nations worked within the UN system, the ability to respond to U.S. Indian policy via reporting requirements in international conventions has become a further means of asserting international human rights standards for American Indian and Alaska Native Tribes.

1. UN Special Rapporteur on the Rights of Indigenous Peoples

In 2001, the Commission on Human Rights appointed a Special Rapporteur on the Rights of Indigenous Peoples (Special Rapporteur) to travel, conduct investigations, and report on the situations of Indigenous peoples. In the mandate issued by the Human Rights Council in Resolution 6/12 of September 28, 2007, the Special Rapporteur was directed to collaborate with the UN Permanent Forum on Indigenous Issues and the Expert Mechanism on the Rights of Indigenous Peoples to protect human rights and provide best practices to nation-states. The Special Rapporteur is empowered to investigate alleged violations of the human rights of Indigenous peoples and to request from the involved governments documents and communications as necessary. In this manner, the Special Rapporteur acts as a frontline representative of the Human Rights Council to be dispatched when a human rights crisis may arise involving Indigenous peoples around the globe.

For Tribal Nations in relations with the United States, the UN Special Rapporteurs over the years have issued reports and statements. From 2008–2014, Professor S. James Anaya held the position as a law trained educator and expert on U.S. Indian policy. The 2017 report following the Special Rapporteur visit to the United States focused on several issues including the updated provisions of the Violence Against Women Act (VAWA) to address sexual and gender-based violence against Indigenous women and girls. A primary topic of the report was the lack of consultation for energy extraction and oil pipelines endangering Tribal Nation lands and waters.

> As is well-documented, the controversy surrounding the Dakota Access Pipeline drew thousands of people to the boundaries of the Standing Rock Sioux Reservation as they sought to protect their land and water and uphold tribal sovereignty. While the actions that took place were mostly non-violent and peaceful, there has been a militarized, at times violent, escalation of force by local law enforcement and private security forces. The previous Special Rapporteur noted that indigenous peoples had the right to oppose extractive activities that impacted their land and resources, free from reprisals, acts of violence or undue pressure to accept or enter into consultations about extractive projects.

A/HRC/36/46/Add.1 (August 9, 2017) at Paragraph 72. The UN Special Rapporteurs hold an important role to address Indigenous issues from a global perspective and hold nation-states accountable through researched reports highlighting both positive developments and areas of ongoing failure to protect Indigenous peoples, their lands, and their waters.

2. UN Permanent Forum on Indigenous Issues

In 2002, the United Nations Permanent Forum on Indigenous Issues (UNPFII) held its first meeting as an advisory body within the UN Economic and Social Council to provide opportunities for Indigenous leadership to give input to the United Nations. The mandate of the UNPFII is threefold according to its website—to "provide expert advice and recommendations on Indigenous issues to the Council, as well as to programmes, funds and agencies of the United Nations, through the Council"; to "raise awareness and promote the integration and coordination of activities related to Indigenous issues within the UN system"; and to "prepare and disseminate information on Indigenous issues."

The twenty-second session of the UN Permanent Forum on Indigenous Issues was held in April 2023 with the theme of "Indigenous Peoples, human health, planetary and territorial health and climate change: a rights-based approach." The 2024 session focus was announced as "Enhancing Indigenous

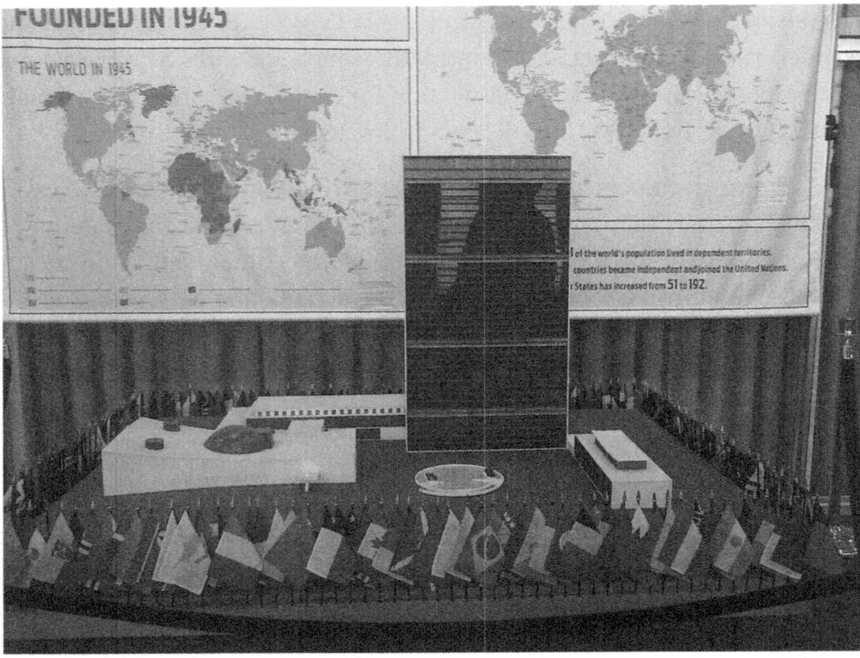

UN Model in NY UN Headquarters. Photo credit: Angelique EagleWoman.

Peoples' right to self-determination in the context of the United Nations Declaration on the Rights of Indigenous Peoples: emphasizing the voices of Indigenous youth." These sessions bring together Indigenous leaders from around the world to join together in solidarity and kinship on common goals and issues.

3. UN Declaration on the Rights of Indigenous Peoples

As Indigenous peoples around the globe continued to give voice to their issues and the demand for basic human rights, the principles in the declaration considered at the 1977 Geneva conference became a focal point for unified action. On September 13, 2007, 30 years after that conference, the UN General Assembly adopted the UN Declaration on the Rights of Indigenous Peoples (UNDRIP), G.A. Res. 61/295, U.N.DOC A/RES/61/295. The original vote was 143 countries in support, 4 countries in opposition, and 11 countries abstaining (including the Russian Federation). The four countries opposed during the adoption vote were Australia, Canada, New Zealand, and the United States of America. All four subsequently have endorsed the UNDRIP in recent years.

The UNDRIP is a historic document and unique human rights instrument that is the first to recognize collective human rights in addition to individual human rights. The Declaration serves as a floor for human rights of Indigenous peoples around the world. Key features of the UNDRIP include: Article 3, recognizing the right to self-determination in pursuing political, economic, social, and cultural direction; Article 8, containing the right "not to be subjected to forced assimilation or destruction of their culture"; Article 19, stating that nation-states shall adhere to the process of obtaining the "free, prior and informed consent" of Indigenous peoples before taking action impacting them; Article 26, acknowledging that "Indigenous peoples have the right to the lands, territories and resources which they have traditionally owned, occupied, or otherwise used or acquired"; and Article 37, calling for enforcement of "treaties, agreements and other constructive arrangements" entered into between Indigenous Peoples and nation-states.

The UN Declaration on the Rights of Indigenous Peoples is a set of guiding principles adopted by a strong consensus of the nation-states around the globe. These minimum standards of human rights for Indigenous peoples will continue to transform the relations between Indigenous peoples and nation-states in the years to come. The impact of the UNDRIP has yet to be fully realized for the Tribal Nations in relationship with the United States. Legal scholars have encouraged Tribal Nations to consider asserting Indigenous collective rights identified in the UNDRIP when defending active claims against the United States to begin bringing those international Indigenous rights to life. As mentioned in Chapter Nine, U.S. Secretary of the Interior Deb Haaland, Laguna Pueblo, while overseeing the federal interagency working group on protection of Indigenous sacred sites referenced the U.S. affirmation of the UNDRIP in 2010 and its guiding principles in current U.S. policy and relations with American Indian and Alaska Native Tribal Nations and with Native Hawaiian organizations.

4. System-Wide Action Plan for the UNDRIP and 2030 Agenda for Sustainable Development

As the UN Declaration on the Rights of Indigenous Peoples has set the standards for collective human rights, efforts have been coordinated with the UN Permanent Forum on Indigenous Issues and other entities within the UN system to implement the UNDRIP's articles. In 2015, the System-Wide Action Plan (SWAP) for the United Nations was launched. In November of 2022, a questionnaire was sent to 52 UN bodies on steps to engage in the SWAP for coherent measures to fulfill the UNDRIP provisions. In February of 2023, a report on some of the responses was announced to detail media releases and coordinated World Indigenous Peoples events by various UN entities, such as the 2022 first ever world-wide "Coalition on Indigenous Peoples' Food Systems." See E/C.19/2023/2 at Paragraph 19. The Office of the UN High Commissioner on Human Rights (OHCHR) reported that the "OHCHR also played an active role in raising the profile of Indigenous Peoples in the context of the Human Rights Council, including by organizing, during the fifty-first session of the Council, an expert workshop on possible ways to enhance the participation of Indigenous Peoples in the work of the Human Rights Council, 15 in November 2022." *Id.* at Paragraph 39.

A second portion of the report relayed responses to shaping the 2030 Agenda for Sustainable Development to comport with the provisions of the UNDRIP. The 2030 Agenda is focused on dealing with poverty and inequality experienced by socioeconomically vulnerable groups throughout the world, including the majority of the 370 million Indigenous peoples worldwide. In the 2023 report, the Secretariat of the Convention on Biological Diversity provided that during the fifteenth Conference of the Parties to the Convention on Biological Diversity the program work would seek "to recognize natural and cultural heritage and diversity as enablers and drivers of the economic, social and environmental dimensions of sustainable development and a pathway to the global biodiversity framework's vision of living in harmony with nature by 2050." *Id.* at Paragraph 94. According to the United Nations Development Programme (UNDP), the "UNDP values the contributions of Indigenous Peoples to humanity's cultural diversity and heritage, climate change solutions and shares their concerns about economic and social disadvantages and weak political representation." *Id.* at Paragraph 98. With consistent monitoring of the work throughout the United Nations on global matters, the implementation of the UNDRIP has provided a significant vehicle for the inclusion of Indigenous peoples from the United States and around the world to be taken into consideration and heard for the good of all.

5. UN Expert Mechanism on the Rights of Indigenous Peoples

The UN Human Rights Council pursuant to Resolution 6/36 on December 14, 2007, formed the Expert Mechanism on the Rights of Indigenous Peoples (EMRIP). The purpose of the EMRIP is to provide research, studies, and recommendations to the Council. The first study of the Expert Mechanism on the Rights of Indigenous Peoples was concluded in 2009 on the right to education for Indigenous peoples with recommendations to further increase educational attainment. In September 2013, the EMRIP released its study regarding access to justice in the promotion and protection of the rights of Indigenous peoples. In 2018, the EMRIP report was "Free, prior and informed consent: a human rights-based approach." The 2022 report by the EMRIP was "Study on treaties, agreements and other constructive arrangements, between indigenous peoples and States, including peace accords and reconciliation initiatives, and their constitutional recognition." The following year in 2023, the EMRIP released the study on "the impact of militarization on the rights of Indigenous Peoples." Each annual report builds on significant issues affecting Indigenous peoples and their collective human rights.

Five members compose the Expert Mechanism through appointment by the Human Rights Council. Both the Special Rapporteur and a member of the Permanent Forum are invited to attend the EMRIP's annual July meeting where representatives of Indigenous organizations, nation-state representatives, Indigenous individuals, and other interested persons and organizations may take part. Through these four developments within the UN structure, Tribal Nations and Indigenous peoples have greater opportunities to be heard on an international level.

6. The United States and UN Conventions Impacting U.S. Indian Policy

For Tribal Nations in relations with the United States, the UN Conventions, also known as treaties, that the United States has agreed to uphold may provide ways to influence U.S. Indian policy. For example, the United States has ratified and joined the UN Convention on the Elimination of Racial Discrimination (UN CERD) on September 28, 1966. The Convention is monitored by the Committee on the Elimination of Racial Discrimination, which periodically requires nation-states bound by the Convention to submit progress reports. In addition, organizations and individuals may file complaints or companion reports to the Committee on the actions of nation-states during the periodic review. The IITC and others have filed companion reports in coordination with the U.S. reporting requirement.

For example, on March 10, 2006, the Committee on the Elimination of Racial Discrimination (CERD) sent out a strongly worded decision to the United States concerning the unlawful seizure of the aboriginal lands of the Western Shoshone Nation and directed the United States to halt further desecration of those lands from military weapon testing, to immediately begin a dialogue with the Western Shoshone Peoples for a resolution to the land claim dispute in accordance with due process requirements, and to stop further imposition of fees on the use of the aboriginal lands by the Western Shoshone Peoples. CERD/C/USA/DEC/1, April 11, 2006.

The Committee has also sent letters of concern over U.S. governmental actions regarding the Ski Resort at the San Francisco Peaks, discussed in Chapter Nine. In a letter dated March 1, 2013, the Committee issued an "early warning and urgent action" communication to the United States government regarding: "the situation of the Kikapoo Traditional Tribe of Texas, the Ysleta del Sur Pueblo (Tigua) and the Lipan Apache (Ndé) Indigenous communities in relation to the construction of the Texas-Mexico border wall." CERD 82nd/GH/CR/MN. On May 17, 2017, a further letter on this situation negatively impacting Indigenous peoples was sent due to the issuance of a January 17, 2017, U.S. Executive Order planning to expand the border wall. CERD 92nd/EWUAP/GH/SK. These letters regarding the U.S. government's actions toward Tribal Nations are available on the Committee on the Elimination of Racial Discrimination—Early Warning Measures and Urgent Procedures website.

The CERD letters demonstrate the international implications of U.S. Indian policy and allow for human rights protections to be accorded through the UN Conventions entered into by the United States. As Tribal Nations continue to work within international forums, the UN Conventions binding upon the United States may be utilized to undo the negative aspects of past and ongoing U.S. Indian policy and law.

In November 2015, the Apache-Ndé-Nnéé Working Group provided a shadow report for the CERD periodic review of the Holy See, the jurisdiction in Rome of the Catholic Church, that provided a collective demand "to no longer be forced to live the lies and the spiritual, moral, judicial, territorial, political, and social discrimination of the Church, the Holy See, and its influences on colonialism, land-grabbing, genocide, theft, and torture that has been felt by Indigenous peoples." In the report, the negative impacts experienced by Indigenous peoples were detailed due to the historical atrocities initiated, condoned, and promoted by the Holy See through the *Inter Caetera* Bull granted to Spain in 1493 by Pope Alexander VI and other related Papal Bulls. The Apache-Ndé-Nnéé Working Shadow Report called for rescinding the *Inter Caetera* and for the creation of a process of working alongside Indigenous peoples to address the resulting legacy of genocide caused by the *Inter Caetera*.

In the concluding observations by the CERD, it was noted that Pope Francis provided an apology statement in Bolivia in July 2015 to Indigenous peoples in the Americas for the role of the Catholic Church in colonialism. The Committee recommended that the Holy See "engage in meaningful dialogue with Indigenous peoples with the aim of effectively addressing their concerns." Concrete steps and information on proposed meetings with representatives of Indigenous peoples was requested by the CERD in the next periodic report. Consequently, the Vatican Committee of the Catholic Church announced in an official statement the repudiation of the "doctrine of discovery" on March 30, 2023. Real world consequences may flow through engagement in the UN Conventions and implementing commissions for the benefit of Tribal Nations and all Indigenous peoples globally.

D. Development of Other International Instruments on the Rights of Indigenous Peoples

While the United Nations continues to be the supreme international body establishing legal principles for member nation-states, there exist many other international and regional organizations that provide standards and conventions for member countries. This section will discuss a few significant developments for Indigenous peoples through the International Labour Organisation, the Organization of American States, and the National Congress of American Indians (NCAI) engagement in international Indigenous issues.

1. The Conventions of the International Labour Organisation

The International Labour Organisation (ILO) in 1957 adopted C107—Indigenous and Tribal Populations Convention, with the goal of integrating these identified populations into the mainstream of national societies. Article 2 contained the provisions directing nation-states to provide for national integration of Indigenous populations and Article 3 included the further guideline that measures adopted should not prolong a state of separation for these populations. Evolution on the understanding of collective human rights for Indigenous and Tribal peoples led the ILO to adopt a new convention in 1989.

In 1989, the ILO adopted C169—Indigenous and Tribal Peoples Convention, with less emphasis on national integration. Article 7 of the 1989 Convention is congruent with respect for Indigenous and Tribal peoples' ability to chart their own economic, social, and political directions. It provides in subsection (1):

> The peoples concerned shall have the right to decide their own priorities for the process of development as it affects their lives, beliefs, institutions and spiritual well-being and the lands they occupy or otherwise use, and to exercise control, to the extent possible, over their own economic, social and cultural development. In addition, they shall participate in the formulation, implementation and evaluation of plans and programmes for national and regional development which may affect them directly.

As international statements of Indigenous and Tribal peoples' rights, the ILO Conventions demonstrate the significant change in perspectives as understandings have developed on the collective nature and persistence of Indigenous peoples worldwide.

In October 2015, the ILO set forth a strategy for action that was developed through a consensus-building approach to promote knowledge of C169 and to include Indigenous peoples in the strategies for the 2030 Agenda for Sustainable Development. In the above mentioned 2023 report for the system-wide action plan on the topic of the 2030 Agenda, the ILO is one of the UN entities mandated to provide updates on initiatives to engage Indigenous peoples for sustainable development practices.

2. Organization of American States' American Declaration on the Rights of Indigenous Peoples

The 35 nation-states in the Western Hemisphere compose the regional Organization of American States (OAS), including the United States of America. In 1948, with the signing of the OAS charter, the member nation-states, including the United States, adopted the American Declaration on the Rights and Duties of Man, which focused on individual rights. In addition, the Inter-American Commission on Human Rights (IACHR) was established in 1959 and its purpose has expanded to provide for consideration of individual petitions, monitoring of human rights situations in nation-states in the Americas, and supporting the thematic priorities of the OAS. The United States has not ratified the 1969 American Convention on Human Rights, which empowers the Inter-American Court of Human Rights to resolve violations under that Convention.

With the international movement toward collective human rights and the issues arising in member nation-states regarding Indigenous peoples in the Western Hemisphere, the OAS established a Working Group on the Draft American Declaration on the Rights of Indigenous Peoples in 1999. Prior to the adoption of the American Declaration, the Inter-American Commission on Human Rights (IACHR) applied other standards binding the nation-states involved in alleged human rights violations. For example, the IACHR issued a final decision, Report No. 75/02, December 27, 2002, in the case brought by Mary and Carrie Dann of the Western Shoshone as Indigenous people against the United States for human rights violations under the American Declaration on the Rights and Duties of Man that the United States was bound by. Other Tribal Nations may seek to have their claims heard in the IACHR.

On June 15, 2016, the American Declaration on the Rights of Indigenous Peoples was adopted by the OAS following 17 years of drafting and negotiations. Encapsulating many of the same rights as the UNDRIP, the American Declaration expands specifically on treaty rights, the rights of Indigenous children and families, and the rights of Indigenous peoples living in isolation to be free of outside interference. In Article XXII of the American Declaration, the following is set forth: "[t]he indigenous law and legal systems shall be recognized and respected by the national, regional, and international-legal systems." The standard of free, prior, and informed consent (FPIC) is carried forward from the UNDRIP into Article XXXIII of the American Declaration regarding nation-state legislative or regulatory actions that may impact Indigenous peoples.

With the American Declaration adopted in 2016, many of the rights asserted in the 1977 Geneva Conference on the Western Hemisphere are actionable as part of international law. The persistent efforts of Tribal Nation leaders, lawyers, and elders have led to these new international legal frameworks. As the American Declaration is relied upon, the fulfillment of better quality of life and greater self-determination for Indigenous peoples in the Western Hemisphere can be attained.

3. NCAI Engagement on Indigenous Issues

The National Congress of American Indians (NCAI) was founded in 1944 in resistance to many of the worst U.S. Indian policy eras, including the termination of federal recognition of Tribal Nations. The NCAI "is the oldest, largest, and most representative American Indian and Alaska Native organization serving the broad interests of tribal governments and communities," according to its website.

> The adoption of the United Nations Declaration on the Rights of Indigenous Peoples (UNDRIP) in 2007, not only marked a significant acknowledgment of Indigenous peoples and their rights worldwide, but it also created opportunities for more action by Tribal Nations in the international sphere. Partially in response to the UNDRIP, in recent years, NCAI has prioritized negotiations at the United Nations (UN) and the Organization of American States (OAS), engaging in a number of substantive policy discussions of particular concern to Indigenous Peoples, including climate change, the protection of Indigenous traditional knowledge and genetic resources, and enhanced participation within international decision making forums.

The NCAI has issued many resolutions urging the leadership of the U.S. to affirm the UNDRIP, to implement the UNDRIP, and to follow the UNDRIP. For example, at the NCAI General Assembly in 2017, resolution MKE-17-049, *Acknowledging the 10th Anniversary of the Passage of the UN Declaration on the Rights of Indigenous Peoples*, set forth that the "NCAI calls upon UN member states to redouble their commitment to ensuring that best intentions to implement UNDRIP result in best practices and meaningful reforms to uphold the rights of indigenous peoples enshrined in UNDRIP." Subsequently, the

NCAI General Assembly held on October 11–14, 2021, resolution SAC-21-023, *Calling on the United States to Take Action to Achieve the Objectives of the United Nations Declaration on the Rights of Indigenous Peoples*, was adopted.

As this chapter demonstrates, the international connections and activity of Tribal Nations as Indigenous peoples of North America continue to build and strengthen bonds around the globe. In addition, the international human rights principles developing to embrace collective rights will likely have potential positive impacts for the relationships between Tribal Nations and the United States. As Indigenous peoples continue to reclaim their voices in the international sphere, attention is being brought to issues of food security, sustainable development practices, enforcement of human rights, and realization of treaty provisions entered into as a basis for government-to-government interactions.

CHECKPOINTS

- Native American leaders have persistently asserted Tribal Nation sovereignty and treaty rights in the U.S. and in international forums. Tribal Nations have not assented to a status as less than full sovereigns.
- Tribal Nation leaders have been engaged with the United Nations and worked with other Indigenous peoples around the world to establish permanent means of communication within the organization.
- One of the most important international documents on Indigenous human rights is the UN Declaration on the Rights of Indigenous Peoples (UNDRIP) approved on September 13, 2007. The UNDRIP will continue to have significant influence on the relationships between Tribal Nations and the United States.
- Alliances and confederacies are traditional governance activities of Tribal Nations and entering into treaties, conventions, and agreements based on mutual peaceful relations is a practice that will continue into the foreseeable future.

Mastering Native American Law Master Checklist

After working through this book, you should be able to understand the following concepts set forth in the preceding chapters.

CHAPTER 1 • INTRODUCTION TO NATIVE AMERICAN LAW

- ☐ Tribal law is formed from Indigenous legal traditions, codified statutes, regulations, and judicial opinions. Tribal Nations have legal histories that extend for thousands of years and continue to exercise their own law. American Indian and Alaska Native Tribal governments compose the over 570 Tribal Nations in mid-North America.
- ☐ Together, Tribal law and federal Indian law form Native American law. Federal Indian law in the United States is derived from concepts developed through European Christian doctrines and early international law. The interaction between Tribal Nations and the United States developed through the treaty-making process.
- ☐ There is an active interaction between Tribal Nation law and the law of the United States. Tribal law has influenced the formation of the United States and concepts such as democracy, dispute resolution principles, and environmental stewardship enacted into law.
- ☐ There are more than 570 federally recognized Tribal Nations in the United States. Each Tribe has its own governance structure and set

of Tribal laws. Almost half of the 570 federally recognized Tribal Nations are Alaska Native Tribes.

- ☐ Federal Indian law is applied generally to all Tribes whether enacted by federal legislation or through a federal judicial opinion. Title 25 of the U.S. Code contains the set of federal laws dealing with American Indians and Alaska Native governments and peoples, with some federal laws including Native Hawaiians. Federal agencies implement many of the federal Indian law provisions. The Bureau of Indian Affairs has a primary role in implementing federal Indian law and policy.
- ☐ The Marshall Trilogy of cases serves as the U.S. interpretation of the foundation of the relationship between Tribal Nations and the United States. Key concepts from the cases include: Tribal Nations characterized as domestic dependent nations, the United States as the successor to the discovery doctrine from the European nation known as Great Britain, the beginning of the federal trust relationship from the announcement of the ward/guardian status, and federal preemption of state law in Native American affairs.

CHAPTER 2 • NATIVE AMERICAN PROPERTY LAW

- ☐ Tribal Nation property ownership concepts continue to inform contemporary Tribal property laws. Tribal realty offices implement Tribal laws and regulations.
- ☐ Native American property law is important to understanding the extent of Tribal regulatory authority. Tribal reservation boundaries provide the basic area of the tribal land base. The allotment process has changed the status of land within reservation boundaries.
- ☐ The Bureau of Indian Affairs, on behalf of the U.S. government, has management authority over the more than 55 million acres of tribal land in trust status. Tribal lands in trust status are recognized under Tribal regulatory authority and are exempt from state property taxation.
- ☐ The Office of Special Trustee within the Department of the Interior has the responsibility of ensuring the accountability of the U.S. government in managing trust fund accounts for Tribal member owners of lands in trust status.

- ☐ The three main types of Tribal property are reservation and trust lands, restricted lands, and fee lands.
- ☐ Alaska Native Villages have been subject to unique federal law on the management of Tribal lands in fee status through regional and village corporations and may utilize the federal fee-to-trust process to increase Tribal land holdings.
- ☐ Reclaiming Tribal lands and stewardship of those lands is part of a social, cultural, and political movement known as "Land Back" across Indian Country.

CHAPTER 3 • CRIMINAL JURISDICTION IN INDIAN COUNTRY

- ☐ Criminal jurisdiction in Indian Country requires an analysis of the land status where the crime allegedly occurred. Next, the determination of whether the perpetrator and/or victim was or was not a Tribal member will establish what authorities have criminal jurisdiction.
- ☐ The U.S. Supreme Court has held that a non-Native perpetrator committing a crime against a non-Native victim in Indian Country is subject to state criminal jurisdiction.
- ☐ Tribal Nations have concurrent jurisdiction with any other prosecuting authority for crimes involving Tribal member perpetrators. Criminal sentencing in Tribal courts is limited by the Indian Civil Rights Act.
- ☐ The U.S. Supreme Court has held that Tribes lack full criminal jurisdiction over non-Native perpetrators committing crimes against Tribal members in Indian Country. Federal legislation has allowed for Tribal Nations to participate in exercising Special Tribal Criminal Jurisdiction over all persons committing specified crimes in Indian Country, which is a removal of limitations on Tribal Nation criminal jurisdiction.
- ☐ Under Public Law 280, certain states have been delegated criminal jurisdiction over Tribal members in Indian Country. Each reservation requires an analysis of this delegated jurisdiction in those states. Tribal criminal jurisdiction is concurrent with those state governments. States may also exercise concurrent prosecutorial authority

with the federal government over non-Indians committing crimes against Tribal members in Indian Country.

- ☐ Prosecution of a Tribal member by a Tribal Nation and a federal or state authority for offenses arising out of the same criminal activity does not constitute double jeopardy under the U.S. Constitution.

CHAPTER 4 • TRIBAL GOVERNMENT, CIVIL JURISDICTION, AND REGULATION

- ☐ Tribal Nation governance is traditionally based upon clan systems and kinship networks that require adherence to high level standards of conduct. With the influence of the U.S., the majority of Tribal Nation governance systems have shifted toward written law codes and constitutionally based governments.
- ☐ Tribal Nation courts resolve disputes involving civil laws. The U.S. Supreme Court has provided that non-members have certain procedural avenues to challenge the civil adjudicatory authority of Tribal courts when actions arise on certain lands within Tribal Nation boundaries.
- ☐ Tribal governments have various administrative agencies and offices to carry out civil regulatory functions, such as: tax offices, personnel agencies, and departments of fishing and hunting.
- ☐ Many Tribal Nation social services are guaranteed under treaty provisions with the U.S. government. These guaranteed services are administered by federal agencies, but may be contracted and operated by Tribal governments.

CHAPTER 5 • TRIBAL NATION CORPORATIONS AND ECONOMIES

- ☐ Tribal Nations have engaged in trading partnerships, and alliances with Europeans prior to the formation of the United States. With the limitations imposed by federal law on Tribal Nation resources and governance, Tribal governments have prioritized economic development.
- ☐ Tribally-owned corporations may be established pursuant to a Tribal constitution, through approval of a federal charter or under state law.

Tribal government officials determine the structure of the corporate leadership.

- ☐ Federal programs, such as Native 8(a), provide incentives to Tribal Nation-owned corporations, Alaska Native Corporations, and Native Hawaiian Organizations to participate in the federal procurement process and federally designated economically depressed areas.
- ☐ The Tribal Nation gaming industry operates pursuant to the federal Indian Gaming Regulatory Act (IGRA) containing many specific requirements that Tribal government licensed gaming facilities must comply with. The National Indian Gaming Commission is the direct federal agency that implements the provisions of the IGRA.
- ☐ Tribal Nation entities have sovereign immunity from lawsuits unless expressly waived in a contract. Best commercial practices are to waive sovereign immunity up to the amount of a contract; designate a specific court and body of law to resolve disputes in the contract; and act with good faith in all commercial dealings.
- ☐ Taxation is a key component to supporting Tribal governmental services. Tribal Nation tax offices and agencies operate under Tribal law overseeing issuance of business licenses, employment preferences, and calculation of Tribal taxes.

CHAPTER 6 • FAMILY LAW IN TRIBAL NATION COMMUNITIES

- ☐ The domestic sphere of Tribal law is an area where Tribal values, culture, and wisdom form the core. Tribal courts generally have exclusive authority in handling domestic issues occurring on Tribal lands involving their citizens.
- ☐ Due to the U.S. Indian policy of assimilation, Tribal members have suffered from the removal of children from Tribal homes and federal conditioning to alter or eliminate Tribal culture and lifeways. Many Tribal Nations have prioritized protection of Tribal languages, Tribal knowledge, and Tribal education systems to remedy the traumas from that policy era.
- ☐ The federal Indian Child Welfare Act (ICWA) was enacted to remedy cross-cultural misunderstandings of state agencies towards Tribal

families and provide a transfer process for cases involving placement of Tribal children from state courts to Tribal courts. Some states have passed their own state laws to further implement the provisions of the ICWA.

- ☐ Tribal family law continues to develop to address contemporary needs of Tribal families. Tribal Healing and Wellness Courts have developed to address family issues in a holistic manner.

CHAPTER 7 • NATURAL RESOURCES IN INDIAN COUNTRY

- ☐ Tribal Nations since time immemorial have developed expertise on reciprocal relationships with the natural world for human quality of life. Tribal stewardship and natural resource use are informed by traditional legal principles and values.
- ☐ Tribal natural resources on trust lands are under the management authority of the U.S. Department of the Interior. An extensive body of federal regulations has been created on the leasing, extraction, and approval processes for commercial use of Tribal natural resources.
- ☐ The federal trust responsibility to Tribal Nations governments and individuals provides guidance on federal decision-making regarding Tribal natural resource extraction and usage.
- ☐ A strong relationship of collaboration has been maintained between many Tribal Nations and the U.S. Environmental Protection Agency (EPA). Several major federal environmental protection statutes have been amended and implemented by the EPA recognizing Tribes as states for federal programs and processes.
- ☐ Tribal governments have invested heavily in the protection of treaty hunting, fishing, and gathering rights. Tribal natural resource departments supply scientific expertise to Tribal conservation efforts. Tribal Nations are experiencing some consequences of the climate change crisis and seeking to respond for the protection of Tribal communities.
- ☐ Recent federal laws have supported the U.S. Indian policy of Indian self-determination by providing for greater Tribal Nation authority over natural resource and energy development.

CHAPTER 8 • TRIBAL NATION-STATE GOVERNMENT RELATIONS

☐ The primary governmental relationship is between the Tribal Nations and the federal government. Due to the proximity between Tribes and state governments, significant areas of collaboration around common concerns have developed in contemporary times.

☐ Tribal members have dual citizenship as citizens of the United States, which incorporates state citizenship. Both Tribal Nations and state governments serve Tribal members through governmental services.

☐ State governments have increasingly sought to tax activities within Tribal Nation territories. While there is no direct enforcement mechanism for such state taxation, the trend has been to enter into Tribal Nation-state government tax agreements to satisfy the legal standards set forth by the U.S. Supreme Court. Federal law mandates Tribal-state gaming compacts for Class III types of gaming on Tribal Nation lands.

☐ State governments may provide a process to grant the status of state recognition for an area Tribe. This state recognition may be a step in the process for a Tribe to meet federal recognition requirements.

CHAPTER 9 • SACRED SITES, CULTURAL PROPERTY PROTECTION, AND REPATRIATION

☐ American Indian and Alaska Native spiritual principles connected to sacred sites are not commonly understood or protected in U.S. law. Cross-cultural understanding is necessary to provide greater legal protections.

☐ Tribal Nations continue to assert legal arguments and seek federal policy changes to protect spiritually, culturally, and historically important geographical sites.

☐ With the enactment of the Native American Graves Protection and Repatriation Act (NAGPRA), the looting of Tribal cemeteries and the unauthorized collection of ancestral remains are federal offenses on Tribal Nation and federal lands. Federally-funded museums have obligations under the law to inventory Tribal items and respond to requests for repatriation of Tribal cultural patrimonial items.

- ☐ Tribal Historic Preservation Officers are operating to ensure that tribal cultural property is recognized and preserved. Tribes are developing and implementing laws on cultural resource protection, the repatriation of Tribal members, the protection of various types of traditional knowledge, and seeking to educate other governments on proper processes.

CHAPTER 10 • INTERNATIONAL INDIGENOUS RIGHTS AND TRIBAL NATIONS

- ☐ Native American leaders have persistently asserted Tribal Nation sovereignty and treaty rights in the U.S. and in international forums. Tribal Nations have not assented to a status as less than full sovereigns.
- ☐ Tribal Nation leaders have been engaged with the United Nations and worked with other Indigenous peoples around the world to establish permanent means of communication within the organization.
- ☐ One of the most important international documents on Indigenous human rights is the UN Declaration on the Rights of Indigenous Peoples (UNDRIP) approved on September 13, 2007. The UNDRIP will continue to have significant influence on the relationships between Tribal Nations and the United States.
- ☐ Alliances and confederacies are traditional governance activities of Tribal Nations and entering into treaties, conventions, and agreements based on mutual peaceful relations is a practice that will continue into the foreseeable future.

Index